C000113096

PROCLAMATIONS,
RULES AND NOTICES

RELATING TO THE

NYASALAND PROTECTORATE

IN FORCE ON THE

31st December, 1914.

COMPILED UNDER THE AUTHORITY OF THE GOVERNMENT OF THE NYASALAND PROTECTORATE

BY

CHARLES J. GRIFFIN,

Late Judge of His Majesty's High Court of Nyasaland

AND

WALTER E. DEMUTH, M.A. (Oxon.)

of the Inner Temple, Barrister-at-Law.

PRINTED AND PUBLISHED BY
THE GOVERNMENT PRINTER, ZOMBA, NYASALAND PROTECTORATE.
1915.

TABLE OF CONTENTS.

No. 12 of 1911.

INTERPRETATION AND GENERAL CLAUSES.

56/1908,—30th April.

Public Holidays.

See Section 2 (30).

THE following days are appointed as Public Holidays throughout the Protectorate :—

Good Friday	King's Birthday	Public holidays.
Easter Monday	Christmas Day	
Empire Day	Boxing Day.	

124/1914,—30th June.

Official Time.

See Section 19.

Zomba mean time is 21 minutes and 10 seconds in advance of South Africa standard time. For general convenience the difference will in future be reckoned as 21 minutes, throughout the Protectorate.

No. 3 of 1906.

HIGH COURT PRACTICE AND PROCEDURE.

See Section 13 (6) (b).

THE following is the text of Section 10 of The Summary Jurisdiction Act, 1879, referred to in the above mentioned section :—

Summary trial of children for indictable offences, unless objected to by parent or guardian.

10. (1). Where a child is charged before a Court of summary jurisdiction with any indictable offence other than homicide, the Court, if they think it expedient so to do, and if the parent or guardian of the child so charged, when informed by the Court of his right to have the child tried by a jury, does not object to the child being dealt with summarily, may deal summarily with the offence, and inflict the same description of punishment as might have been inflicted had the case been tried on indictment :

Provided that—

(*a*). A sentence of penal servitude shall not be passed, but imprisonment shall be substituted therefor ; and

(*b*). Where imprisonment is awarded, the term shall not in any case exceed one month ; and

(*c*). Where a fine is awarded, the amount shall not in any case exceed forty shillings ; and

(*d*). When the child is a male the Court may, either in addition to or instead of any other punishment, adjudge the child to be, as soon as practicable, privately whipped with not more than six strokes of a birch rod by a constable, in the presence of an inspector or other officer of police of higher rank than a constable, and also in the presence, if he desires to be present, of the parent or guardian of the child.

(2). For the purpose of a proceeding under this section the Court of summary jurisdiction, at any time during the hearing of the case at which they become satisfied by the evidence that it is expedient to deal with the case summarily, shall cause the charge to be reduced into writing and read to the parent or guardian of the child, and then address a question to such parent or guardian to the following effect: "Do you desire the child to be tried by a jury, and object to the case being dealt with summarily?" with a statement, if the Court think such statement desirable for the information of such parent or guardian, of the meaning of the case being dealt with summarily, and of the assizes or sessions (as the case may be) at which the child will be tried, if tried by a jury.

(3). Where the parent or guardian of a child is not present when the child is charged with an indictable offence before a Court of summary jurisdiction, the Court may, if they think it just so to do, remand the child for the purpose of causing notice to be served on such parent or guardian, with a view so far as is practicable of securing his attendance at the hearing of the charge, or the Court may, if they think it expedient so to do, deal with the case summarily.

(4). This section shall not prejudice the right of a Court of summary jurisdiction to send a child to a reformatory or industrial school.

(5). This section shall not render punishable for an offence any child who is not, in the opinion of the Court before whom he is charged, above the age of seven years and of sufficient capacity to commit crime.

No. 2 of 1907.

FUGITIVE CRIMINALS SURRENDER.

Application of Ordinance to certain Foreign States.

Under Section 2.

IN EXERCISE of the powers conferred by Section 2, the above Ordinance has been applied as from the undermentioned dates in the cases of the undermentioned Foreign States and their Protectorates during the continuance of the arrangements made between His Majesty the King and the Rulers of such States under which the Protectorate is to surrender fugitive criminals to such States and their Protectorates :—

STATES TO WHICH ORDINANCE APPLIES.

104/1908,—31st July.

Argentine Republic	Hayti	Roumania
Austria-Hungary	Italy	Russia
Bolivia	Liberia	Salvador
Chile	Luxemburg	San Marino
Colombia	Mexico	Servia
Cuba	Monaco	Spain
Denmark	Nicaragua	Sweden
Ecuador	Norway	Switzerland
France	Panama	United States of America
Guatemala	Peru	Uruguay.

95/1911,—12th June.

All German Protectorates.

57/1912,—30th April.

Germany.

104/1912,—5th June.

Greece.

107/1912,—21st June.

Siam.

162/1912,—30th September.

Tunis.

No. 10 of 1905.

PRISONS.

Notices.

214/1911,—30th December.

Buildings set apart as Prisons.

Under Section 2.

THE following buildings are set apart as Prisons :—

For Long Sentence Prisoners :—Zomba Central Prison. Prison
For European Long Sentence Prisoners :—Blantyre Buildings.
Central Prison.

For Short Sentence Prisoners :—The buildings at present
used as prisons at the head-quarters of each administrative
district and sub-district.

125/1908,—1st August.

Appointment of Prison Officers.

Under Section 3.

To be Keeper of the Central Prison, Zomba :—The Officer Prison
Commanding the Troops. Officers.

To be Assistant Keeper of the Central Prison, Zomba :—
An Officer of the King's African Rifles to be appointed by
the Officer Commanding the Troops. *

29th June, 1907.

To be Keeper of the Central Prison, Blantyre :—The
District Resident.

215/1911,—30th December.

To be Keeper of the District and Sub-district Prisons
(for short sentence prisoners) :—The District Residents and
Assistant Residents for the prisons situate in their respective
Districts and Sub-districts.

---

* Though this notice has not been cancelled, the post of Deputy
Superintendent of the Central Prison, Zomba, has been created and the
post has been filled (100/1913, 31st May and 139/1913, 30th June.)

30th December, 1905.

R u l e s.

GENERAL.

Under Section 4.

Prisoners in legal custody of Superintendent.

1. Every prisoner confined in any prison shall be deemed to be in the legal custody of the Superintendent or Keeper and shall be subject to the prison discipline and Rules during the whole term of his imprisonment. Every criminal prisoner shall continue in custody until he becomes entitled to his freedom or shall be absolutely or conditionally pardoned or shall be either removed to some other prison or discharged with licence to be at large on such conditions as the Governor may prescribe.

Prisoners in course of transference.

2. The period spent by a prisoner in transference after conviction to any prison or from one prison to another shall be deemed to be part of the period of his imprisonment.

Warrant.

3. (*a*). The officer or constable commanding the escort in charge of a prisoner committed or transferred to any prison for custody shall be duly provided by the Judge or Magistrate by whom the prisoner has been committed or before whom the conviction has been obtained, with a proper warrant setting out:—

(1). The name.

(2). The village, tribe and district or, in the case of Europeans or Asiatics, the nationality and place of residence of the prisoner.

(3). The nature of the offence or charge and, in case of conviction, (4) the duration of the sentence, and (5) the nature of the sentence, *e.g.*, whether imprisonment with hard labour or penal servitude or otherwise.

(*b*). Such warrant shall be delivered with the prisoner to the Superintendent of the prison, and shall be filed by him with the prison records.

(*c*). No prisoner shall be received into custody by the Superintendent of any prison unless accompanied by such warrant except in case of arrest without warrant by a Constable or other proper officer or person upon some sufficient charge and then only for such period as may be absolutely necessary pending production of accused before a Magistrate empowered to inquire into the charge.

(*d*) No civil prisoner shall be received by the Superintendent of the Central Prison at Zomba unless the accompanying warrant bears the seal of the High Court or is signed by a Judge of the High Court.

4. (*a*). The High Court may order any prisoner to be removed to any other prison whenever such removal is necessary in the course of any proceedings pending in the said High Court or for the purpose of any Assize of Gaol Delivery.

Removal of prisoners in other cases.

(*b*). Whenever any prisoner is removed to any other prison than that referred to or named in the warrant or order under which he shall have been imprisoned, the said warrant or order together with an order of removal either endorsed on the warrant or order or separate therefrom shall be sufficient authority for the removal of such prisoner to the prison named in the order of removal, and his detention therein, and for carrying out the sentence described in the warrant or order of imprisonment, or any part thereof which may then remain unexecuted.

5. European prisoners shall in no case be confined in the same cells as Asiatics or natives and shall where possible be confined only in a Central Prison.

Europeans.

6. (*a*). Male and female prisoners shall be kept absolutely separate from each other and shall where possible be confined in separate buildings.

Females.

(*b*). Native female prisoners shall not be detained in any prison outside the district to which they belong or in which the offence has been committed except by the written directions of the Governor or of a Judge of the High Court.

(*c*). Juvenile prisoners shall as far as possible be kept separate from adults and they shall not be detained in any prison outside the district to which they belong or in which the offence has been committed except by the written directions of the Governor or of a Judge of the High Court.

Children.

7. (*a*). Hard labour for the purposes of sentences of imprisonment or penal servitude shall consist of work at the necessary service of the prison or at any trade or may consist of such other description of hard industrial labour as the Governor may direct, and in every prison where prisoners sentenced to hard labour are confined, adequate means shall be provided for enforcing hard labour in accordance with these provisions.

Occupations of prisoners.

(*b*). Prisoners may be employed in hard industrial labour (*e.g.* road making, brick making or sanitary work) .

outside the walls of the prison under the control of a prison officer belonging to such prison.

(*c*). Prisoners shall be employed in useful work and where possible shall be taught useful trades.

(*d*). Where possible, religious and secular instruction shall be provided for such prisoners as may desire the same.

Distribution of prisoners.

* **8.** (*a*). Native prisoners sentenced to more than six months' imprisonment by any Court shall be deemed to be long-sentence prisoners, and shall upon confirmation of sentence be forthwith transferred to the Central Prison at Zomba.

(*b*). No long-sentence prisoner shall be received by the Keeper of the Central Prison at Zomba unless the accompanying warrant bears the seal of the High Court or is signed by a Judge of the High Court. .

(*c*). With the above exceptions no prisoners shall be confined outside the district in which they have been convicted unless by the direction of the Governor or of a Judge of the High Court.

No detention of prisoners beyond expiration of original sentence.

9. No prisoner can in consequence of misconduct while in prison be detained in prison beyond the expiration of the term of imprisonment to which he was sentenced by a court of law, unless he has been again brought before a court of law and has received a fresh sentence.

MEDICAL INSPECTION.

Medical inspection and treatment.

10. (*a*). Every prison shall be subject to the periodical inspection of a Government Medical Officer or in his absence of some other duly qualified medical practitioner;

(*b*). Sick prisoners shall be segregated for treatment, and shall where practicable be removed to a prison hospital, or may in the absence of a prison hospital be removed by the Superintendent of a prison to some other hospital upon the written certificate of a medical officer;

(*c*). Prisoners removed to hospital shall remain therein under such safeguards for their custody as may be advisable until their discharge by the Medical Officer as cured and shall be brought back to the prison by the Superintendent if still liable to be confined therein;

(*d*). The Medical Officer shall at the end of every month transmit to the officer in charge of the prison a report setting forth the names of the prisoners under medical treat-

---

* Rule 8 as amended by Notice of 31st January, 1912. (No. 3 of 1912).

ment and in case of a prisoner in hospital a certificate signed by him stating that it is in his opinion necessary that such prisoner should remain in the said hospital.

11. The Medical Officer shall report in writing to the Superintendent the case of any prisoner whose mind appears likely to be injuriously affected by the discipline or treatment, with such directions as he may think necessary.

Report of special cases.

12. He shall report in writing to the Superintendent the case of any prisoner appearing to be insane.

To report insanity of prisoners.

13. Whenever he shall be of opinion that the life of any prisoner is endangered by his continuance in prison, he shall state in writing such opinion and the grounds thereof to the Superintendent who shall without delay transmit such report to the Governor.

To report on life of prisoner endangered.

14. He shall forthwith on the death of any prisoner, enter in his case book the time when the illness was first observed, when it was reported to him, and when it assumed a dangerous character; the nature of the disease, the time of death and an account of the appearances after death together with any special remarks that appear to him to be required.

Death of prisoner.

15. Every prisoner shall, as soon as possible after committal, be examined by the Medical Officer, who shall enter in the Prisoners' Register to be kept by the Keeper or Superintendent a record of the state of the health of the prisoner and any observations he may deem it expedient to make.

Examination by Medical Officer.

16. The Medical Officer shall have general supervision, and shall inspect from time to time the sanitary conditions of the prison, the clothing, bedding and food of the prisoners; and shall give all necessary instructions in writing with reference to the same.

Medical Officer to supervise in sanitary matters and give directions.

17. An inquest shall be held on the body of every prisoner who may die in a prison. Whenever possible a Medical Officer shall attend or send a medical certificate of the cause of death.

Inquest to be held on a death in prison.

VISITORS.

18. (a). The Judge or Judges of the High Court, the Chief Secretary or the officer holding the equivalent position and the Principal Medical Officer, with such other persons as the Governor may appoint for such period and for such district or districts as he may specify, shall have in respect of any prison all the powers of the Visiting Justices or Committee under the Prisons Act 1877 in England or under any Act amending or substituted for the said Act.

Visiting Justices.

(*b*). Visiting Justices shall from time to time at frequent intervals visit all prisoners and hear any complaints which may be made to them by the prisoners and shall report on any abuses within the prisons or any repairs that may be required and shall further take cognizance of any matters of pressing necessity and do such acts and perform such duties in relation to prisons as they may be required to do or perform by the Governor.

(*c*). A Visiting Justice may make recommendations for the pardon of any prisoners or for the enlargement of any prisoner upon ticket-of-leave or otherwise for good and sufficient cause or for the transfer of any prisoner to another prison on the ground of health or for any other reason.

(*d*). A Visiting Justice shall have power to require the attendance of a Government Medical Officer or in his absence of some other duly qualified practitioner during his inspection of any prison.

(*e*). The Governor may appoint one or more European women to act as Visiting Justices in the case of female prisoners upon such terms as he may deem advisable.

(*f*). Ministers of religion shall be allowed access to prisoners desiring their assistance at convenient hours to be determined by the Superintendent.

DUTIES OF PRISON OFFICERS.

Hour of locking and unlocking prisons.

19. The outer gates of the part of the prison where prisoners are confined shall be locked and the key delivered to the Keeper or Superintendent or commander of the guard at six o'clock each night, he having first ascertained that the Officers resident in the prison are all present. No ingress or egress shall be allowed into or out of the prison between the hours of six at night and five in the morning except to the Medical Officer and persons furnished with an order in writing under the hand of the Superintendent.

Visitors not to be in the prison at night.

20. No persons other than the officers of the prison, the medical officer and the prisoners shall be in the prison between the hours of six at night and five in the morning without the permission in writing of the Superintendent.

21. No person shall convey or attempt to convey in or out of any prison to or from any prisoner any letter, food or other article save with the consent of the Keeper or Superintendent.

22. No prison officer shall strike a prisoner except in self-defence or in defence of some one else. Prison officers who carry arms shall only use them when absolutely necessary and in such a way as to disable—not to kill.

23. The Superintendent or Keeper shall give to the Medical Officer the names of any prisoners who are ill, or who complain of illness or who appear to him to require attention in mind or body, or who are in solitary confinement; and he shall carry into effect whatever written instructions may be given to him by the Medical Officer. Cases of sudden illness shall be reported to the Medical Officer without delay.

24. He shall occasionally from time to time test the quantity and quality of the rations supplied to the prisoners. He shall investigate the complaints of the prisoners and hear their applications on any point as soon as practicable, and shall take care that any prisoner wishing to appeal to an authorized visitor shall have an opportunity of doing so. Not less than two pounds of grain or one-and-a-half pounds of rice per head, together with salt, and, if possible, some condiments, should be issued as food to native prisoners.

Should, however, repeated complaints of a groundless nature be made under this rule, the matter may be treated as a breach of prison discipline and the offender shall be liable to punishment accordingly.

25. In case of the death of a prisoner he shall at once notify the same to the Medical Officer and an inquest shall be held and if the death is certified by the Medical Officer to be from natural causes he shall deliver up the body of the deceased to the relatives for the purpose of burial, provided that they desire to have it, and that there is on sanitary grounds no objection to such a course.

*26. (1). The following books shall be kept by the Keepers of Prisons :—

(*a*). By the Keeper of a Long Sentence Prison :

(i). A Roll of Convicted Prisoners.

(ii). A Visiting Justices' Record.

(iii). A Prison Work Record.

(iv). A Journal of any matters by any Rules directed to be recorded and of any important occurrences connected with the Prison.

(v). A general Mark Account for prisoners committed for more than six months.

---

* Rule 26 as amended by Notice of 30th March, 1912, (No. 40 of 1912), and further amended by Notice of 26th April, 1912, (No. 59 of 1912).

(vi). A Punishment Book in which shall be recorded all punishments ordered for breach of prison discipline, with the reasons therefor, date and signature of the Keeper of the Prison.

(b). By the Keeper of a Short Sentence Prison :

(i). All the books specified in paragraph (a) hereof except the general Mark Account, and in addition :

(a). A Remand Book.

(b). A Prison Calendar.

(2). The Roll of Convicted Prisoners shall contain the following particulars of each prisoner :—

(a) Serial number on the roll, (b) name, (c) sex, (d) age, (e) tribe, (f) village, (g) district, (h) offence for which imprisoned, (i) Court or authority by which confined, (j) date of conviction, (k) duration and nature of sentence, (l) date, of release, (m) behaviour while in prison, (n) occupation while in prison, (o) state of health, (p) remarks. If prisoner dies, escapes, is transferred to another prison or is released before expiry of sentence, here insert fact of such death, escape transference or release, with date and cause of or reason therefor.

In the case of non-native prisoners the nationality and place of residence shall be substituted for (e) and (f).

(3). The Remand Book shall contain the following particulars of each prisoner remanded :—

(a). Serial number in Remand Book, (b) name, (c) sex, (d) age, (e) tribe, (f) village, (g) district, (h) nature of charge, (i) date of remand or remands, (j) date or dates to which remanded, (k) if subsequently convicted, serial number on roll of convicted prisoners.

In the case of non-native prisoners the nationality and place of residence shall be substituted for (e) and (f).

(4). The Prison Calendar shall contain the following particulars of each convicted prisoner :—

(a) Serial number on Roll of convicted prisoners, (b) name.

The entry in the Prison Calendar shall be made in the space reserved in the Calendar for the date upon which the prisoner is due for release.

(5). New Rolls of Prisoners, whether convicted or under remand, shall be commenced each year on the 1st April. All prisoners in custody shall be entered anew on that date in order, beginning with the prisoner whose conviction or detention is of earliest date.

(6). The names of all female prisoners on the Roll of Convicted Prisoners and in the Remand Book shall be entered in red ink.

(7). The date of release of each prisoner shall be entered in red ink.

(8). At the end of each month a line shall be drawn immediately below the name of the last prisoner appearing on the Roll or in the Remand Book and the number of prisoners then in custody shall be recorded in red ink.

(9). Where a Government Medical Officer is available a certificate shall be signed by such Medical Officer to the effect that all prisoners have been medically inspected during the month. Such certificate shall be entered immediately below the entry of the particulars required by (8) hereof.

REMISSION FOR GOOD CONDUCT MARKS.

* **27.** Every criminal prisoner under a first sentence of imprisonment for more than six months may earn remission of sentence by industry accompanied by good conduct.

Remission of sentence.

28. The maximum remission obtainable shall be one-third of the sentence.

Maximum remission.

29. The amount of remission shall be determined by marks, as follows:—

Remission: how determined.

(*a*). Every day of imprisonment shall be represented by four marks, irrespective of conduct or industry.

(*b*). One additional mark shall be given for a fair day's work; two additional marks for steady hard work and full performance of the task allotted for the day.

† (*c*). A prisoner must obtain a number of marks equal to four times the number of days of the term of imprisonment to which he has been sentenced; thus, if he obtains only four marks per diem he earns no remission; whereas, if he obtains six marks per diem and none are forfeited for misconduct, he earns the full remission of one-third of the sentence.

(*d*). No marks shall be allowed for mere good conduct except on Sunday, Christmas Day and Good Friday. Every prisoner entitled to marks who conducts himself well on these days shall receive six marks.

30. Prisoners in hospital if injured while engaged at their work or in the performance of their duty (without any fault of their own) shall be allowed six marks per diem. If in hospital for any other cause they shall be allowed the average number of marks which they have earned in the past week.

Marks allowed prisoners in hospital.

---

* Rules 27—34 inclusive as amended by Notice of 11th May 1906.
† Rule 29 (*c*) as further amended by Erratum Notice of 1st July, 1906.

Marks for light labour.

31. Prisoners who have been certified by the Medical Officer to be only capable of light labour shall be allowed marks in proportion to their industry on the same scale as other prisoners.

Marks for prisoners in solitary confinement.

32. Prisoners in solitary confinement for breaches of prison discipline shall be allowed only four marks a day during the time of such confinement.

Prisoners previously convicted may earn marks in second year.

33. Criminal prisoners who have been sentenced a second time to imprisonment for two years or upwards shall not be allowed the privilege of earning any remission of their sentence during the first year of such second sentence; but if their conduct and industry during the first year be reported upon favourably by the Superintendent or Keeper of the prison, they shall be allowed the privilege of earning a remission of the third part of the remainder of their sentence on the same terms as prisoners under a first sentence.

Prisoners thrice convicted may not earn marks.

34. (a). Prisoners sentenced a third time or oftener to imprisonment, for two years and upwards, shall not be allowed to earn any remission of sentence.

(b). Prisoners who have earned a remission of a part of their sentence shall receive a ticket-of-leave, which shall be subject to all the conditions endorsed thereon, and to the provisions of any law in force relating to tickets-of-leave.

(c). The earning of marks and grant of remission shall extend to re-convicted holders of a ticket-of-leave serving the remanents of former sentences.

Life sentence.

* **35.** The case of a prisoner under sentence of imprisonment for life will be specially considered at the end of fifteen years.

PUNISHMENTS.

† **36.** (a). The Superintendent or Keeper may hear and decide all complaints respecting prison discipline and may punish any prisoner found guilty by him of an offence against prison discipline by ordering the offender to be kept in solitary confinement for not more than twenty-four hours or by keeping such offender upon reduced diet for any time not exceeding three days or by loss of marks or by whipping not exceeding ten lashes.

† (b). The Medical Officer shall examine every prisoner sentenced to be whipped or flogged before the punishment is inflicted and shall be present while it is being carried out. He shall give such orders for preventing injury to health as he may deem necessary, and it shall be the duty of the Superintendent or Keeper to carry out such orders.

† (c). No prisoner shall be whipped or flogged until the Medical Officer has certified in writing that he is fit to undergo the punishment.

---

* Rule 35 an additional Rule, made 22nd April 1912. (No. 139/1912.)
† Sub-rules (b) and (c) additional Rules made 11th May, 1906.

RETURNS.

§ **37.** (*a*). The Keeper or Superintendent of each prison shall on the 30th September and the 31st March of each year transmit to the Judge of the High Court a copy of the roll of convicted prisoners in his custody during the previous half year.

(*b*). He shall transmit also a list of all prisoners sentenced to three years or upwards who have already served two years of their term of imprisonment and shall inform the Judge of the High Court whether there are any circumstances in regard to the said prisoners which may warrant special consideration of their cases.

(*c*). The Judge of the High Court shall after inspection transmit all prison returns to the Governor for his consideration and shall prepare such statistics as may from time to time be required.

§ Rule 37 made 30th March, 1912. (No. 40/1912.)

No. 19 of 1908.

KING'S AFRICAN RIFLES RESERVE FORCES.

43/1913,—28th February.

Rules.

Under Section 21.

Removal from one district to another.

1. Should a reservist desire to move from his own district to another he shall inform the District Magistrate of his district to that effect. His name shall then be transferred from the records of the district in which he was residing to those of the district to which he proceeds : provided that a reservist may temporarily leave his district but in the event of his so doing he shall notify the District Magistrate of his district at the time of his departure. Should such reservist remain away from his district for a period exceeding three months he shall again inform the District Magistrate of his district by letter or messenger of his whereabouts.

Receipt of pay.

2. Under no circumstances shall a reservist receive pay except from the District Magistrate of his own district or from the Military Authorities.

Payment shall only be made direct to the reservist and not by letter.

No. 18 of 1908.

VOLUNTEER RESERVE.

21/1914,—2nd February.

Rules.

Under Section 7.

1. These Rules may be cited as " The Volunteer Reserve Rules, 1914." Short title.

2. Before any Section of the Volunteer Reserve can be formed under " The Volunteer Reserve Ordinance, 1908," the names of not less than ten persons over the age of 16 wishing to form the Section must be submitted for the approval of the Governor, through the Resident of the district within which its headquarters are to be fixed. Formation of Section.

On the approval of the Governor being signified by notice in the *Gazette*, the Section shall be deemed to be duly formed.

3. The Section shall cease to exist if its numerical strength falls below ten registered members. In such case all arms and other articles issued to the members must be returned, unless the members are specially allowed by Government to retain them pending the reorganization of the Section. When Section ceases to exist.

4. A Candidate for membership shall be nominated by two members, such nomination to be considered by the Committee and if approved by them the person proposed for membership to be declared elected subject to the approval of the Governor, and notification of such election when so approved shall be published in the *Gazette*. Method of election of Members.

5. There shall be an Annual General Meeting of each Section to be held in the second week of January of each year, or such other date as the Governor may determine. Annual general meeting.

6. A person can be a registered member of one Section only, but may attend Range practices and Instructional classes with any Section. Restriction on registered members.

7. Subject to modifications sanctioned by the Governor, the Musketry Course shall be conducted in accordance with Army Musketry Regulations, and competitions shall be regulated by the Rules of the National Rifle Association, or as decided by the Committees of local rifle meetings. Musketry and Rifle Competitions.

Capitation
Grants and
Qualification
for efficiency.

8. The conditions of efficiency are as follows :—

(1) Completing the Musketry course set forth in Schedule ' A ' hereto and—

(2) Undergoing 15 hours military instruction at Section headquarters or under special arrangements made by the Staff Officer.

Liability for
failing to
qualify.

9. Any member failing to make himself efficient in any year shall be liable to the funds of his section in the sum of £1. This payment may be remitted at the discretion of the Governor on the recommendation of the Staff Officer.

Supplemental
Grant.

10. The Governor will supplement the Capitation grant by an extra grant of 5/- in respect of each efficient member of the Volunteer Reserve who undergoes an additional 15 hours' military instruction and by extra grants in respect of each efficient member who passes an examination in any of the following subjects :—

> Semaphore Signalling,
> Morse Code Signalling,
> Maxim, Nordenfelt or Field Gun,
> Map-making and Reconnaissance,

at the rate of 5/- for each subject.

Capitation
grants, how
drawn.

11. The annual Capitation and extra grants will be drawn by the Section Secretary on a list certified by the Organizing Secretary. Before these grants can be drawn in any year a statement must be furnished by the Section Secretary to the Organizing Secretary showing how the grants for the previous year have been expended.

Prize Meetings.

12. Prize Meetings shall be held from time to time as arranged by the Committee, who shall fix the amount of entrance fees payable. Such entrance fees shall be paid to the Range Officer on the range before a Member is allowed to compete, and the winner or winners of the competition shall be paid the amount of prize money so won on the day of competing. Provided always that any Member not desirous of entering for a prize competition shall be allowed to fire on the range as if he were a competitor.

No money paid into the funds by Government shall be expended on prizes for competitions without the sanction of the Governor.

Ammunition
allowance.

13. Each Section shall be entitled to draw 200 rounds of ammunition per annum free of charge, on account of each registered member who shall have fired 30 rounds on a range. Each Section may with the permission of the Governor purchase additional ammunition, at cost price, up to 300 rounds per annum or such greater quantity as the Governor may sanction, on account of each registered member as described above.

14. Ammunition must be drawn by Members as required from the Range Officer, who shall duly record the amount drawn and the name of the member drawing it. The ammunition so drawn must be fired on a range under the supervision of the Section Secretary, his Deputy, or a registered member detailed to act as Range Officer. Ammunition unfired must be returned to the Range Officer on the Range. Any member failing to return the ammunition as aforesaid, or obtaining or attempting to obtain more ammunition than the amount to which he is entitled under these rules shall be liable to a fine not exceeding £5.

Ammunition, how drawn on Range.

15. The Section Secretary shall draw rifles, ammunition and equipment from the Organizing Secretary, who shall be reponsible to the Quartermaster of the King's African Rifles for them. Arms and equipment issued by Government will be repaired free of cost unless damaged through neglect or carelessness.

Rifles, ammunition and equipment, how drawn and repaired.

16. Every registered member of a Section shall be provided with a Government rifle on his entering into a bond with or without sureties in the form set forth in Schedule ' B ' hereto in the presence of the Section Secretary or a Magistrate. Only Government rifles shall be used for the Musketry Course and for competitions.

Rifles, issue to members.

17. Rifles and other equipment remain Government property. No rifle issued by the Government for the use of a member of any Section shall be transferred by such member to any other member of the Section without the sanction of the Section Secretary.

Rifles, retention by member.

18. A member in possession of a Government rifle on resignation or on being removed from the Reserve shall return his rifle to the Section Secretary.

Rifles, return on resignation.

19. A rifle or any other article issued by the Government to a member of a Section shall not be removed from the Protectorate, nor may any ammunition purchased or received under these Rules be taken from the Protectorate. Any person contravening this Rule shall be liable to a fine not exceeding £10 and, in addition, to make good the value of the article so removed.

Rifles and Ammunition not to be taken from the Protectorate.

20. The Governor may appoint a Staff Officer who shall arrange all details connected with the military training of the Members and efficiency and other examinations.

Staff Officer.

Organizing
Secretary.

21. The Governor may appoint the Staff Officer to be Organizing Secretary.

Section Secretary's Accounts and Returns.

22. It shall be the duty of the Section Secretary to keep—

(1). Registers of all shooting practices conducted on the Section range, whether forming part of the Musketry Course or Competitions. The registers must give the place and the date, names of the firers, description of the practices, scores obtained, and the amount of ammunition expended on the day and the total per firer since the commencement of the year. Registers must be signed by the superintendent of the practice: the originals retained by the Section Secretary, and a copy forwarded to the Organizing Secretary. A record of the total points made by each member at the different practices will be kept in a separate book.

(2). Equipment accounts showing the distribution of all arms, equipment and stores on charge of the Section with receipts for all issues to members.

(3). Ammunition accounts :—

(*a*). Members' accounts of ammunition used.

(*b*). A general account of all ammunition, (reserve and practice) received from Government, issued to members and balance in hand.

(4). An account of money received from Government and the manner of disbursement.

The above accounts shall be submitted for Government audit at the close of each calendar year, and the cash balance and bank pass book checked.

(5). The Section Secretary shall also furnish the Organizing Secretary with the following quarterly returns :—

(*a*). A nominal roll of all registered members of his Section showing the consecutive number of the Government rifle in the possession of each.

(*b*). An account showing all receipts and issues of ammunition to date and the balance (reserve and practice) remaining on hand.

Inspection.

23. Any Section and the arms, ammunition and equipment issued to it may be inspected at any time by an Officer appointed by the Governor for the purpose.

Schedule A.

MUSKETRY COURSE.

TABLE A.—PRELIMINARY COURSE.

PART I. INSTRUCTIONAL PRACTICES.

No.	Practice	Target	Yards	Rounds	Instructions for Conduct of Practice
1	Grouping	2nd Class Elementary Bull's eye	100	5	Lying with rest.
2	Application	do.	200	5	Do. do.
3	do.	do.	200	5	Kneeling or sitting.
4	do.	1st Class Figure Target	300	5	Lying with rest.
5	do.	do.	300	5	Lying.
6	do.	do.	300	5	Kneeling or sitting.
				30	

PART II. STANDARD TEST.

No.	Practice	Target	Yards	Rounds	Instructions for conduct of Practice	Standard to be reached before passing to next practice
7	Grouping	2nd Class Elementary Bull's eye.	100	5	Lying	All shots in 12-inch ring.
8	Application	do.	200	5	Lying	Score 12 points.
9	do.	1st Class Figure Target.	300	5	Lying	,, ,, ,,
10	do.	do.	300	5	Kneeling or Sitting	,, 10 ,,
				20		

TABLE B.—ANNUAL COURSE.

PART I. INSTRUCTIONAL PRACTICES.

No.	Practice	Target	Yards	Rounds	Instructions for conduct of Practice
1	Grouping	2nd Class Elementary Bull's eye	100	5	Lying with rest.
2	Application	2nd Class Figure Target	300	5	Lying with rest.
3	Rapid	do.	300	5	Lying. 35 seconds allowed.
4	Snapshooting	do.	200	5	Kneeling or sitting. 6 seconds exposure.
5	Application	do.	200	5	Standing.
6	do	1st Class Figure Target	500	5	Lying with rest.
				30	

PART II. STANDARD TEST.

No.	Practice	Target	Yards	Rounds	Instructions for conduct of Practice	Standard to be reached before passing to next practice
7	Grouping	2nd Class Elementary Bull'seye.	100	5	Lying.	All shots in 12-inch ring.
8	Snapshooting	2nd Class Figure Target.	200	5	Lying. Taking cover behind stones or sand bags and firing round them, with side of rifle only rested. Exposure 6 secs. for each shot.	Score 10 points.
9	Rapid	do.	200	8	Lying. 1 minute allowed. Chamber and magazine empty until the command "Rapid Fire."	Score 15 points.
10	Slow	1st Class Figure Target.	500	5	Lying with rest.	Score 8 points.
				23		

The dimensions of the targets shall be as described in Musketry Regulations, Part II, 1910.

Members who have not qualified under previous Nyasaland Volunteer Reserve Rules before 1st January, 1914, or have not served in any branch of the Army, Auxiliary or Colonial Forces, will fire Table 'A' and the passing of its standard tests will qualify them in musketry. After qualifying in Table 'A' in one year, they will be required to fire Table 'B' in subsequent years.

All the instructional practices of Part I. must be fired before commencing Part II, and as the practices in each part are progressing they should be fired in the sequence of the Table as far as circumstances admit.

The standard tests may be repeated as often as necessary to reach the proficiency required.

Schedule B.

BOND TO BE EXECUTED BY A MEMBER BEFORE RECEIVING A GOVERNMENT RIFLE.
Nyasaland Volunteer Reserve.

...................Section.

....

I   a member of the above Section, in consideration of the receipt from His Majesty's Government of a rifle numbered   do hereby acknowledge myself bound to His Majesty's Government in the sum of Twenty Pounds sterling, to be recovered in the Court of any Magistrate, not to damage in any manner or alter or sell or part with the said Rifle to any person except in accordance with the Rules of the Volunteer Reserve: to return the Rifle, Ammunition and other equipment issued to me to the Section Secretary when called upon to do so, and at no time to take or allow the removal of the same beyond the borders of the Protectorate nor to use Government ammunition for other purposes than duties connected with the Volunteer Reserve.

Signed and sealed by the
above named at   } (Signature and
on the   day of   } seal of Member).
in my presence   }
                                            Section Secretary or Magistrate.

Notice.

23/1914,—5th February.

NOTIFIED that His Excellency the Governor has been pleased to approve of the division of the Volunteer Reserve into the following Sections:—

Port Herald	Blantyre
Mlanje ·	Magomero
Mikalongwe	Zomba

Fort Johnston.

Members of any Section must reside within 30 miles of Section Head-quarters.

No. 1 of 1902.

SHIPPING.

118/1913,—31st May.

Notice.

Under Section 3.

Ports of
Registry.

PORTS OF REGISTRY of ships approved by the Governor :—

Port Herald.
Fort Johnston.

No. 7 of 1905.

WEIGHTS AND MEASURES.

Proclamation.

99/1914,—30th May.

Local Standards of Weight.

Under Section 4.

PROCLAIMED THAT—

The following sets of weights and measures shall be the local standards of weight and measurement for the Protectorate, viz :—

(1) A set of weights and measures in the joint custody of the Officer of Customs and of the District Resident (Lower Shire District) at Port Herald :

(2) A set of weights and measures in the joint custody of the Registrar of Deeds and of the District Resident (Blantyre District) at Blantyre :

(3) A set of weights and measures in the joint custody of the Treasurer and of the District Resident (Zomba District) at Zomba.

Notices.

Appointment of Inspectors.

Under Section 12.

THE FOLLOWING officers are appointed Inspectors of Weights and Measures :—   Inspectors.

156/1910,—4th October.

The Comptroller of Customs.

For each District—The District Resident.

For each Sub-District—The Officer in charge of the Sub-district.

100/1914,—30th May.

The Officer of Customs, Port Herald.

No. 8 of 1906.

CUSTOMS.

Notice.

192/1910,—31st December.

Appointment of Customs Officers.

Under Section 7 (d).

IN PURSUANCE of the powers in him vested by Section 7 (d) of the above Ordinance, His Excellency the Acting Governor doth Hereby appoint the District Residents and Assistant Residents or such other Officers as may from time to time perform the duties of their office, of the districts set forth in Schedule I hereto to be Customs Officers in the district specified.

FURTHER IN PURSUANCE of the power in him by the said section vested His Excellency doth HEREBY appoint the Postmasters, who may from time to time be stationed in the places or districts set forth in Schedule II hereto, or such other Officers as may from time to time perform the duties of such Postmasters to be Customs Officers in such places or districts.

SCHEDULE I.

Lower Shire	Zomba	South Nyasa	West Nyasa
Ruo	Chikala	Dedza	Mombera
West Shire	Blantyre	Lilongwe	North Nyasa.
Mlanje	Upper Shire	Marimba	

SCHEDULE II.

Lower Shire	Blantyre	South Nyasa	Ruo	Zomba.

202/1911,—30th November.

To be a Customs Officer for the whole Protectorate :—The Superintendent of Native Affairs.

34/1914,—14th February.

To be a Customs Officer in the South Nyasa District :—The Clerk and Storekeeper, Marine Transport Department.

Proclamations.

79/1909,—28th June.

Prohibition of Import of Cotton Seed, other than Cotton Seed grown in Egypt.

Under Section 21 (f).

WHEREAS owing to the prevalence of a cotton pest known as the Cotton Weevil or Boll-Weevil (*Anthonomus Grandis*), it has been made to appear to me that the importation of cotton seed, except cotton seed grown in Egypt and such other cotton seed as may be imported for purposes of scientific research or experiment by the Director of Agriculture should be prohibited :

NOW THEREFORE in exercise of the powers conferred on me in that behalf by Section 21 (*f*) of the above Ordinance, I DO HEREBY declare and proclaim that the importation of cotton seed except cotton seed grown in Egypt is prohibited from the date of publication hereof; save and except such seed as may be imported for purposes of experiment by the Director of Agriculture, which must be packed in double linen bags, sent through the post and addressed to the Director of Agriculture, Zomba.

131/1909,—8th October.

Restriction on Import of Potatoes.

Under Section 21 (f).

WHEREAS BY PROCLAMATION dated the first day of April one thousand nine hundred and nine in exercise of the powers conferred by Section 21 (*f*) of the above Ordinance, and owing to the prevalence in the United Kingdom and elsewhere of the disease in potatoes known as *Chryso-phlyctis Endobiotica* (black scab) I did declare and proclaim that the importation of potatoes was prohibited from the date of publication thereof :

AND WHEREAS it has now been made to appear to me that the total prohibition of importation of potatoes is no longer necessary but that they may be safely imported if certain precautionary measures be taken :

NOW THEREFORE in exercise of the powers conferred on me in that behalf by Section 21 (*f*) of the above Ordinance, I DO HEREBY declare and proclaim that from the date of publication hereof the importation of potatoes is permitted but only under the following conditions, viz.,—that each consignment be accompanied by a certificate from the consignor that the potatoes were grown in a particular locality, and by a further certificate from the Board of Fisheries and Agriculture in the case of potatoes imported from the United Kingdom, that *Chryso-phlyctis Endobiotica* has not been declare to exist in that locality, and in the case of potatoes imported from other countries or colonies by a similar certificate from the equivalent authority in the country or colony of export.

3/1913,—31st January.

Prohibition of Import of Naval or Military Uniforms.

Under Section 21 (f).

WHEREAS it has been made to appear to me expedient that the importation of the uniform of His Majesty's Naval or Military Forces or any dress having the appearance or bearing any of the regimental or other distinctive marks of any such uniform for purposes of sale to persons not serving in His Majesty's Naval or Military Forces should be prohibited :

NOW THEREFORE by virtue of the powers in me as Acting Governor-in-Council vested I DO HEREBY declare and proclaim that the importation of any uniform of His Majesty's Naval or Military Forces or any dress having the appearance or bearing any of the regimental or other distinctive marks of any such uniform for purposes of sale to persons not serving in His Majesty's Naval or Military Forces shall be and is HEREBY prohibited.

40/1913,—28th February.

Prohibition of Re-Export of Opium.

Under Section 61.

WHEREAS it has been made to appear to me expedient that the re-export of opium imported into the Protectorate for use or sale under "The Sale of Drugs and Poisons Ordinance, 1912," should be prohibited :

NOW THEREFORE by virtue of the powers in me as Acting Governor-in-Council vested I DO HEREBY proclaim and declare that the re-export of opium as aforesaid shall be and is HEREBY prohibited.

Notice.

207/1913,—30th August.

Interpretation of Port of Shipment.

IT IS HEREBY NOTIFIED for general information that the term Port of Shipment in Section 1 of Schedule I to The Customs Ordinance, 1906, is taken to mean the place at which goods are finally shipped for direct conveyance to the Nyasaland Protectorate, irrespective of the Country of Origin of such goods.

109/1910,—27th July.

Rules.

I. Goods in Transit.

1. Goods in transit shall be deemed to be goods in transit outwards or inwards according to their place of entry or exit.

Entry and exit.

2. A bond or other satisfactory security may be accepted by the Comptroller of Customs for the full import duty and other charges on goods declared on entry to be in transit, such bond or security to remain in force until the goods are certified to have left the Protectorate, but in all cases such certificate must be produced to the Comptroller of Customs within six calendar months from the date of first entry, otherwise the bond or security will be enforceable.

Bonds and other securities for payment of dues.

When the security tendered is not considered satisfactory by the Comptroller or other Officer of Customs he may, at his discretion, demand payment of the full import duties and other charges, which payment shall be refunded on the goods being certified to have left the Protectorate within six calendar months as aforesaid.

3. In respect of all goods in transit the importer or his agent shall present to the Customs Officer at the port or station of entry a Transit Warrant in triplicate giving a full description of the goods and their weight and value and shall pay any charges due thereon. The original copy, when examined and certified by the Officer, shall be handed back to the importer or agent to accompany the goods, the duplicate copy shall be sent by post to the port or station of exit and the triplicate shall be retained by the Officer.

Transit Warrants.

4. Packages declared to be in transit or cleared in transit from a bonded warehouse may be wired and sealed at the discretion of the Officers of Customs.

Sealing of packages.

5. On the arrival of goods at the port or station of exit the importer or his agent shall present the goods for inspection together with the original copy of the Warrant as aforesaid to the Officer of Customs who shall endorse the Warrant with the number and description of the packages produced and passed out of the Protectorate. The Warrant, duly endorsed, shall be the certificate of export required under Rule 2. Goods subject to export duty will be treated as exports from the Protectorate unless accompanied by the Transit Warrant.

Procedure at station of exit.

All packages must be produced in the same condition as originally specified on the Warrant with wires and seals intact, where such packages have been wired and sealed.

Breaking bulk, etc.

6. The importer or his agent shall be permitted if he so desires to break bulk at the port or station of entry, or to repack goods, before such goods have been described on the Transit Warrant.

II. Goods in Bond.

Bonded Warehouse.

7. The Governor may approve of buildings to be used as bonded warehouses and on satisfactory bond or other security being furnished, may permit goods on which duty has not been paid to be deposited in such warehouses and cleared either for home consumption or in transit. All bonded warehouses shall be under the supervision of an Officer of Customs or other Officer appointed by the Governor for the purpose.

Locks and keys.

8. Bonded warehouses shall be securely locked with two locks one of which shall be the property of the Customs and the key thereof shall remain in the possession of the Officer having charge of the warehouse; the key of the other lock shall remain in the possession of the proprietor of the warehouse or his agent.

Duration of Bond.

9. When goods are entered at any Customs station for warehousing they shall be removed under bond to their destination without delay. Such bond shall remain in force until advice is received by the Comptroller of Customs that the goods have been cleared for home consumption or in transit under a fresh bond. If such advice is not received within twelve months from the date of first entry the bond shall be enforced. When goods are cleared from a bonded warehouse in transit the bond becomes enforceable unless proof is received that they have left the Protectorate within six months from the date of clearance, but in no case shall the period exceed twelve months from the date of first entry.

Notice of removal of goods.

10. When it is intended to clear goods from bond the Officer having charge of the warehouse shall be entitled to demand two days' notice of such intention and all duties and other charges shall be paid prior to the carrying into effect of such intention.

Removal by rail of goods under bond.

11. The Comptroller of Customs may permit goods on which duty has not been paid to be removed by rail from Port Herald or other place of entry below Port Herald that may be in future determined, to Blantyre, in closed trucks duly approved and sealed by an Officer of Customs, and under bond as aforesaid. On the goods being delivered to an Officer of Customs in Blantyre at the place appointed by the Comptroller of Customs for the unlading and examination of such goods the bond shall be discharged and the goods shall be subject to the Customs laws governing goods landed at a port of entry.

12. No claim for rebate on account of breakages or shortages shall be entertained after the goods have been removed from a port or station of entry under bond, unless removed in a sealed railway truck as provided for in the preceding Rule.

Claims for rebate.

13. In all other respects bonded goods shall be subject to the existing or any future Customs laws in force in the Protectorate and all Rules and Regulations made thereunder.

Bonded goods subject to ordinary law.

14. The open Customs shed at Port Herald shall be used to facilitate the examination, landing or shipping of cargo, and goods shall not be stored in the shed for a longer period than three days without the consent of the Comptroller of Customs. Any Officer of Customs may, when such consent has been given and after the expiration of three days, order the removal of goods and if such order is not complied with rent may be charged for the goods at the same rate as that charged for goods deposited in the King's Warehouse.

Customs shed at Port Herald.

III. DISTILLED LIQUORS.

15. (a). The duty on whisky, brandy, rum and gin shall be calculated on the proof strength as shown by Sikes' Hydrometer at as low a temperature as possible. When such spirits are mixed with colouring, sweetening or other matter in solution tending to conceal the actual strength, an addition of 5 per cent shall be made to the apparent strength as shown by the Hydrometer in lieu of the test for obscuration.

Calculation of duty on Liquors.

(b). The strength of all liqueurs and other spirits so mixed or sweetened that they cannot be tested with the Sikes' Hydrometer shall be assumed to be proof strength and duty shall be charged on the proof gallon accordingly: Provided that Imperial Customs Certificates as to strength may be accepted.

(c). Six reputed quart bottles or twelve reputed pints shall be assumed to contain one liquid gallon.

IV. SHIPPING.

16. Manifests of cargo or ships' reports shall not be required for vessels proceeding from Chiromo to Katungas or other port on the Shire River above Chiromo. For vessels returning from such port to Chiromo no clearance shall be necessary but a detailed list of passengers and cargo shall be prepared by the Master of the vessel or his agent and handed in to the Customs House at Chiromo on arrival. Vessels leaving Chiromo or Port Herald for ports outside the Protectorate must deposit at the Custom House two copies of the manifest or ship's report before a clearance is obtained.

Internal navigation.

Customs examination at Port Herald.

17. The Masters of all vessels passing Port Herald or other place of entry below Port Herald that may in future be determined shall bring-to there and have their manifests, ships' reports and other papers relating to the cargo *visé* by an Officer of Customs.

Regulation of shipping.

18. The Officers of Customs shall have power to regulate the shipping in any port or harbour and may assign berths or order the removal of any vessel the cargo of which has been discharged or shipped to make room for another or any vessel that may be obstructing the fair-way.

V. Miscellaneous.

Hours of attendance of Customs Officers.

19. The following hours of attendance of Customs Officers are hereby prescribed—On Mondays, Tuesdays, Wednesdays, Thursdays and Fridays from 8 a.m. to 11 a.m. and from 1 p.m. to 4 p.m.; Saturdays, 8 a.m. to 12 noon.

Charges for attendance of Customs Officers at other times.

20. There shall be charged in respect of attendance of Customs Officers at hours other than those prescribed, and on Sundays and public holidays, for attendance at any hour, the following fees :—

(1). Customs charge, £1 per hour or fraction thereof with a maximum of £5 per diem.

(2). Fees personal to each Customs Officer engaged :—5/- per hour or fraction thereof with a maximum of £1 5s. per diem.

Extraordinary attendances.

21. The Comptroller of Customs may at his discretion direct the attendance at any hour of Customs Officers without remuneration in the case of ships arriving or departing carrying His Majesty's mails, or for such other duty as the exigencies of the public service may require.

Attendance of Customs Officers on public holidays.

22. The following are prescribed as public holidays on which days there will be no attendance of Customs Officers except by direction of the Comptroller of Customs :—Good Friday, Easter Monday, Empire Day, King's Birthday, Christmas Day and Boxing Day.

Offences.

23. Any person committing an offence against any of the provisions of these Rules shall be liable on conviction to a fine not exceeding fifty pounds and in addition to the forfeiture of any goods in respect of which such offence may have been committed.

No. 15 of 1911.

LAND TAX.

12/1912,—31st January.

Forms.

Under Section 7 (1).

Directed by the Governor—

(1). That the Return (Form 1) herein specified shall in the case of every owner or occupier resident in the Protectorate be supplied to the Land Tax Office, Treasury, Zomba, on the 1st. day of April, 1912.

.(2). That the said Return shall in the case of every owner or occupier absent from the Protectorate be supplied as aforesaid on or before the 1st day of June, 1912.

(3). That the Return (Form 2) herein specified shall be supplied by every owner or occupier to the Land Tax Office, Treasury, Zomba, in respect of every transfer or lease of land taking place after the 1st day of April, 1912; and such Return shall be rendered within one month of the date of every such transfer or lease.

(4). Blank forms will be sent to every registered owner from the Land Tax Office, Treasury, Zomba, or may be had on application to that office or to a District Resident.

FORM 1.
Land Tax Register.
Folio No.

DECLARATION.

To be rendered to the Land Tax Office, Treasury, Zomba, on the 1st day of April, 1912, by owners, or occupiers of estates.

(A separate declaration is required for each estate).

---

1. Name of Estate.
2. Name of Owner, or Occupier, in full.
3. Interest (i.e., fee simple, leasehold, or other).
4. Registered number in the Registry of Deeds.
5. If leasehold, Name of Lessor.
6. Number of acres.
7. District in which situate.

8.   Nearest Government Station.

9.   Address in full of Owner, or Occupier.

10.   Name of Local Representative in full (in case of absentee landlord).

11.   Address of Local Representative in full.

12.·   Amount of Land Tax payable   acres @ ½d. per acre. **£**
    (Minimum rate 1/- per annum).

I HEREBY CERTIFY that to the best of my knowledge and belief the above is a true statement.

Signature of Owner, Occupier or Representative

Profession

Place

Date

When the Estate or any interest therein has been disposed of, the following Schedule shall be filled in and certified.

Number of acres originally transferred, or leased by Government, or by registered owner.	Number of acres since transferred or leased.	Name of transferee or lessee.	Deed Reg. No. (if any).	Date of registration (if registered)

Total.

Balance   acres declared on the reverse side for assessment.

I HEREBY CERTIFY that to the best of my knowledge and belief the above is a true statement.

Name

Date

FORM 2.

Land Tax Register.

Folio No.   Registration No.

NOTIFICATION to be rendered to the Land Tax Office, Treasury Zomba, of any land transfers or leases included in the Declaration rendered under terms of the Ordinance (Form 1).

All owners or occupiers of estates are required to render this notice in respect of any transactions taking place after 1st April, 1912.

---

1. Name of Estate.
2. Name of Owner or Occupier.
3. Registration number of Original Deed.
4. Acreage of Estate originally declared for assessment.
5. Acreage now transferred.
6. Name of Transferee or Lessee.
7. Address in full.
8. Registration number of New Deed of Transfer.
9. Acreage of the above estate remaining for re-assessment.

I HEREBY CERTIFY that to the best of my knowledge and belief the above is a true statement.

Signature of Transferor or Representative

Profession

Place

Date

Signature of Transferee or Representative

Profession

Place

Date

Proclamations.

56/1912,—25th April.

Exempted Lands.

European and Asiatic Cemeteries.

Under Section 8.

By the Governor in Council—

European and Asiatic Cemeteries.

WHEREAS it has been made to appear to me both just and expedient that certain lands in use as cemeteries and burial grounds for Europeans and Asiatics should be exempt from the provisions of the above Ordinance :

NOW THEREFORE in virtue of tho powers vested in me by section 8 I DO HEREBY declare and proclaim that all plots of land which have been reserved for the exclusive purpose of burial of Europeans and Asiatics and are in use as cemeteries and have been approved by me as such, shall be exempt from the provisions of the said Ordinance.

42/1913,—28th February.

Lands of the Shire Highlands Railway (Nyasaland), Ltd.

Shire Highlands Railway Co. permanent way, etc.

WHEREAS it has been made to appear to me both just and expedient that certain lands in the occupation of The Shire Highlands Railway (Nyasaland) Limited (hereinafter called the Company) and actually used by the said Company for permanent way, yards, sheds and buildings for the purposes of traffic only, should be exempt from the provisions of the said Ordinance :

NOW THEREFORE by virtue of the powers in me as Acting Governor in Council vested as aforesaid I DO HEREBY proclaim and declare that lands in the occupation of and actually used by the said Company for permanent way, yards, sheds and buildings for the purposes of traffic only shall be and are HEREBY exempted from the provisions of the said Ordinance.

No. 10 of 1911.

INTOXICATING LIQUOR.

174/1913,—31st July.

Rules.

Sale of Native Beer, etc.

Under Section 1.

1. Where it has been proved to the satisfaction of a District Resident that the sale of native beer or other native intoxicating liquor or the manufacture thereof for sale in any place in his district is attended or is likely to be attended with abuses he may, subject to the approval of the Governor, prohibit such sale or manufacture in such place.

Prohibition of sale of native intoxicating liquor.

2. Any person knowingly and wilfully selling native beer or other native intoxicating liquor or engaging in the manufacture thereof for sale in a prohibited place shall be deemed to have committed an offence and all native beer or other native intoxicating liquor and all vessels and their contents employed in connexion with such illegal sale or manufacture shall be liable to be forfeited.

Sale of native intoxicating liquor in prohibited place.

No. 9 of 1906.

REGISTRATION OF MEDICAL PRACTITIONERS.

N o t i c e .   *31st October, 1906.*

Under Section 2.

THE FOLLOWING Officer is appointed to the Medical Council by Order of the Governor :—

The Government Medical Officer for the time being resident in Zomba.

No. 20 of 1912.

SALE OF DRUGS AND POISONS.

Proclamation.

41/1913,—28th February.

Prohibition of Growing or Cultivating Opium Poppy.

Under Section 18.

WHEREAS it has been made to appear to me that the growing or cultivating of the opium poppy (*Papaver somniferum*) should in the public interest be prohibited :

NOW THEREFORE by virtue of the powers in me as Acting Governor-in-Council vested I DO HEREBY proclaim and declare that the growing or cultivating of the opium poppy (*Papaver somniferum*) shall be and is HEREBY prohibited.

No. 4 of 1903.

EPIDEMIC AND CONTAGIOUS DISEASES.

Rules.

117/1911,—21st July.

Sleeping Sickness.

I. GENERAL.

Under Section 2.

Definition.
1. The following words and expressions shall, unless the context otherwise requires, have the meanings hereby assigned to them.

"District" means a District specified in Schedule I.

"Medical Officer" means the Government Medical Officer or Officers or other Medical Practitioners duly authorized to act by the Governor.

"Medically examined" means examined by a Medical Officer as herein defined.

Infected Areas.
2. For the purposes of these Rules the areas specified in Schedule II are declared to be areas infected with "Sleeping Sickness," and hereinafter referred to as "infected areas."

Stations of Entry.
3. In each District Stations of Entry shall be established at the places specified in Schedule III, and no person shall enter or leave a District save by one of such Stations.

Procedure on entering District.
4. (1). Every person seeking to enter a District shall be detained at a Station of Entry, and shall be medically examined.

(2). Every person who upon examination as aforesaid is certified as free from infection from human trypanosomiasis shall be given a Special Pass by the Local Authority or Medical Officer, and shall forthwith be permitted to enter the District.

(3). Every person who upon examination as aforesaid is certified as infected with human trypanosomiasis shall be detained at such place and for such period as the Governor may from time to time decide.

Proviso in the case of Europeans entering a District.
(4). Provided always that in the case of a European seeking entry into a District he shall not be liable to examination as aforesaid, unless he fails to satisfy the Local

Authority or Medical Officer that he has not come from an infected area. The Local Authority may require evidence on oath as to the locality whence such person has come, the route travelled and such other particulars as are deemed fit. Upon failure to satisfy the Local Authority as aforesaid he shall be liable to be detained and medically examined. Every European found upon medical examination to be infected with human trypanosomiasis shall be refused entry, and shall forthwith be required to leave the limits of the Protectorate under Section 2 (4) of "The Immigration Restriction Ordinance, 1905." Every such case shall be immediately reported to the Governor.

5. A European or Asiatic seeking entry into a District shall furnish the Local Authority or Medical Officer at the Station of Entry at which he presents himself with a list of his employés accompanying him. Such employés shall be dealt with as in Rule 4 provided. *Employés accompanying Europeans or Asiatics.*

6. All natives and Asiatics desiring to leave the District shall be required to provide themselves with a Pass signed by the Local Authority and they shall be required to state their destination and such other details as may from time to time be required. Provided that this Rule shall not be deemed to apply to the West Nyasa and Mombera Districts notwithstanding anything contained in the Schedules hereto. *Issue of Pass.*

7. The Local Authority as aforesaid may refuse at his discretion to issue such Pass. *Refusal of Pass.*

8. Natives or Asiatics employed by trading firms or individuals within the District for the transport of goods shall not be permitted to carry such goods beyond the limits of the Protectorate. *Transport of goods.*

9. Asiatics and Natives in transit through a District shall, after having passed through a Station of Entry, be required to report themselves to the District Resident and they must obtain a permit to leave the District; and they shall be required to furnish the District Resident with their place of destination and such other details as may be required from them; and they shall travel through the District only by such routes as the District Resident shall specify. *Asiatics and Natives in transit to report themselves.*

10. At each Station of Entry a Pass Register shall be kept in which shall be entered the description and destination and such other details as may be from time to time specified concerning all persons passing through or presenting themselves at Stations of Entry. The form of such register shall be as laid down in Schedule IV. *Pass Register.*

11. The Local Authority or Medical Officer may detain and examine or order the examination for human trypano- *Detention of suspected persons.*

somiasis of any person or persons suspected of having come from an infected area or of being infected by human trypanosomiasis.

Local Authority may search any district.

12. Any Medical Officer for the purpose of these Rules may, notwithstanding anything contained in the Rules or the Schedules thereto enter any house, village, compound or inclosure in any district and examine every inmate thereof or any person found therein : Provided that on or before entering any district he shall without delay notify the District Resident. Any inmate or person wilfully absenting himself from such examination or obstructing such entry or examination or assisting other persons to escape shall be considered as having acted in contravention of these Rules.

Removal of infected persons.

13. Any person found infected with human trypanosomiasis shall be removed by order of the Local Authority or Medical Officer to such segregation settlement, hospital or other place as may from time to time be determined upon.

Removal of inhabitants from one area to another by District Resident.

14. The District Resident shall have power to order the removal of the inhabitants of any hut, settlement or village who may be declared by a Medical Officer to be infected with human trypanosomiasis, or to be situated within the " Fly " range, or in proximity thereto, to such place or places as may may be selected, and they shall so remove forthwith.

Disobedience of District Resident's order.

15. In case of disobedience to such an order the District Resident may, after due warning, destroy such hut, settlement or village and remove the inhabitants thereof in custody.

Responsibility of Headmen and owners of huts.

16. Headmen of villages and owners of huts shall be held responsible that natives coming from outside the Protectorate from an infected area do not remain in the vicinity of such villages or huts unless in possession of a permit certifying that they are free from infection. Headmen of villages shall report the arrival of all such natives without delay to the nearest District Resident.

Rule applicable to Dowa Subdistrict only.

17. No person shall be allowed to enter or leave the Dowa *Sub-District of the Lilongwe District specified in Schedule I hereto until such time as a census and complete medical examination of the district have been carried out, with the following exceptions :—

(1). Natives returning to their homes, who will be permitted to enter only by the Dowa or Mvera Stations of Entry specified in Schedule III.

(2). Government Officers on duty and their native employés.

---

* Now Dowa District.

(3). Police, and persons employed on Sleeping Sickness duty, who shall be provided with Passes to enter and leave the district by the District Resident or by an Officer engaged on Sleeping Sickness duty.

(4). Persons employed on vessels plying on the Lake may land at Domira Bay for the purpose of loading firewood and for transmission of telegrams but for no other purpose. Masters in charge of vessels are held responsible for the due observance of this Rule.

II. RULES FOR LAKE TRAFFIC.

18. The master shall on arrival at the ports or roadsteads of Fort Johnston and Karonga furnish the Local Authority with a certificate list of all persons on board, both passengers and crew, which list shall specify the place from which they originally started, destination, and such other details as may from time to time be required.

Duty of master to furnish list of persons on board at Fort Johnston and Karonga.

19. (1). Any person travelling on a ship on Lake Nyasa who is suspected by the master of being infected with human trypanosomiasis may be detained at any port intermediate between Karonga and Fort Johnston by order of the District Resident or any person duly authorized by the Governor. Every person so detained shall be dealt with in the manner provided in Rule 4 or as near thereto as may be.

Case of Sleeping Sickness suspected by master.

(2). Every master shall, when called upon so to do at any port, produce for the inspection of the District Resident or any person duly authorized by the Governor the list of all persons on board prescribed in Rule 18.

List of persons on board may be required at any port.

20. In the event of any person travelling on a ship on Lake Nyasa being found infected with human trypanosomiasis and for that reason refused entry into the Protectorate, the master shall be required to carry such infected person back to the port (other than a British port) at which he embarked.

Infected persons to be carried back to port of embarkation.

21. No dhow or canoe navigated by Asiatics or natives shall ply in the waters adjoining the District or Districts specified in Schedule I, unless it has been registered by and a permit to ply obtained from the District Resident. Such permit shall state the period during which and the purpose for which it is valid, together with such other details as may be required, and the owner of any dhow or canoe plying without having been registered as aforesaid shall be liable to the penalties provided for a breach of these Rules.

Registration of dhows and canoes.

22. A dhow or canoe registered under the preceding Rule shall have its registration number on some conspicuous part thereof in numerals of not less than six inches in length.

Registration Number to be painted on dhows and canoes.

Stations of entry for dhows or canoes trading with German territory.

23. All dhows or canoes navigated by Asiatics or natives trading with German territory shall land their passengers at the following Stations of Entry only, viz :—Songwe, Karonga.

Dhows and canoes plying to foreign ports.

24. Owners of dhows or canoes wishing to ply to foreign ports shall be required to obtain from the District Resident an authorization in writing to do so.

III.—GENERAL POWERS AND PENALTIES.

Powers of every District Resident and local authority.

25. The Resident of any District not specified in Schedule I or the Medical Officer may, on having reason to believe that any person within any such District is infected with human trypanosomia‹is, order such person to be detained and medically examined, and in such case shall follow the procedure laid down in Rule 4 hereof as near as may be thereto.

Penalty.

26. Any person whether European, Asiatic or Native, who

(1). wilfully violates any of the above Rules or any amendments thereof ; or

(2). wilfully obstructs any person acting under the authority or in the execution of these Rules or any amendments thereof ;

shall be liable on conviction to a fine not exceeding £100, or to imprisonment with or without hard labour for a term not exceeding one year, or to both fine and imprisonment as in "The Epidemic and Contagious Diseases (Amendment) Ordinance, 1908, provided.

Schedule I.

DISTRICTS TO WHICH RULES SHALL BE APPLICABLE.

1. North Nyasa.

† 2. That portion of the Dowa Sub-District * of the Lilongwe District which is bounded as follows :—

Commencing at a point on the western shore of Lake Nyasa about 1¼ miles north of the Lintipe River at Mtonda's village where the old hoed road which divides the villages of Chief Pemba from those of Chief Maganga reaches the Lake shore, the boundary shall be carried along the said road in a north-westerly direction for a distance of about 7 miles until it reaches th left bank of the Lintipe river : thence it shall be carried along the left bank

† Amended by Notice of 30th December, 1911. (No. 213/1911).
* Now Dowa District.

of the Lintipe river, up stream, to a point some 9½ miles above its confluence with the Lilongwe river; thence it shall be carried in a north north-westerly direction to a point some 3 miles east of the Mvera Mission; thence it shall be carried in a straight line with Mchisi mountain as far as the right bank of Chirua stream; thence it shall be carried along the right bank of Chirua stream, down stream, to its mouth on the western shore of Lake Nyasa; thence it shall be carried along the western shore of Lake Nyasa, in a southerly direction, to the point of commencement.

3. West Nyasa.
4. Mombera.

Schedule II.

INFECTED AREAS.

The Congo Free State.
German East Africa.
The Infected Areas of Northern Rhodesia, Portuguese East Africa (east of and in the vicinity of Lake Nyasa).

Schedule III.

PLACES WHICH SHALL BE STATIONS OF ENTRY WITHIN THE MEANING OF THESE RULES.

NORTH NYASA DISTRICT :—
  (1). At the mouth of the Songwe river.
  (2). Fort Hill.
  (3). Karonga.
  (4). Livingstonia.

LILONGWE DISTRICT (Dowa Sub-District).*
  (1). Dowa.
  (2). Mvera.

WEST NYASA DISTRICT.
  (1). Nkata.
  (2). Chintechi.

* Now Dowa District.

Schedule IV

(White Paper.)   PASS I.

No...... . (Consecutive).

PERMIT TO LEAVE DISTRICT.

....Father,...... . ...Chief,

....Village,... ... ...Headman,

.... .has permission to leave the... ....

District for the purpose of proceeding to......... ....

He is to proceed by... ....road and to report himself at.........Station

of Entry. He $\frac{\text{has}}{\text{has not}}$ been medically examined for trypanosomiasis.

........................District Resident

Left thumb mark.   Date................................

(Red Paper.)   PASS II.

ENTRY PASS.

No......... ..(Consecutive).

.............................Father,...........................Chief,

.... Village,...........................Tribe,

....Race,... ....

has been medically examined for trypanosomiasis and has been found free from infection. He is hereby permitted to enter... ... .District

He states he intends to reside at ....Chief....... ... ...

....

Left thumb mark.   Medical Officer or other Officer
                            in charge of Entry Station

Date...... ... .

Schedule V.

DHOW AND CANOE PERMIT.

No............   ....District.

....Station of Entry.

This is certify that... ... .of

................has registered one $\frac{\text{Canoe}}{\text{Dhow}}$ (Registered Number).........and is

hereby permitted, subject to the Laws and Rules now and hereafter in force, to ply on Lake Nyasa, for a period of...... ....months from the date of this Permit, for the purpose of... ....

Date.................   ....Resident.

The Rules affecting the plying of vessels on Lake Nyasa have been explained to the above owner.

Additional Rules.

141/1912,—22nd August.

Under Section 2.

1. A person infected with human trypanosomiasis (hereinafter called a "patient") shall not travel in the Protectorate without the Governor's permission.

Restriction of travelling of sleeping sickness patient.

2. On such permission being obtained the Medical Officer in charge of the patient or other person appointed for the purpose by the Principal Medical Officer shall notify in writing the Transport Agent or other person by whom it is intended that the patient's journey shall be conducted, of the intention of such person to travel and of the place of departure and the destination of such patient.

Notification to transport agent of travelling of sleeping sickness patient.

3. No Transport Agent or other person shall conduct the journey of any patient until he shall have received such notice.

4. Every person conducting the journey of a patient shall be responsible that the patient is accompanied by an attendant. The person conducting the journey and the attendant shall be severally responsible that the patient is properly protected against biting flies either by an efficient mosquito net or by a head net, leather gloves and thick clothing.

Precautions to be taken.

Additional Rules.

233/1913,—31st October.

Under Section 2.

1. These Rules may be cited as The Sleeping Sickness Rules, 1913.

2. If the Governor shall by notice in the Gazette declare that any District not scheduled in the Rules made under the above Ordinance and published in the Gazette of 31st July, 1911, is a District infected with Sleeping Sickness the following of the said Rules shall automatically apply in any District so notified, namely :—

Rules 11, 12, 13, 14, 15, 16, and 26.

Notice.

234/1913,—31st October.

Under Section 2.

The undermentioned Districts declared to be Districts infected with Sleeping Sickness within the meaning of the above Rules :—

The Marimba District.
The Dedza District.
The South Nyasa District.
The Upper Shire District.

207/1912,—30th November.

Venereal Diseases.

Under Section 2.

1. In Townships and other European settlements and on plantations, Europeans, Asiatics and Natives shall notify the District Resident of any natives whom they have reason to believe to be suffering from venereal disease.

2. Principal and Village Headmen and Chiefs of villages shall notify the District Resident of any cases of venereal disease found to exist in their villages.

3. All cases so notified to the District Resident shall be notified by him to the District Medical Officer, and as far as possible all such cases shall be treated in Government Hospitals and Dispensaries, either as in-patients or out-patients.

No. 2 of 1908.

INFECTIOUS DISEASE (NOTIFICATION).

Rule.

103/1908,—7th July.

Payment to Medical Practitioners for Certificates.

Under Section 5.

There shall be paid to every duly registered Medical Practitioner not being a Government Medical Officer, for each certificate sent by him in accordance with the provisions of the Ordinance, a fee of two shillings and six-pence if the case occurs in his private practice and of one shilling if the case occurs in his practice as Medical Officer of any hospital or other institution not being a Government hospital or institution or not being a hospital or institution to which the Government makes any contribution : Provided that whenever a Medical Practitioner attends on or is called in to visit at one and the same time more than six patients suffering from a similar infectious disease to which the Ordinance applies he shall include their names in the same certificate and shall be paid at the rate of sixpence for every ten names contained in the certificate exclusive of the first six names for which he shall be paid as hereinbefore provided.

Fee on
Certificates.

No. 7 of 1903.

DISEASES OF ANIMALS.

Proclamations.

104/1909,—5th August.

Removal of Cattle from South Nyasa District.

Under Section 9.

WHEREAS under the provisions of Section 9 of the above Ordinance, the Governor; may at any time by Proclamation in the Gazette declare any place in the Protectorate to be a place infected with disease within the meaning of the above Ordinance; and may further for the purpose of preventing such disease prohibit the removal of cattle from one district to another :

NOW THEREFORE in virtue of the power vested in me as aforesaid I DO HEREBY declare and proclaim from the date of publication hereof in the Gazette, the SOUTH NYASA DISTRICT of this Protectorate to be a place infected with disease within the meaning of above Ordinance.

AND I DO FURTHER declare and proclaim that from and after the said date of publication all removal of cattle out of or into the said SOUTH NYASA DISTRICT is hereby prohibited.

140/1910,—16th September.

Removal of Cattle from South Nyasa District to Zomba District.

Under Section 9.

WHEREAS by Proclamation made under the provisions of Section 9 of the above Ordinance, on 5th August, 1909, and published in the Gazette of 31st August, 1909, the Governor did declare and proclaim all removal of cattle out of or into the South Nyasa District to be prohibited :

AND WHEREAS it has been made to appear to me that it is expedient to allow the said removal of cattle from the South Nyasa District under certain restrictions :

NOW THEREFORE in virtue of the powers in me to that end vested I DO HEREBY declare and proclaim from the date of publication hereof in the Gazette, that cattle may be removed from the said South Nyasa District into the Zomba District subject to the following conditions being observed :—

(1). That all such cattle be embarked at Fort Johnston after inspection by a Veterinary or Medical Officer of the Protectorate, and on it being certified by him that they are free of all infectious disease :

(2). That the said cattle be conveyed in a fly-proof barge to Liwonde, or as near thereto as the said barge can be brought:

(3). That they be disembarked after and within one hour of sundown:

(4). That they be immediately driven without halting to a point on the Liwonde-Zomba road not less than ten miles from Liwonde:

(5). That they be quarantined for twenty-five days thereafter at a place to be selected by the Veterinary Officer of the Protectorate in the vicinity of the Domasi Mission:

(6). That they be inspected by the said Veterinary Officer before proceeding to their destination, and that any animal which may show signs of disease may be destroyed by his orders without compensation.

38/1912,—14th March.

Removal of Cattle from Mombera District and Movement of Cattle within District.

Under Section 9.

WHEREAS under the provisions of Section 9 of the above Ordinance, the Governor in Council may at any time by Proclamation in the Gazette declare any place in the Protectorate to be a place infected with disease within the meaning of the aforesaid Ordinance; and may further for the purpose of preventing such disease prohibit the removal of cattle from one district to another:

AND WHEREAS the Governor in Council may further in exercise of the powers conferred on him as aforesaid prescribe by Rules all necessary steps to suppress the said disease or to prevent the further spread of the said disease and may appoint all necessary officers to carry the same into effect:

NOW THEREFORE by virtue of the powers in me as Governor in Council vested as aforesaid I DO HEREBY declare and proclaim, from the date of publication hereof in the Gazette, the MOMBERA DISTRICT of this Protectorate to be a place infected with disease within the meaning of the above Ordinance.

AND I DO FURTHER declare and proclaim that from and after the said date of publication all removal of cattle out of or into the said Mombera District shall be and is HEREBY prohibited and the movement of cattle from any one place to any other place within the said District shall be subject to the following Rules:—

(1). No person shall remove cattle from any one place to any other place within the aforesaid District without the permission of the Government Veterinary Officer, or, in his absence, the District Resident first had and obtained.

(2). Such permission may be granted subject to such restrictions as the Government Veterinary Officer or in his absence the District Resident may deem fit to impose.

Diseases of Animals.

Removal of Cattle from North Nyasa and West Nyasa Districts, and Movements of Cattle in said Districts.

Under Section 9.

WHEREAS under the provisions of Section 9 of the above Ordinance, the Governor in Council may at any time by Proclamation in the Gazette declare any place in the Protectorate to be a place infected with disease within the meaning of the above Ordinance; and may further for the purpose of preventing such disease prohibit the removal of cattle from one district to another:

AND WHEREAS the Governor in Council may further in exercise of the powers conferred on him as aforesaid prescribe by Rules all necessary steps to prevent the further spread of the said disease and may appoint all necessary officers to carry the same into effect:

NOW THEREFORE by virtue of the powers in me as Governor in Council vested as aforesaid I DO HEREBY declare and proclaim, from the date of publication hereof the WEST NYASA and NORTH NYASA DISTRICTS to be places infected with disease within the meaning of the above Ordinance.

AND I DO FURTHER declare and proclaim that from and after the said date of publication all removal of cattle out of or into the said West Nyasa and North Nyasa Districts shall be and is HEREBY prohibited and the movement of cattle within the said Districts shall be subject to the following Rules :—

(1). No person shall remove cattle within the aforesaid Districts without the permission of the Government Veterinary Officer or the District Resident first had and obtained.

(2). Such permission may be granted subject to such restrictions as the Government Veterinary Officer or the District Resident may deem fit to impose.

Swine Fever in Lilongwe District.

Under Section 9.

WHEREAS under the provisions of Section 9 of the above Ordinance, the Governor in Council may at any time by Proclamation in the Gazette declare any place in the Protectorate to be a place infected with disease within the meaning of the above Ordinance; and may further prescribe by Rules all necessary steps to prevent the further spread of the said disease and may appoint all necessary officers to carry the same into effect:

NOW THEREFORE by virtue of the powers in me as Governor in Council vested as aforesaid I DO HEREBY declare and proclaim from the date of publication hereof the LILONGWE DISTRICT to be a place infected with swine fever within the meaning of the above Ordinance, and I DO FURTHER declare and proclaim that from and after the said date of publication the following Rules shall be of full force and effect.

(1). No person shall remove swine out of or into the aforesaid District :

(2). No person shall move swine from any one place to any other place within the aforesaid District without the permission of the District Resident or of the Government Veterinary Officer first had and obtained.

(3). Such permission may be granted subject to such restrictions as the District Resident or the Government Veterinary Officer may deem fit to impose.

111/1913,—31st May.

Inter-movement of Cattle between Mombera and North Nyasa Districts.

Under Section 9.

WHEREAS the Governor in Council by Proclamations Nos. 2 and 4 of 1912 made by virtue of Section 9 of the above Ordinance, *inter alia* prohibited the movement of cattle out of or into the Mombera and North Nyasa Districts :

AND WHEREAS it has been made to appear to me expedient that the prohibition as aforesaid should be modified by allowing the inter-movement of cattle between the said Districts subject to such restrictions as the Government Veterinary Officer, or, in his absence, the District Residents of the said Districts may deem fit to impose :

NOW THEREFORE by virtue of the powers in me vested by Section 9 of the above Ordinance, I DO HEREBY declare and proclaim that the said Proclamations shall be and are HEREBY modified so as to allow the inter-movement of cattle between the Mombera and North Nyasa Districts subject to such restrictions as the Government Veterinary Officer, or, in his absence, the District Residents of the said Districts shall deem fit to impose.

Rules.

143/1912,—22nd August.

Demodectic Mange.

Separation of diseased animals and notice to Resident.

1. Every person having in his possession or under his charge an animal infected with the disease known as demodectic mange shall :—

(1). Keep that animal separate from animals not so infected.

(2). Within twenty-four hours give notice of the fact of the animal being infected to the District Resident of the district in which the animal is.

Notice to Veterinary Officer.

2. The District Resident shall immediately notify the Veterinary Officer.

Power to Veterinary Officer to slaughter animals.

3. The Veterinary Officer may cause to be slaughtered or may order the owner of any animal infected with demodectic mange to slaughter it and to dispose of the carcase in such manner as may be best calculated to prevent the spread of the disease.

The owner shall not be entitled to any compensation in respect of animals so destroyed.

4. * The Veterinary Officer may order the owner of any animal infected with demodectic mange to take such measures to disinfect any animal or any enclosure in which such animal has been as may, in the opinion of the Veterinary Officer, be necessary to prevent the spread of the disease.

5. * Any person who is bound under these rules to give notice of the existence of disease or to segregate or slaughter any animal or to dispose of the carcase or to disinfect any animal or enclosure as hereinbefore provided and who fails to do so shall be liable to a fine not exceeding five pounds in respect of each offence.

22/1914,—22nd February.

Importation of Animals from Portuguese East Africa.

1. No animals shall be imported except by the Contractor in charge of the construction of the Central Africa Railway and only for use as draught or riding animals in connexion with such construction.

2. Such animals shall be imported into the Lower Shire District only and shall not be removed therefrom unless they are certified free from disease by a Government Veterinary Officer.

---

* Rules 4 and 5 as replaced by Notice of 31st March 1914 (No. 64/1914).

3. Animals of the following kinds only shall be imported :—Horses, mules, donkeys, trek oxen.

4. ·No animal shall be imported until a Government Veterinary Officer has certified that in his opinion it does not suffer from any disease which would render its importation undesirable.

196/1914,—23rd October.

The importation of horses, mules and donkeys from Portuguese East Africa and Northern Rhodesia other than those imported from Portuguese East Africa under the provisions of Notice No. 22 of 1914 shall be permitted subject to the following conditions :—

(1). The importation of any horse, mule or donkey shall be subject to the previous consent in writing of the Government Veterinary Officer or in his absence of the District Resident into whose District such horse, mule or donkey is to be imported, and to such restrictions as the Government Veterinary Officer or in his absence the District Resident may impose.

(2). Such consent shall be liable to be withdrawn without notice thereof or any reason being assigned therefor.

No. 4 of 1912.

TOWNSHIPS.

28th September 1897.

BYE-LAWS.

Townships Regulations, 1897.

See Section 27. *

Short title.

1. These Regulations may be cited as "The Townships Regulations, 1897."

Interpretation.

2. In these Regulations, unless the context otherwise requires—

"Street" includes any road, alley, or thoroughfare, and any open space not being the property of a private owner; .

† "Surveyor" means in the case of a Township where no Surveyor has been appointed, the Council of such Township or a Committee of such Council.

"Cattle" includes oxen, heifers, bulls, cows, horses, asses, mules and swine, but not goats or sheep;

"Health Officer" includes every Officer appointed by the Governor by that designation;

"Daily penalty" means a penalty for every day during which an offence is continued after conviction thereof.

Application to townships created by Proclamation.

3. Whensoever the Governor by Proclamation declares any settlement or place to be a township, and fixes the boundaries thereof, these Regulations, or such part or parts thereof as the Governor may by the Proclamation determine, shall apply to such township: Provided that the Governor may also suspend the operation of these Regulations, or any part thereof, within any township so created, or within any part of such township.

Constructive application of ancillary clauses.

Whenever, by any such Proclamation, any part of these Regulations is applied to any township, all penal and other ancillary clauses applicable for the due enforcement of the part so applied shall, although not mentioned in such Proclamation, be deemed to be applied and be in form in such town or place or part thereof.

PART I.—REGULATION OF STREETS AND BUILDINGS.

Streets to be under supervision of Surveyor.

4. All streets within the township shall be under the immediate supervision and control of the Surveyor, subject to such instructions as he may receive from the Governor.

* See note p. 75.

† As amended by Section 2 of the Ordinance.

The Surveyor shall, when authorized by the Governor, cause any such street to be levelled, drained, altered and repaired as occasion may require.

5. Any person who, without the written consent of the Surveyor, wilfully displaces or takes up or injures the pavement stones or material of any such street, or changes or attempts to change or obstruct any watercourse, shall be liable to a fine not exceeding 40s.

Injuring road-way, &c., of streets, pro-hibited.

6. Any person who, without the permission of the Surveyor, cuts, breaks down, uproots, lops, or in any other manner destroys or injures any tree growing in any street shall be liable to a fine not exceeding 10l.

Cutting trees, &c., in streets, prohibited: penalty.

7. The Governor, upon making such compensation to the persons entitled thereto as may be determined in cases of difference by arbitration, may acquire any lands or premises for the purpose of widening, opening, enlarging or otherwise improving any street, or for the purpose of making any new street : Provided that nothing in this Regulation shall entitle any person to compensation where the lands or premises so acquired are held subject to the right of the Government of the Protectorate to take or resume possession of such lands or premises for such purposes as aforesaid without compensation.

Power to pur-chase lands and premises for forming new streets, &c.

8. When any house or building situated in any street or the front thereof, has been taken or has fallen down, the Surveyor may prescribe the line in which any such house or building, or the front thereof, to be built or rebuilt in the same situation, shall be erected, and such house or building or the front thereof shall be erected in accordance therewith.

Power to regulate line of buildings.

The Surveyor shall pay or tender compensation to the owner or other person immediately interested in such house or building for any loss or damage he may sustain in consequence of his house or building being set back or forward. Any question concerning such compensation or its payment shall be settled, in case of difference, by arbitration.

Compensation to owners, &c.

9. It shall not be lawful, without the written consent of the Surveyor, to erect or bring forward any house or building forming part of any street, or any part or outbuilding thereof, beyond the front wall of the house or building on either side thereof, nor to build or make any addition thereto beyond the said front wall, nor to make any paved or other footway of greater or less width or of higher or lower level than the pavement which may be in front of the said house or building on either side.

Buildings not to be brought forward, &c.

Any person offending against this Regulation shall be liable to a penalty not exceeding 40s. for every day during

Penalty on con-travention.

which the offence is continued after written notice in this behalf from the Surveyor.

10. The Surveyor may, with the sanction of the Governor in writing, give notice to the occupier or owner of any house or building to remove or alter any porch, shed, verandah, projecting window, step, or pavement, sign-post, show-board, or any other obstruction or projection erected against or in front of such house or building whilst the same has been within the operation of this enactment, and which is an obstruction to the safe and convenient passage along any street, and such occupier or owner shall, within fourteen days after the service of such notice upon him, remove such obstruction, or alter the same in such manner as shall have been directed by the Surveyor and in default thereof shall be

liable to a penalty not exceeding 40s.; and the Surveyor may then remove such obstruction or projection, and the expense of so doing shall be recoverable as a debt from such occupier or owner. If the obstruction or projection was not made by the occupier, and is removed by him, he shall be entitled to deduct the expense of such removal from the rent payable by him to the owner of the house or building.

If any such obstruction or projection was erected or placed against or in front of any house or building in any street whilst such house or building was not within the operation of this enactment, the Surveyor may, with the sanction of the Governor in writing, cause the same to be removed or altered as he thinks fit, after giving notice of such intended removal or alteration to the occupier or owner, if the occupier is not found, of the house or building against or in front of which such obstruction or projection shall be, thirty days before the alteration or removal is begun; and if such obstruction or projection shall have been lawfully made, reasonable compensation shall be made by the Governor to any person who may suffer damage by such alteration or removal.

11. Where these Regulations provide for the determination of any question by arbitration, the following provisions shall have effect :—

(*a*). The parties shall be the persons claiming compensation and the Resident of the district.

(*b*). The reference shall be to two arbitrators, one appointed by each party, and their umpire.

(*c*). The award shall be final and conclusive, and may, on the application of either party, be made a rule of Court.

(*d*). All matters in relation to the appointment of the arbitrators or umpire, and to the reference and award, shall be conducted in such a manner as a Magistrate may, on the application of either party or his arbitrator, or the umpire, direct.

12. The Surveyor may, subject to the approval of the Governor, make rules with respect to—

    (i). The level, width, and construction of new streets.

    (ii). The structure of foundations and walls of new buildings for securing stability and preventing fire.

    (iii). The spaces to be left unbuilt around buildings to secure free ventilation.

    (iv). The watercourses of streets and the drainage of buildings.

    (v). The form and structure of the roofs of buildings where covered with thatch or other inflammable materials, to the effect that the lowest part of the roof shall not be nearer the ground than 7 feet.

Regulations for new buildings, watercourses, roofs &c.

Such rules may be either general or with respect to particular streets or buildings or classes of buildings, and shall be published in such manner as the Governor may direct.

Mode of notifying Regulations.

Any person who fails to comply with any rules made under this Regulation shall be guilty of an offence and liable to a penalty not exceeding 40s. for every day during which the offence is continued, and the Surveyor upon such notices as shall be fixed by the rules, or approved by the Governor, may remove, alter or pull down any work begun or done in any contravention of the rules, and the expenses incurred shall be a debt due from the person so in default hereby to the Governor.

Work contrary to Regulations may be removed.

The fourth and fifth sub-sections of this section shall apply notwithstanding that any watercourse, or drain, or building effected thereby has been made or erected before the making of the rules.

Application of clauses respecting drains, roofs, &c.

13. For the purposes of these Regulations, the re-erecting of any building taken or fallen down to or below the top of the ground-floor, or of any frame building of which only the framework is left down to the top of the ground-floor, or the conversion into a dwelling-house of any building not originally constructed for human habitation, shall be considered the erection of a new building.

What to be deemed a new building.

14. If in any township any building or wall, or anything affixed thereon, is deemed by the Surveyor to be in a ruinous state and dangerous to passengers, or to the occupiers of such building or neighbouring buildings, the Surveyor shall immediately take sufficient means, by fencing or otherwise

Ruinous or dangerous buildings &c., to be taken down or secured.

for the protection of passengers, and shall cause notice to be given to the owner of such building or wall, if he is known and resident in or within one day's journey from the township, and also to the occupier if any, requiring such owner or occupier forthwith to take down, secure, or repair such building, wall, or other thing as the case shall require; and if such owner or occupier do not begin to repair, take down, secure, or repair such building, wall, or other thing within four days after service of such notice, and complete the work as speedily as the nature of the case will admit, or if no owner or occupier is found the Surveyor shall subject to any order of the Governor, cause all or so much of such building, wall or other thing as shall be in a ruinous or dangerous condition to be secured or to be taken down, and may rebuild or repair the same; and all the expenses of protecting passengers, and of securing, taking down, repairing, or rebuilding such building, wall, or other thing, shall be a debt due by the owner or occupier thereof to the Governor, and be recoverable accordingly.

Building may be sold for expenses. 15. If no owner shall be found within the said limits, or appear and pay such expenses within six months after the completion of such repairs or rebuilding, the Surveyor may cause the building and the site thereof to be sold by public auction, and the price shall be applied in defraying the said expenses and the balance, if any, paid over to the owner, if he shall establish his claim thereto within twelve months after the date of such sale, failing which such balance shall be paid to the Governor, and become part of the revenue of the Protectorate.

Persons from whom expenses may be recovered. 16. Where the Surveyor incurs expense in or about the removal or alteration of any work executed contrary to these Regulations, or to any rule or instruction prescribed or given in pursuance of these Regulations, he may, with the sanction of the Governor, recover the amount of such expense as a debt either from the person executing the work removed or altered or from the person causing the work to be executed or failing to cause the required alteration to be made thereon or from the occupier or owner of the premises.

Materials of buildings taken down may be sold. 17. Whenever any building or part thereof is pulled or taken down by virtue of any powers conferred by these Regulations the Surveyor may sell the materials thereof, or so much of the same as shall be pulled down, and apply the proceeds of such sale in payment of the expenses incurred in respect of such building, and the balance, if any, shall be disposed of in the manner prescribed by Regulation 15.

Saving clause. Although the Surveyor sells such materials for the purposes aforesaid, he shall have the same remedies for compelling the payment of so much of the said expenses as may remain due after the application of the proceeds of such sale as are hereinbefore given to him for compelling the payment of the whole of the said expenses.

18. Every occupier of any lot or parcel of land within the township, or the owner thereof if unoccupied, shall fence such lot or parcel, and maintain such fence in good repair to the satisfaction of the Surveyor, and every fence erected or renewed after the application of this enactment shall not exceed 6 feet in height, and all live fences shall be kept carefully cropped of all superfluous branches.

Lots to be fenced.

If such occupier or owner shall make default in commencing to make or repair such fence after fourteen days' notice in that behalf from the Surveyor, or shall not complete such fence or the repairs thereof with as little delay as the nature of the work admits, every such offender shall incur a fine not exceeding 10s., and a daily penalty not exceeding 2s.

Penalty in default.

19. If any such fence shall be erected or raised to a greater height than 6 feet, the person causing such fence to be so erected or raised shall be liable to a penalty not exceeding 10s. and to a daily penalty not exceeding 2s.

Fences not to exceed 6 feet in height.

The Surveyor may, with the sanction of the Governor, after fourteen days' notice to the occupier of the lot, or the owner thereof if unoccupied, or without notice in case no owner is found in or within one day's journey from the place or town where the lot is situated, cause any fence which, after the application of this enactment shall be erected or raised to a greater height than 6 feet, to be taken down to that height, and may recover the expense of doing so in the manner provided by Regulation 17.

Surveyor may reduce height of new fence upon notice.

20. Whoever shall wilfully or maliciously break down or injure any fence shall for each offence incur a fine which may extend to 10l.

Maliciously injuring fences: penalty.

The Court imposing such fine may, if it thinks fit, direct the whole or any part thereof to be applied in compensating the occupier or owner sustaining damage by the act in respect of which the fine is imposed.

Compensation for damage.

21. In every township every occupier of any building, and every owner of any parcel of land whereupon no building is erected, or where the building thereon is unoccupied, shall keep the footway and roadway bounding such building or land, to a distance of 12 feet from the boundary of such building or land, or to the centre line of the street if not at a greater distance than 12 feet from such boundary, clear of all loose dirt, weeds, grass, or other incumbrances, filling up all holes with stones, gravel, or other like materials.

Occupier or owner to clear footways, &c.

Penalty.

Every owner or occupier who shall make default in complying with any rule made as aforesaid, or with the provisions of this enactment, shall for each offence incur a penalty not exceeding 10*s.*

Rules for removal of house refuse.

22. The Governor may make rules imposing on the occupiers of premises the duty of removing therefrom soil, ashes, and house-refuse of whatever nature, at such intervals and to such receptacles or places as he thinks fit, and may also make rules for the prevention of the keeping of animals on any premises so as to be injurious to health.

Penalty on non-compliance with rules.

Whoever makes default in complying with any such rule, or wilfully obstructs any person acting under the authority thereof, shall for each offence, incur a penalty not exceeding 10*s.*

Surveyor to provide receptacles for temporary deposits.

The Surveyor, with the approval of the Governor, may provide in proper and convenient situations receptacles for the temporary deposit and collection of dust, ashes, rubbish, or other refuse.

23. *   .   .   .   .   .*

Penalties on certain offences.

24. If any person commits any of the following offences, that is to say :—

Throwing out rubbish, filth, &c.

(i). Throws or lays on any street, or lot or parcel of town land, or on any yard or garden, whether occupied or not, or on any place declared an open space under these Regulations (except at such places as may be set apart by the Surveyor for such purpose), any carrion, filth, rubbish, or any offensive or unwholesome matter; or

Pigstyes in front of streets.

(ii). Keeps any pigstye to the front of any street not being shut out from the street by a sufficient wall or fence, or who keeps any swine or other cattle in or near any street so as to be a nuisance; or

Impediment on footway.

(iii). Without the consent of the Surveyor, places or leaves any lumber, bricks, stones, iron, timber, cable, anchor, bale, puncheon, cask, box, or other impediment whatsoever in any footway or street to the obstruction, danger, or annoyance of the residents or passengers; or

Riding or driving furiously.

(iv). In any street rides or drives furiously any horse or other animal, or drives or propels furiously any carriage, cart, or other vehicle, or drives furiously any cattle; or

---

* Regulation 23 is repealed by Section 27 of the Ordinance.

(v). Throws or discharges any stone or other missile in or into any street or place of public resort; or

Throwing missiles.

(vi). In any street or place of public resort, or in any place within sight or hearing of the persons then being in such street or place, disturbs the peace by quarrelling with any other person, or uses or applies to any other person then being in such street or place, or within sight or hearing thereof, any violent, scurrilous, or abusive term of reproach; or

Quarrelling and scolding.

(vii). In any street or place of public resort, or in any place within sight or hearing of the persons therein, shall, with intention of annoying or irritating any other person, sing any scurrilous or abusive song or words, whether any person be particularly addressed therein or not; or

Singing offensive song.

(viii). Is drunk in any street or place of public resort, and guilty of any violent or indecent behaviour; or

Being drunk and violent.

(ix). Is guilty of any violent or indecent behaviour in any police office, or station-house or lock-up house, or in any building used as a police office, station, or lock-up house; or

Behaving violently in police station.

(x). Commits any nuisance in any street or place of public resort or in any place declared an open space under these Regulations, or in any place being an appurtenance of or adjoining a dwelling-house; or

Committing nuisance.

(xi). Behaves irreverently or indecently in or near any church, chapel, or other building appropriated for religious worship; or

Behaving irreverently in churches.

(xii). Wilfully defaces or removes any milestone or board or any public lawful notice or posting-bill from any building or place where such notice or bill may lawfully be affixed;

Wilfully defacing public notices.

He shall, for each offence, in addition to any liability for damage at the suit of any person aggrieved, incur a fine not exceeding 40s., or in default of payment be imprisoned, with or without hard labour, for a period not exceeding four weeks.

Penalty.

Any person found committing any offence punishable under this Regulation may be taken into custody without warrant by any constable or person whom he may call to his aid, or by the owner or occupier of the property on or with respect to which the offence is committed, or by his servant or any person authorized by him, and may be detained until he can be delivered into the custody of a constable, who shall carry such person, as soon as conveniently may be, before a Magistrate, to be dealt with according to law; Provided that

Apprehension of offenders.

no person arrested under this Regulation shall be detained by any constable or other person longer than necessary for bringing him before a Magistrate.

Discharging fire-arms, &c., prohibited: Penalty.

25. Whoever discharges any fire-arms, or throws or sets fire to any fire-work in any street, or in any house or building or within the curtilage thereof shall, for each offence, in addition to any liability for damage at the suit of any person aggrieved, incur a fine which may extend to 10*l.*, or, in default of payment, be imprisoned, with or without hard labour, for a period which may extend to three months, and may be taken into custody without warrant, as provided in the last preceding Regulation.

Liability of occupier of house in which fire-arms discharged.

If it is proved that a fire-arm has been discharged in or within the curtilage of any house or building, and the person doing so has not been identified or discovered, the occupier of such house or building, if within the premises at the time the offence was committed, shall be liable for each offence to a fine which may extend to 10*l.*, or, in default of payment, to be imprisoned, with or without hard labour, for a period which may extend to thirty days.

Beating drums &c., without permission unlawful.

26. It shall not be lawful for any person, without the permission in writing of the Governor or a Magistrate to assemble or be in any street, house, building, garden, yard, or other place beating any drum, gong, tomtom, or other instrument, or dancing thereto; and any constable by himself, or with such assistance as he may take to his aid, may warn the persons so unlawfully assembled to depart, and for this purpose may enter into such house, building, garden, yard, or place in which persons are assembled as aforesaid.

Penalty on persons refusing to desist.

Any person who, after being so warned, shall not depart forthwith (except the persons actually dwelling in such house or building), may be apprehended without warrant by any constable or person acting in his aid, and shall incur a fine which may extend to 10*s.*

Penalty on occupier of house, &c.

The occupier of such house, building, garden, yard, or place who shall have permitted such persons unlawfully to assemble or be therein as aforesaid, shall incur a fine which may extend to 40*s.*, and every drum, gong, tomtom, or other such instrument found in the premises shall be liable to forfeiture.

Court may prohibit drumming &c., during its sittings.

27. Any Court may prohibit, during the hours of its sitting, and at any place within a radius of 300 yards from the building where such sitting is held, any beating of drums, gongs, tomtoms or other instruments, or other loud noises of any kind or description; and whosoever, being required by any constable or officer of the Court to desist from beating drums, gongs, tomtoms or other instruments, or from making any other noise as aforesaid, fails to comply with such requisition, shall, for every offence, incur a penalty not exceeding 40*s.*, and may be apprehended by any constable without warrant.

28. If any house or building catches or is on fire, it shall be lawful for any officer of police, Magistrate, or Surveyor to order, with the purpose of staying the spreading or communication of the fire, that any near or adjacent houses or premises to which the fire is likely to communicate shall be demolished, or the roofs thereof broken down, or the thatch or other inflammable roofing pulled or broken from the roofs or other suitable means used for interrupting the communication; but no order for the demolition of any house or premises, or for breaking down the roof, or pulling the roofing material therefrom, shall be given, unless the officer is present at the fire and satisfied to the best of his judgment, upon personal view, that such order appears necessary for staying the progress or communication of the fire.

Demolition or unroofing of building during fires.

Such orders may be carried out by any constable or other person; and if any person obstructs in any manner of way the execution of any such order, he shall be liable to a fine which may extend to 10*l.*, or to imprisonment, with or without hard labour, which may extend to sixty days, or to both.

Penalty on obstruction[1]

No occupier, owner, or other person interested in any house or premises demolished or unroofed, or from which the roofing materials shall have been pulled as aforesaid, shall be entitled on account thereof to compensation of any sort whatsoever.

No compensation due to owner, &c., of houses so demolished.

29. Whoever, being called by any Magistrate or Surveyor or by any constable to assist in extinguishing or staying the progress of any fire, refuses or delays to do so, or fails to use his best endeavours in carrying out the directions given for that purpose by any Magistrate, Surveyor, or constable, shall be liable to a fine which may extend to 5*l.*

Penalty on persons refusing to assist in extinguishing fires.

PART II.—STRAY CATTLE.

30. If any cattle are found at large and unattended in any township, any constable or person assisting him may seize and impound such cattle in any common pound provided by the Surveyor, with the approval of the Governor, and may detain the same therein until the owner thereof pays to the pound keeper or the District Resident a fine not exceeding

Power to impound stray cattle.

2*s.* for each head of cattle, besides the expenses of keeping the same at rates not exceeding 6*d.* a-day for each head of swine, and 1*s.* a-day for each head of other cattle.

Power to sell stray cattle.

If the said penalty and expenses are not paid within four days after such impounding, the pound keeper or other person appointed by the Surveyor for that purpose may sell or cause to be sold any such cattle; but previous to such sale six days' notice thereof shall be given or left at the dwelling-house of the owner of such cattle, if he is known, or, if not, then notice of the intended sale shall be conspicuously posted in some usual place for the posting of public notices in the township.

Disposal or proceeds of sale.

The money arising from such sale, after deducting the said fine and expenses, shall be paid by the Surveyor on demand to the owner of the cattle sold. If within three months after the sale no demand is made, or no person appears entitled to such money, the same shall be paid to the Governor, and become part of the revenue of the Protectorate.

Penalty for pound breach.

31. Whoever releases, or attempts to release, any cattle from any pound or place where the same are impounded under these Regulations, or who pulls down, damages, or destroys the said pound or place, or any part thereof, with intent to procure the unlawful release of such cattle, shall incur a penalty not exceeding 5*l.*

Owners of stray cattle may be fined.

32. It shall be lawful, in lieu of impounding the cattle found at large as aforesaid, to summon the owner thereof before the Magistrate, who may, on conviction, impose a fine on such owner for each animal so found not exceeding 2*s.*, besides costs of the summons and service thereof.

Furious dogs; penalty on owner.

33. If any dog, either at large in any street or public place, or in charge of any person, shall attack, worry, or put in fear any person, or any horse or other animal, the owner or person in charge of the dog shall incur a fine which may extend to 10*s.*, and such dog may, by order of the Court making the conviction, be destroyed.

Rabid dogs at large may be destroyed; penalty on owner.

34. It shall be lawful for any constable to destroy any dog going at large which shall be reasonably suspected to be in a rabid state, or which shall have been bitten by any other dog reasonably suspected to be in a rabid state, and the owner or person in charge of such dog who shall permit the same to go at large shall incur a fine which may extend to 10*l.*

When slaughter-house provided, cattle not to be slaughtered elsewhere.

PART III.—SLAUGHTER-HOUSES, MARKETS, &c.

35. When the Governor provides any public slaughter-house for any town or place, it shall not be lawful, unless

by the licence of the Health Officer, to slaughter any cattle or dress any carcase for the food of man within the limits for which such slaughter-house is provided, except in such slaughter-house; and any person contravening this enactment shall incur a penalty which may extend to 40*s.* for every offence, and to a daily penalty which may extend to 40*s.*

36. For the purposes of this Regulation the Health Officer may issue licences for slaughtering elsewhere than in the public slaughter-house, for any period not exceeding one year, and every such licence shall be subject to such stamp duty not exceeding 1*l.* for a whole year, as the Governor may by rule prescribe. The Governor may make rules for all or any of the following purposes :—

With respect to the structure and management of slaughter-houses, and the charges for the use thereof ;

For preventing cruelty in slaughter-houses ;

For keeping slaughter-houses in a cleanly and proper state, and providing them with a sufficient supply of water ;

For restricting or prohibiting the keeping of dogs in any slaughter-house or in any premises appurtenant thereto ;

For regulating the butchers, labourers, and others resorting to or employed about slaughter-houses.

Any person contravening any such rules, or obstructing any person acting in the execution thereof, shall be liable to a penalty not exceeding 40*s.*, and to a daily penalty not exceeding 10*s.*

37. Whenever the Governor provides any public market, he may make rules for all or any of the following purposes :—

For regulating the use of the market, and the several parts thereof, and for keeping order therein, preventing nuisances or obstructions therein, or in the immediate approaches thereto ;

For regulating the stallages, rents, or tolls payable by the vendors in such markets, and the collection thereof ;

For fixing the days and the hours during each day on which the market shall be held ;

For regulating the carriers and labourers resorting to or employed about the market, and fixing the rates for carrying articles thereto or therefrom, within the limits of the town or place where such market is situated ;

For preventing the use of false or defective weights scales or measures.

Rules for slaughter-houses.

Penalties on breach of rules.

Rules for markets.

Penalties on breach of rules.

And any person contravening any such rules, or obstructing any person acting in the execution thereof, shall be liable to a penalty not exceeding 40s., and to a daily penalty not exceeding 10s., and any false or defective weights, scales, or measures which may be used or found in such market shall be forfeited.

Officers of Health to inspect meat, &c.

38. Any Health Officer, or person authorized by the Governor to act as Inspector of Provisions, in any place in which this enactment at any time applies, may at all reasonable hours inspect and examine any animal, carcase, meat, poultry, game, fish, vegetables, corn, bread, flour, or other provisions exposed for sale, or deposited in any place for the purpose of sale or of preparation for sale, or remaining in the custody of the seller after being sold and intended for the food of man, the proof that the same was not exposed or deposited for any such purpose, or was not intended for the food of man, resting with the party charged; and if any such animal, carcase, meat, poultry, game, fish, vegetables, corn, bread, flour, or other provisions appear to such Health Officer or Inspector to be diseased or unsound, or unwholesome, or unfit for the food of man, he may seize and carry away the same in order to its being brought before a Magistrate.

Unsound meat, &c., to be destroyed: penalty on owner &c.

If it appears to the Magistrate that any animal, carcase, meat, poultry, game, fish, vegetable, corn, bread, flour, or other provisions so seized is diseased or unsound, or unwholesome, or unfit for the food of man, he shall condemn the same and order it to be destroyed or so disposed of as to prevent it from being exposed for sale or used for the food of man; and the person to whom the same belongs, or did belong at the time of exposure for sale, or in whose possession or premises the same was found, shall be liable to a penalty not exceeding 10s. for every article condemned.

Penalty on hindering Officer from inspection &c.

Any person who in any manner obstructs any Health Officer or Inspector, when carrying into effect the provisions of this Regulation, shall be liable to a penalty not exceeding 5l.

Search warrant.

39. On complaint made on oath by a Health Officer or by an Inspector of Nuisances, or by any Constable, any Magistrate may grant a warrant to enter any building or part of a building in which such complainant has reason for believing that there is kept or concealed any animal, carcase, meat, poultry, game, fish, vegetables, corn, bread, flour, or other provisions intended for sale for the food of man which is diseased, unsound, or unwholesome, or unfit for the food of man; and to search for, seize, and carry away any such animal or other article, in order to have the same dealt with by a Magistrate:

Any person who obstructs any such officer in the performance of his duty under such search warrant shall, in addition to any other punishment to which he may be subject, be liable to a penalty not exceeding 10*l.*, or to be imprisoned, with or without hard labour, for a period not exceeding sixty days.

Penalty on hindering execution of warrant.

PART IV.—NUISANCES.

40. For the purpose of these Regulations—

Definition of nuisance.

(1). Any house or premises in such a state as to be a nuisance or injurious or dangerous to health :

(2). Any house or part of a house so overcrowded as to be injurious or dangerous to the health of the inmates, whether members of the same family or not :

(3). Any pool, ditch, gutter, watercourse, privy, urinal, cesspool, cistern, drain, or ashpit, so foul or in such a state as to be a nuisance or injurious or dangerous to health :

(4). Any animal so kept as to be a nuisance or injurious or dangerous to health :

(5). Any accumulation or deposit which is a nuisance or injurious or dangerous to health :

(6). Any growth of weeds, long grass, or wild bush of any sort in any garden or yard :

shall be deemed to be nuisances liable to be dealt with under these Regulations.

41. It shall be the duty of every Inspector of Nuisances to make from time to time inspection of his district, with a view to ascertain what nuisances exist calling for abatement, and to enforce these Regulations.

Duty of Inspectors of Nuisances.

42. Whenever an Inspector of Nuisances or any Surveyor or Health Officer has reason, by inspection or otherwise, to believe that any nuisance exists on any premises, he shall by notice require the occupier or owner of the premises, or any person by whose act or default the nuisance arises, to abate the same.

Notice to abate nuisance.

43. If the person to whom such notice shall have been given makes default in complying with any of the requisitions thereof within the time specified by the notice, or within five days if the time is not specified, or fails to satisfy the Inspector of Nuisances, or Health Officer, or Surveyor that he has used all due diligence to carry out the requisition, or if the nuisance although abated since the date of the notice, is, in the opinion of the Inspector of Nuisances, Health Officer, or Surveyor, likely to recur on the same premises, he shall take proceedings before a Court.

On non-compliance complaint to Court.

Order of Court on complaint.

If the Court is satisfied that the alleged nuisance exists, or that, although abated, it is likely to recur on the same premises, the Court shall make an order on the person in default, requiring him to comply with all or any of the requisitions of the notice, or otherwise to abate the nuisance within the time specified in the order, or such time as the Court may deem sufficient, or an order prohibiting recurrence of the nuisance, or an order both requiring abatement and prohibiting recurrence of the nuisance.

Penalty for nuisance.

The Court may impose a penalty not exceeding 20s. on the person on whom the order is made in respect of the nuisance existing previously to such order.

Penalty for contravention of order of Court.

Any person not obeying an order requiring abatement or prohibiting the recurrence of the nuisance shall, if he fails to satisfy the Court that he has used all due diligence to carry out such order, be liable to a penalty not exceeding 5s. per day during his default; and any person acting knowingly and wilfully contrary to an order of prohibition shall be liable to a penalty not exceeding 20s. per day during such contrary action: moreover, the Surveyor or Inspector of Nuisances, or his assistants may enter the premises to which the order relates and abate the nuisance, and do whatever may be necessary in execution of such order, and recover the expenses incurred by them as a debt from the person on whom the order is made.

Power to abate nuisance where owner or occupier of premises not known.

44. Where it appears to the satisfaction of the Court that the person by whose act or default the nuisance arises, or the owner or occupier of the premises, is not known or cannot be found, then the necessary work for abating such nuisance may, subject to any order of the Governor, be executed by the Inspector of Nuisances or Surveyor.

Prohibition in case of houses unfit for human habitation.

45. Where any house or building, by reason of any nuisance, or of its insecurity and liability to fall down in whole or in part, is, in the judgment of the Court, unfit for human habitation, the Court may prohibit the using thereof for that purpose until in its judgment the house or building is rendered fit for habitation; and, if necessary, may authorize any constable to remove the inhabitants therefrom.

Penalty on contravention of prohibition.

Any person inhabiting or using any house or building in contravention of this enactment shall be liable to a penalty not exceeding 10s., and to a daily penalty not exceeding 5s.

Power of entry to examine or abate nuisances.

46. Any Surveyor, or Health Officer, or Inspector of Nuisances, or any persons employed by them or by any of them, such last mentioned persons showing any badge, or token, or written notice of such employment, shall be admitted into any premises for the purpose of examining as to the existence or continuance of any nuisance therein, at any time between the hours of six in the morning and six in the afternoon, and also for the purpose of abating any nuisance·

If admission to premises for any of the purposes of this section is refused, any Magistrate may, by order under his hand, require the person having custody of the premises to admit the Surveyor, Health Officer, or Inspector of Nuisances, or any person employed by them, or by any of them as aforesaid, into the premises during the hours aforesaid; and if no person having custody of the premises is found, the Magistrate shall authorize the aforesaid persons, or any of them, if necessary, to break and enter on such premises.

Any such order shall continue in force until the nuisance has been abated, or the work for which the entry was necessary has been done.

Any person who fails to obey such order, or obstructs the Surveyor or Inspector of Nuisances, or other person in carrying this Regulation into effect, shall be liable to a penalty not exceeding 5*l.*

47. Whoever by any act or default causes or suffers to be brought or to flow into any well, stream, tank, reservoir, aqueduct, pond, or place used or intended for supplying water to man, or into any conduit communicating therewith, any substance, or does any act whereby the water in or which may enter such well, stream, tank, reservoir, aqueduct, pond or place is fouled, shall be liable to a penalty not exceeding 10*l.* and to a daily penalty not exceeding 40*s.* Such penalties shall not be recoverable unless sued for during the continuance of the offence, or within one month after it has ceased.

48. The provisions of these Regulations relating to nuisances shall be deemed to be in addition to and not to abridge or affect any right, remedy, or proceeding under any other provisions of these Regulations or under any other law.

Provided that no person shall be punished for the same offence both under these Regulations relating to nuisances and under such other law.

Part V.—Infectious Diseases.

49. Where any Health Officer or Surveyor considers that the cleansing and disinfecting of any house, or part thereof, and of any articles therein, or the destruction of such articles, would tend to prevent or check infectious disease it shall be the duty of such Health Officer or Surveyor to give notice to the occupier or owner of such house, or part thereof, that the same and any such articles therein will be cleansed and disinfected or (as regards the articles) destroyed, unless he informs the Health Officer or Surveyor (as the case may be)

Marginal notes:

If admission refused or premises vacant, order for admission to be made.

Duration of order.

Penalty on disobeying order.

Penalty for causing water to be fouled.

Provision relating to nuisances not to affect other remedies.

Proviso.

Cleansing and disinfecting premises on notice.

within twenty-four hours from the receipt of the notice that he will cleanse and disinfect the house or part of such articles or destroy such articles to the satisfaction of the Health Officer or Surveyor within a time fixed by the notice.

If within such twenty-four hours the owner or occupier does not so inform the Health Officer or Surveyor, or having so informed him or without so informing him fails to cleanse or disinfect the house or articles, or destroy the articles within the time fixed in the notice, the house or part and articles may be cleansed and disinfected and the articles may be destroyed by or by direction of the Health Officer or Surveyor.

Prohibition on letting houses in which infected persons have lived.

50. Any person who knowingly lets, either for hire or otherwise, any house, room, or part of a house in which any person has been suffering from any dangerous infectious disorder, without having such house, room, or part of a house and all articles therein properly disinfected to the satisfaction of a Health Officer or Surveyor, shall be liable to a penalty not exceeding 10*l.*

For the purposes of this section the keeper of an inn shall be deemed to let for hire part of a house to any person admitted as a guest into such house.

Prohibition on exposure of infected persons or things.

51. Any person who—

(1). While suffering from any dangerous infectious disorder wilfully exposes himself without proper precautions against spreading the disorder in any street, public place shop, or inn, or public conveyance ; or

(2). Being in charge of any person so suffering so exposes such sufferer ; or

(3). Gives, lends, sells, transmits, or exposes without previous disinfection any bedding, clothes, or other things which have been exposed to infection from any such disorder

Penalty.

shall be liable to a penalty not exceeding 5*l.*

Penalty on infected persons entering public conveyance without information to persons in charge.

52. Any person who, while suffering from any such disorder, enters any public conveyance without previously notifying to the person in charge thereof that he is so suffering, shall be liable to a penalty not exceeding 5*l.*, and, in addition, may be ordered to pay to the owner of the conveyance the amount of any expense he may incur in disinfecting the conveyance.

Disinfection of public conveyances.

53. Every person in charge of a public conveyance shall immediately provide for the disinfection of such conveyance after it has to his knowledge conveyed any person suffering from a dangerous infectious disorder, and if he fails to do so he shall be liable to a penalty not exceeding 5*l.*

54. Where any suitable hospital or place for the reception of the sick is provided, any person who is suffering from any dangerous infectious disorder, and is without proper lodging or accommodation, or is lodged in a house so overcrowded as that in the opinion of the Health Officer the continuance of such sick person therein may probably lead to the spread of the disorder, may, with the consent of the superintending authority of such hospital or place, be removed thereto by order of a Magistrate.

Removal of infected persons to hospital in certain cases.

Any person who wilfully disobeys or obstructs the execution of such order shall be liable to a penalty not exceeding 5*l.*

55. The Governor may from time to time make such Regulations as to him may seem fit with a view to the treatment of persons affected with small-pox, cholera, yellow fever, or any other epidemic, endemic, or infectious disease, and for preventing the spread of small-pox, cholera, yellow fever, and such other diseases, and may declare by what authority or authorities such Regulations shall be enforced and executed.

Governor to make Regulations as to epidemics.

Any person wilfully neglecting or refusing to obey or carry out, or obstructing the execution of any Regulation made under this section, shall be liable to a penalty not exceeding 20*l.*

Penalty on disobeying Regulations.

PART VI.—RATING.

56. The Governor may once in every year, on a day to be fixed by him, assess all lands and tenements within the township, and levy a rate on such assessment: Provided that no rate shall be levied or be charged upon any lands or tenements for the time being in the occupation of any department of His Majesty's Government or of the Government of the Protectorate, or appropriated exclusively to public worship, public roads, public schools, public libraries, public hospitals, public lunatic asylums, or public burial-grounds, or, with the approval of the Governor, appropriated to public gardens.

Assessment of property in township.

57. The valuation roll, when prepared, shall be exhibited for public inspection for the period of one week, and any objection to the valuation shall be heard and determined by a Magistrate on such day or days and at such place as the Governor, or a Magistrate, may by any public notice similarly exhibited, appoint.

Objections to valuation.

58. After the determination of the objections, if any, the Governor may by public notice appoint a day, not less than fourteen days after the day or last day appointed for

Appointment of day for payment of rates.

the hearing of objections, on which the rate is to become due and payable.

Rate to be a charge upon property.

59. Subject to the provisions of these Regulations, every rate shall from the day so appointed by the Governor, be deemed to be a charge on the property on which it is assessed and be recoverable from the owner or occupier of the property, or any subsequent owner or occupier, or the agent of any such owner or occupier.

Application of rate.

60. The township rate shall be applied in defraying any expenses incurred by the Governor in carrying these Regulations into effect, in providing lighting, watching, and police, or otherwise in promoting the well-being of the township.

61. The owner or occupier of any land outside but adjoining the limits of the township shall be liable to pay in aid of the township rate a contribution of 4*d.* for every yard of so much of his land as is coterminous with the township.

Any lands which would if situate within the township be exempt from the township rate shall be exempt from such contribution.

The list of contributories and the amounts payable by each shall be appended to the valuation roll of the township, and the four last preceding Regulations shall apply to such list as if the contributions were rates.

PART VII.—FORMS, LEGAL PROCEEDINGS, &c.

The Governor may make rules as to notices &c.

62. The Governor may make rules as to the form and method of services of notice and orders under these Regulations, and in what cases, and for what purposes notices to the Chief or Headman of any place, or part thereof, may be deemed to be notice to the native inhabitants of the same.

Service until rules made.

Subject to such rules, and until such rules are made, any notice or order served in the manner prescribed for the service of summonses and other documents by " The Africa Order in Council, 1889," shall be sufficiently served.

Limitation of time for prosecutions.

63. Any complaint or information in pursuance of these Regulations shall be made or laid within two months from the time when the matter of such complaint or information arose and not afterwards.

Recovery of penalties.

64. All penalties, forfeitures, costs and expenses the recovery of which is not otherwise provided for, shall be recovered upon summary trial and conviction; and upon non-payment the same shall be enforced under the provisions of " The Africa Order in Council, 1889."

The term for which any person may be imprisoned in default of payment of any penalty under these Regulations shall not, except where otherwise herein expressed, exceed thirty days.

Limitation of imprisonment.

65. Where any nuisance under these Regulations appears to be wholly or partially caused by the acts or defaults of two or more persons, it shall be lawful for the complainant to institute proceedings against any one of such persons, or to include all or any two or more of such persons in one proceeding, and any one or more of such persons may be ordered to abate such nuisance, so far as the same appears to the Court to be caused by his or their acts or defaults, or may be prohibited from continuing any acts or defaults which the Court finds as matter of fact contribute to such nuisance, or may be fined or otherwise punished, notwithstanding the acts or defaults of any one of such persons would not separately have caused a nuisance; and the costs may be distributed as to the Court may seem fair and reasonable.

Joinder of parties in proceedings for nuisance.

66. When in any proceeding under these Regulations an inmate of any house is summoned or otherwise dealt with as the occupier of such house, if he alleges that he is not the occupier the proof of such allegation shall be upon the person making it.

Burden of proof in certain cases.

N.B. It is important to note the effect of these Regulations. Being Queen's Regulations made under the authority of the Africa Order in Council 1889, they had the same force and effect as an Ordinance made under the British Central Africa Order in Council 1902. The Regulations could not, therefore, be repealed by any Rules, Regulations or Bye-laws made under an Ordinance. [B. C. A. Order in Council 1902, Article 12 (10).] The Town Councils Ordinance (No. 5 of 1908) was intended to supplement The Townships Regulations 1897 and conferred on Town Councils a large measure of self-government including an extensive power to make Bye-laws. Many of the matters in respect of which Town Councils were thus empowered to make Bye-laws were already dealt with in the 1897 Regulations and therefore any Bye-laws made by Town Councils which were at variance with the provisions contained in the 1897 Regulations were, by virtue of Article 12 (10) referred to above, *ultra vires*—and bad . It became necessary therefore to adjust the relative positions of the 1897 Regulation and of the 1908 Ordinance. This was done by repealing the Ordinance and by re-enacting it with certain modifications and additions as The Townships Ordinance (No. 4 of 1912). By Section 27 of this latter Ordinance (Ordinances p. 371) it was provided that the Queen's Regulations 1897 were repealed *as Queen's Regulations but re-enacted with the force of Bye-laws only.* The effect of this section and of Section 4 (2) (Ordinances p. 363) is to validate all Bye-laws made under The Town Councils Ordinance 1908, even where inconsistent with the 1897 Regulations, and to enable Town Councils to amend, repeal, etc. by the enactment of new Bye-laws, any of the provisions of the 1897 Regulations. The 1897 Regulations are in force therefore with the effect of Bye-laws only in so far as they have not been affected by subsequent legislation either by way of Ordinance or Bye-law. The 1897 Regulations still in force apply to all Townships in the Protectorate.

Regulations.

24th September, 1901.

Native Locations.

Regulations additional to Parts IV and V of The Townships Regulations 1897.

1. The following Bye-laws are ancillary to the Nuisances and Infectious Diseases Byelaws of the 28th September, 1897.

2. The Governor in Council may authorize any Council or District Resident to select and acquire suitable sites in the neighbourhood of any Township or Settlement for the purpose of Native Locations for imported native labourers employed in such Township or Settlement.

3. The Governor in Council may empower any Council or District Resident to levy all such rents, rates or charges and to make all such Bye-laws as may be necessary for the purchase, upkeep and control of the said Native Locations, the same to be approved of by him.

4. The expenses incurred in connexion with such Locations shall be defrayed by the employers of the labourers using the same or by the residents of the Township or Settlement in such proportions as the Governor in Council shall approve.

5. The Governor in Council may by Proclamation forbid the settlement of native labourers within a certain distance of any European Township or Settlement except within such Locations: the prohibited area shall be prescribed by him in such Proclamation.

6. The Council and District Residents set out in the Schedule hereto are hereby empowered to acquire such Native Locations from the Townships and Settlements therein mentioned and it is hereby forbidden to settle imported labourers within the area set opposite the names of such Townships or Settlements in the said Schedule. The Governor in Council may from time to time by Notice add the names of other Councils or District Residents to the said Schedule or may remove the name of any Council or District Resident from the same.

Schedule.

Name of Council or District Resident.	Name of Township.	Prohibited Area.
Blantyre Town Council and District Resident Blantyre, jointly.	Blantyre Township.	Within half a mile of Township.

Proclamations

Of Townships and Boundaries.

FORT JOHNSTON.—   *24th February, 1899.*
DECLARED A TOWNSHIP.

158/1908—5th October.

BOUNDARIES FIXED AS FOLLOWS :—

COMMENCING at a point on the right bank of the Shire River which
point is distant 10 chains in a southerly direction from where the south
side of Manning Street meets the right bank of that River, the boundary
shall be carried on a bearing of 247 deg. 30 min. for a distance of 30 chains
21 links to the prolongation of the west side of India Street; thence it shall
be carried along the prolongation of the west side of India Street on a
bearing of 337 deg. 30 min. for a distance of 62 chains 44 links; thence it
shall be carried on a bearing of 67 deg. 30 min. for a distance of 30 chains
more or less or until it reaches the right bank of the Shire River; thence it
shall be carried along the right bank of the Shire River, in a southerly
direction, down stream, to the point of commencement.

ZOMBA.—   *30th September, 1900.*

BOUNDARIES FIXED AS FOLLOWS :—

COMMENCING at a point on the right bank of the Mlungusi river, where
that river is crossed by the road from Zomba to Mlungusi house, the
boundary shall be carried along the south side of that road in a westerly
direction for a distance of 40 chains, or until it reaches the right bank of the
Mponda stream; thence it shall be carried along the right bank of the
Mponda stream, down stream, in a south-easterly direction for a distance
measured in a straight line of 25 chains 52 links to the south-east corner beacon
of the African Lakes Corporation's Mandala (Zomba) estate; thence it shall be
carried along the southern boundary of that estate, on a bearing of 258° 21',
for a distance of 31 chains 48 links, to the south-west corner beacon of the
African Lakes Corporation's Mandala (Zomba) estate; thence it shall be
carried, on a bearing of 253° 4', for a distance of 45 chains 95 links or until
it reaches the left bank of Bwaila stream; thence it shall be carried along
the left bank of the Bwaila stream, up stream, in a northerly direction for a
distance of 4 chains to the confluence of the Mirola and Bwaila streams;
thence it shall be carried along the left bank of the Mirola stream, up stream,
in a northerly direction for a distance of 49 chains, or until it reaches the
high road from the Residency to the Camp; thence it shall be carried on a
bearing of 346° 30', for a distance of 97 chains or until it reaches the edge of
the mountain road at Zomba plateau; thence it shall be carried along the
edge of Zomba plateau in an easterly and then north-easterly direction until
it reaches the right bank of the Mlungusi river; thence it shall be carried

along the right bank of the Mlungusi river, down stream, in a south-easterly direction for a distance measured in a straight line of 95 chains to the point of commencement.

CHIROMO.—   *114/1914,—2nd June.*

BOUNDARIES ALTERED AND CONSTITUTED AS FOLLOWS :—

COMMENCING at the confluence of the Shire and Ruo rivers the boundary shall be carried along the left bank of the Shire River, upstream, until it reaches the centre line of the Port Herald-Blantyre railway ; thence it shall be carried in a more or less easterly direction along the centre line of that railway until it reaches the west side of the Chiromo-Cholo road; thence it shall be carried along the west side of that road in a more or less southerly direction until it reaches the south side of the Lake road at the large tree marking the boundary of the Chiromo Estate ; thence it shall be carried along part of the western boundary of that estate on a true bearing of 149° 55′ 22″ for a distance of 18 chains 60 links or until it reaches the right bank of the Ruo River ; thence it shall be carried along the right bank of the Ruo River, downstream, in a westerly direction to the point of commencement.

BLANTYRE.—   *31st August, 1903.*

BOUNDARIES FIXED AS FOLLOWS :—

COMMENCING at a beacon which is situated on the east side of the road which connects the Blantyre Mission and Blantyre-Zomba roads, and which beacon is distant 3 chains 50 links from the north-east corner of the house now occupied by the Blantyre Mission Secretary, the boundary shall be carried along the east side of this road for a distance of 13 chains, to a beacon which is 50 yards south of the southern side of the Blantyre-Zomba road ; thence it shall be carried along the south side of this road (but distant 50 yards from it) in a westerly direction, for a distance, measured in a straight line, of 10 chains or until it reaches the junction of the Mandala-Mission road with the Blantyre-Zomba road ; thence it shall be carried along the east side of the Mandala-Mission road (but distant 50 yards from it) in a south-westerly direction, for a distance, measured in a straight line, of 48 chains 70 links, or until it meets the Blantyre-Cholo road, thence it shall be carried along the east side of the Blantyre-Cholo road (but distant 50 yards from it) in a southerly direction, for a distance, measured in a straight line, of 13 chains 50 links or until it reaches the Mandala-Katunga road ; thence it shall be carried along the south side of the Mandala-Katunga road (but distant 50 yards from it) in a southerly and westerly direction for a distance, measured, in a straight line, of 81 chains 40 links, or until it reaches a beacon which is situated 50 yards west of the junction of the Mandala-Katunga road with the Blantyre-Katunga road ; thence it shall be carried on a bearing of 0° 34′ 30″ for a distance of 19 chains 10 links, to a beacon which is 2 chains 30 links north of the north side of the African Transcontinental Telegraph Co's., Ltd., house ; thence it shall be carried on a bearing of

344° 51′ 30″ for a distance of 84 chains 46 links, to a beacon which is situated on the south side of the Blantyre-Mitsidi road, 35 yards west of its junction with the Michiru office and Manager's house road; thence it shall be carried along the west side of this office road (but distant 50 yards from it) in a northerly direction, for a distance, measured in a straight line, of 46 chains 50 links to a beacon which is 20 yards north of the north side of the house at present occupied by the Secretary of the Blantyre and East Africa Co. Ltd.; thence it shall be carried on a bearing of 87° 30′ 30″ for a distance of 34 chains 29 links to a beacon which is 22 yards from the Blantyre Building Company's new workshop; thence it shall be carried on a bearing of 111° 13′ 30″ for a distance of 81 chains 50 links to the point of commencement.

PORT HERALD.— *31st January, 1905.*

PROCLAIMED A TOWNSHIP AND BOUNDARIES FIXED AS FOLLOWS :—

COMMENCING at a beacon situated at the north-west side of the Zambesi Road and 14 links from its intersection with the west side of Hunt Road, which beacon bears 10° 28′ 50″ and is distant 1 chain 12 links from the north-east corner of Abraham Kassam's plot No. 191 the boundary shall be carried on a bearing of 17° 38′ 10″ for a distance of 34 chains 42 links; thence it shall be carried on a bearing of 1° 37′ 10″ for a distance of 22 chains 11 links; thence on a bearing of 91° 37′ 10″ for a distance of 37 chains 88 links; thence on a bearing of 191° 37′ 10″ for a distance of 31 chains 70 links or until it meets the right bank of the Shire River; thence the boundary shall follow the right bank of the Shire River downstream for a distance measured in a straight line of 45 chains 70 links; thence it shall be carried on a bearing of 233° 48′ 10″ for a distance of 3 chains; thence on a bearing of 287° 38′ 10″ for a distance of 58 chains 20 links, or until it meets the prolongation of Zambesi Road; thence it shall be carried on a bearing of 334° 37′ 10″ for a distance of 90 links; thence on a bearing of 64° 37′ 10″ for a distance of 14 chains 79 links (following the North side of Zambesi Road) to point of commencement.

All the foregoing bearings are from True North.

The boundaries so drawn include an area of 177 acres 0 roods 10 perches exclusive of all roads, lanes and wharf.

Plots Nos. 149 to 250 inclusive, lying to the South of Zambesi Road and the Government Reserve (with the exception of the Railway Plot No. 184) will comprise the " Indian Township."

LIMBE.— *19/1909,—26th February.*

PROCLAIMED A TOWNSHIP AND BOUNDARIES FIXED AS FOLLOWS :—

COMMENCING at a beacon situated 12 links north of the northern side of the Blantyre-Mlanje road from which beacon the most southerly verandah corner of Mr. James Lindsay's Bungalow bears 6° 25′ 00″ and is distant 2 chains 94 links; the boundary shall be carried on a bearing of 273° 16′ 35″

for a distance of 62 chains 40 links till it reaches a beacon situated on the left bank of the Limbe river; thence it shall follow the left bank of the Limbe river, up stream, for a distance measured in a straight line of 117 chains 5 links or until it reaches a beacon situated on the left bank of the Limbe river; thence it shall be carried on a bearing of 93° 16′ 35″ for a distance of 35 chains 42 links; thence it shall be carried on a bearing of 183° 16′ 35″ for a distance of 107 chains 50 links; thence it shall be carried on a bearing of 273° 16′ 35″ for a distance of 19 chains 45 links to the point of commencement.

Notices.

Appointment of Health Officers.

31st August, 1907.

The following Officers were appointed Health Officers for the Townships of Zomba, Blantyre, Chiromo, and Fort Johnston respectively :—

The Government Medical Officers for the time being for the Zomba, Blantyre, Ruo and South Nyasa Districts.

106/1912,—17th June.

For the Townships of Limbe and Port Herald respectively :—

The Government Medical Officers for the Blantyre and Lower Shire Districts.

Rules.

Election of Councillors.

110/1912,—29th June.

Under Section 6.

Qualifications entitling to vote.

1. (1). The qualifications entitling to vote at the election of Councillors shall be as set forth in the Schedule hereto.

(2). No person shall be eligible for election who is not upon the Township Roll or who being upon such Roll has failed to pay the rates lawfully due by him.

Nomination of candidates.

2. Every candidate for election as a Councillor shall be nominated in writing by two persons (of whom the candidate shall not be one), whose names are on the Township Roll of Voters. All nominations shall be in the hands of the Town Clerk not later than three clear days before the day of election.

3. Voting shall be open and may be by proxy.

(margin: Method of voting.)

4. (1). The District Resident of the District in which the Township is situate (or some officer duly appointed by such District Resident) shall be the officer charged with the conduct of the election.

(2). The Town Clerk shall be present and shall present for the inspection of the District Resident or other officer as aforesaid, the Township Roll and the nomination papers.

(3). If the number of valid nominations is the same as that of the vacancies, the persons nominated shall be deemed to be elected.

(4). If the number of valid nominations is less than that of the vacancies, the persons nominated shall be deemed to be elected and the deficiency shall be made up by co-option at the first meeting of the newly elected Council from among the retiring Councillors who are willing to hold office and failing such, by co-option of such other persons as are qualified.

(5). If there be no valid nominations the retiring Councillors shall be deemed to be re-elected.

(6). If the number of valid nominations exceeds that of the vacancies, the Councillors shall be elected from among the persons nominated.

(7). Every person entitled to vote may vote for any number of candidates not exceeding the number of vacancies.

(8). Where an equality of votes is found to exist between any candidates and the addition of a vote would entitle any of those candidates to be elected, the District Resident or other officer presiding may give such additional vote by word of mouth or in writing.

5. The annual election shall be on the last Thursday in March of each year and shall take place between the hours of 4 p.m. and 6 p.m. The election shall be held at the office of the District Resident or at the office of the Town Council, as the District Resident may appoint.

(margin: Date and place of election.)

6. (1). The number of Councillors who shall go out of office each year shall be as set forth in the Schedule.

(margin: Number of Councillors to go out of office each year.)

(2). Such Councillors shall retire by rotation and in the event of two or more Councillors of equal seniority being due to retire by rotation, it shall be resolved by vote of the Council which Councillors shall retire.

(3). Seniority in the Council shall be computed from the date on which a Councillor last presented himself for election.

Casual vacan-
cies.
> **7.** Vacancies on the Council occurring in the interval between two elections shall be filled up by co-option. Any Councillor so co-opted shall retire at the next annual election.

Penalty for
illegal nomina-
tion or vote.
> **8.** Every person who signs any nomination papers or votes without being legally entitled so to do shall be guilty of an offence and upon summary conviction therefor shall be liable to a fine not exceeding £25.

Schedule.

Name of Township.	No. of Members of Council.	No. of Members to go out of Office Annually.	Chairman.	Persons qualified to vote	Maximum No. of Votes that may be exercised by one person.
Blantyre.	12, 2 of whom shall be Asiatics.	6, 1 of whom shall be an Asiatic.	Elected by Council.	Inner Ward: Owners or occupiers of buildings and land in the Inner Ward assessed at a value of not less than £100 Where the assessed value exceeds £200 an additional vote shall be allowed in respect of every tenant for each £200 of assessed value over and above the first £200.	5
				Outer Ward: Owners or occupiers of buildings in the outer ward assessed at a value of £100 or upwards. Where the assessed value exceeds £200 an additional vote shall be allowed in respect of every tenant for each £200 of assessed value over and above the first £200.	5

SCHEDULE—*Continued.*

Name of Township.	No. of Members of Council.	No. of Members to go out of Office Annually.	Chairman.	Persons qualified to vote	Maximum No. of Votes that may be exercised by one person.
Blantyre *Continued.*				Asiatic Ward: Asiatics owning or occupying buildings and land in the Asiatic Ward assessed at a value of £50 or upwards. Where the assessed value exceeds £100 one additional vote shall be allowed in respect of one additional tenant. Note. In respect of business premises there shall not be more than one vote which shall be vested in the owner or manager of such business.	5
Port Herald	5, one of whom shall be an Asiatic.	2, one of whom shall be an Asiatic.	Resident.	Same as Blantyre Inner Ward.	5
Chiromo *	3, (including Resident) one of whom shall be an Asiatic.	2, one of whom shall be an Asiatic.	Resident.	Same as Blantyre Inner Ward.	5
Zomba.	5, (including Resident) one of whom shall be an Asiatic.	2, one of whom shall be an Asiatic.	Resident.	Same as Blantyre Inner Ward.	5
Fort Johnston.	5, (including Resident) one of whom shall be an Asiatic.	2, one of whom shall be an Asiatic.	Resident.	Same as Blantyre Inner Ward.	5
Limbe.	5, one of whom shall be an Asiatic.	2, one of whom shall be an Asiatic.	Elected by Council.	Same as Blantyre Inner Ward. If an Asiatic Ward is created the qualifications shall be as in Blantyre Asiatic Ward.	5

* As amended by Notice of 2nd June 1914, (No. 1171-1914)

No. 3 of 1912.

STAGE PLAYS AND CINEMATOGRAPH EXHIBITIONS.

163/1912,—10th September.

Rules.

Under Section 15.

Form of licences.

1. The form of licences to be issued under the Ordinance shall be as set forth in the Schedule hereto.

Table of Fees.

2. The following fees shall be payable in respect of licences for Stage Plays or Cinematograph Exhibitions.

	£
For a period of one month or less ...	5
For a period exceeding one month but not exceeding three months	10
For a period exceeding three months but not exceeding six months	15
For a period exceeding six months but not exceeding twelve months	20

Schedule.

LICENCE FOR PLAY OR EXHIBITION.

The Stage Plays and Cinematograph Exhibitions Ordinance, 1912.

In pursuance of the powers in me vested by section 3 of "The Stage Plays and Cinematograph Exhibitions Ordinance, 1912" I do hereby license :—

(1).   in respect of

(2).   ·   in accordance with the provisions of the said Ordinance and subject to the terms and conditions endorsed on the back hereof.

Nyasaland

191   Licensing Officer.

(1). State name of applicant.

(2). State name of stage plays or cinematograph exhibition as the case may be.

THEATRE LICENCE.

The Stage Plays and Cinematograph Exhibitions Ordinance, 1912.

In pursuance of the powers in me vested by Section 7 of "The Stage Plays and Cinematograph Exhibitions Ordinance, 1912," I do hereby license the (*1*)

from the   day of   191 , to the   day of
          191   for the performance of (*2*)

in respect of which a licence under the hand of the Licensing Officer has been produced to me for inspection.   The licence hereby granted is issued subject to the terms and conditions endorsed on the back hereof.

Nyasaland
          191   District Resident.

(1). State name of theatre (if any) and particulars as to place of representation.

(2). State the name of stage play or kind of cinematograph exhibition as the case may be.

Notices.

Exemptions.

Under Section 14.

The provisions of the Ordinance shall not apply to :—

128/1912,—29th July.

(1). Stage plays given by the Blantyre Sports Club subject to the following condition :— Blantyre Sports Club.

No fee shall be charged for admission to the performance of such plays.

161/1912,—30th September.

(2). Lantern exhibitions of pictures, concerts and entertainments given under the superintendence of European members of the Church of Scotland Mission for educational and religious purposes to the pupils under their charge. Church of Scotland Mission.

No fee shall be charged for admission to such exhibitions, concerts and entertainments.

9/1913,—1st January.

(3). (*a*) Stage plays given by the Zomba Gymkhana Club. Zomba Gymkhana Club.

(*b*). Lantern exhibitions of pictures, concerts and entertainments given under the superintendence of European members of the Zambezi Industrial Mission and The Dutch Reformed Church Mission for educational and religious purposes to the pupils under their charge. Zambezi Industrial Mission.

Dutch Reformed Church Mission.

No fee shall be charged for admission to such stage plays, exhibitions, concerts and entertainments.

United Free
Church of
Scotland.

87/1913,—30th April.

(4). Lantern exhibitions of pictures, concerts and entertainments given under the superintendence of European members of the United Free Church of Scotland Mission for educational and religious purposes to natives.

No fee shall be charged for admission to such exhibitions, concerts and entertainments.

No. 4 of 1913.

IMMIGRATION RESTRICTION.

143/1913,—20th June.

Rules.

1. In these Rules the term "The Ordinance" shall mean "The Immigration Restriction Ordinance, 1913," and all Ordinances for the time being in force amending or adding to the said Ordinance.

> Definition.

2. Whenever any Immigration Officer shall, under the powers conferred by Section 11 of the Ordinance, allow a person appearing to be a prohibited immigrant to enter the Protectorate upon conditions, he shall grant to such person a permit in the form set out in Schedule A of these Rules.

> Conditional permit.

3. Every person to whom such permit has been granted shall report himself personally or by letter, as the issuer of the permit shall decide, at the office of issue of such permit or to such person in the service of the Government as the issuer of the permit shall direct, at least once in every fourteen days during the currency of the permit.

> Holder of permit to report himself

4. The transit pass contemplated by Section 18 of the Ordinance shall be in the form set out in Schedule B of these Rules.

> Transit pass.

5. The issuer of a transit pass shall immediately on the issue of each pass notify the Immigration Officer at the station named in the pass.

> Notification by issuer.

6. Each holder of a transit pass shall, before leaving the Protectorate, report himself at the office of the Immigration Officer at the station named in the pass within the period specified in the pass.

> Production of pass.

7. Any person who shall enter the Protectorate at any place to which an Immigration Officer is not appointed shall forthwith proceed to and appear before the nearest Immigration Officer who shall inform such person whether he is a prohibited immigrant or not, and if he is not a prohibited immigrant the Immigration Officer shall furnish him with the certificate set out in Schedule A to the Ordinance.

> Persons entering the Protectorate where no Immigration Officer.

Production of certificates, permits and passes.
8. Every person who shall enter the Protectorate after the date of the publication of these Rules shall retain the certificate, permit or pass issued to him under the Ordinance and shall on demand being made by an Immigration Officer produce the same for inspection.

Any such person who shall without lawful excuse fail to produce the certificate, permit or pass or a duplicate of such certificate, permit or pass issued as hereinafter provided, on demand being made as aforesaid, shall be liable to a fine not exceeding £5 and in default of payment to imprisonment, for a term not exceeding one month.

Duplicate of certificate, permit or pass.
9. Any person who shall satisfy the Principal Immigration Officer that he has obtained a certificate, permit or pass on his last entry into the Protectorate and has lost or destroyed the same may obtain from him a duplicate of the certificate permit or pass lost or destroyed.

Fees of certificates, etc.
10. Persons to whom certificates, permits and passes are issued under the Ordinance or any Rule thereunder, shall be charged and shall pay fees in accordance with Schedule C hereto.

Thumb prints.
11. Any person who is required to sign any certificate, permit, pass or other document to be issued to him under the Ordinance or any Rule thereunder, shall, if he is unable to sign his name in the characters of the English language, in lieu of signing the certificate, permit, pass, or other document, impress thereon the prints of both his right and left thumbs.

Schedule A.

(FACE.)

CONDITIONAL PERMIT.

Issued under the provisions of " The Immigration Restriction Ordinance, 1913."

No
Issued at
Sum deposited £
Deposit made by
(or if a bond has been taken) Amount of Bond £
Date of Bond   day of   191
Names and addresses of Sureties.

PERMISSION is hereby granted to the person or persons named below to enter the Nyasaland Protectorate and to remain therein for a period of six months from the date of this permit, and no longer, unless the person named as the holder of the permit shall within such period of six months obtain from the Immigration Officer at the office of issue a certificate that he is not a prohibited immigrant.

This permit is granted subject to the condition that the holder reports himself at least once in every fourteen days to the   at

Immigration Officer.

Name of Holder of the Permit
Nationality   Sex and Age
Usual place of Residence   Occupation
Height and general Description
Distinctive Marks, etc
Postal Address in the Protectorate
Names and Ages of Wife and Children if included
Signature of permit holder

(BACK.)

Left thumb print.	Right thumb print

RECEIPT.

This is to acknowledge the receipt of the sum of   (£   )
being refund of deposit named on the face thereof:

Signature
Witness

Place
Date

Schedule B.

(FACE.)

TRANSIT PASS

Issued under the provisions of " The Immigration Restriction Ordinance 1913."

No
Issued at
Date
Sum deposited £
Deposit made by
PERMISSION is hereby granted to the person named below to enable him to proceed without delay to
being his destination outside the Protectorate on condition that he leaves the Protectorate within   days from the date of issue of this pass, and that before leaving he reports himself at the office of the Immigration Officer at

Any breach of the conditions attaching to the issue of this pass or of the Ordinance or of the Rules printed on the back hereof involves the forfeiture of the deposits in addition to any other punishment prescribed by the Ordinance.

Immigration Officer.

Name of Holder of Pass
Nationality   Sex and Age
Usual Place of Residence   Occupation
Height and General Description
Distinctive Marks
Postal Addresses in the Protectorate during stay
Names and Ages of Wife and Children, if included
Destination outside Protectorate
Signature of Pass Holder

(BACK.

Left thumb print.	Right thumb print.

(ENDORSEMENT).
Entered Protectorate per   on
Reported at Office of the Immigration Officer at   on
   Extensions :—

RECEIPT.

This is to acknowledge receipt of the sum of   (£
being refund of deposit named on the face hereof.

                                            Signature
                                            As Witness

Place
Date
Left Protectorate per   on

Schedule C.

FEES PAYABLE IN RESPECT OF CERTIFICATES, PERMITS AND PASSES.

For a conditional permit 5/-
For a transit pass 5/-
For a duplicate of any certificate, pass or permit ...   5/-

No. 3 of 1902.

MARRIAGES.

Notices.

Under Section 57.   *14th January, 1903·*

DATE of commencement.

Notified that the first day of February 1903 is appointed as the date on which the Marriage Ordinance shall come into operation in the Protectorate

Order.

29th June, 1907.

Under Section 3.

ORDERED that the districts into which the Protectorate is now or may be hereafter divided for administrative purposes shall be Marriage Districts for the purposes of the above Ordinance.

AND FURTHER that the District Resident of each district as approved is appointed to be Registrar of Marriages for each such Marriage District.

AND FURTHER directed that for the purposes of the above Ordinance the office of the Registrar shall be the District Resident's Office at the chief Station of each District.

Licensed Buildings.

Under Section 6.

The following places of public worship have been licensed for the celebration of marriages under the above Ordinance :—

1st April, 1903.

The Church of Scotland Mission Churches at Blantyre, Zomba and Domasi.

6th August, 1903.

"White Fathers" Mission Church, Likuni, Lilongwe District.

12th December, 1903.

Mkoma Mission Station Schools Church, of the Dutch Reformed Church Mission.

14th January, 1904.

Mvera Church of the Dutch Reformed Church Mission.

1st April, 1904.

The Free Church of Scotland Mission Churches at Bandawe and Livingstonia.

76/1908,—26th May.

Dutch Reformed Church Mission Building at Mlanda, Upper Shire District.

706/1908,—4th July.

The Seventh Day Adventist Church, Malamulo Station, Cholo, Ruo District.

31/1910,—7th March.

The Dutch Reformed Church Mission Church at Kongwe, near Dowa, Dowa District.

91/1910,—30th June.

The Church of Scotland Mission Church at Mlanje.

138/1912,—30th July.

St. George's Church, Zomba.

114/1913,—7th May.

The Cathedral Church of St. Peter, Likoma.
The Church of All Saints, Kota-Kota.
The Church of St. Peter and St. Paul, Mpondas, Fort Johnston.
The Church of St. Martin, Malindi.
The Church of the Ascension, Likwenu.

No. 15 of 1912.

CHRISTIAN NATIVE MARRIAGES.

Licensed Buildings.

Under Section 5.

THE following places of public worship have been licensed for the celebration of Marriages under the above Ordinance:—

86/1913,—17th April.

ZAMBESI INDUSTRIAL MISSION CHURCHES AT

Chiole, near Ncheu	...	Upper Shire District.
Chipande	...	Blantyre District.
Mitsidi	...	Do. do.

NYASA INDUSTRIAL MISSION CHURCHES AT

Cholo	...	Ruo District.
Likabula	...	Blantyre District.

117/1913,—17th May.

CHURCH OF SCOTLAND MISSION CHURCHES AT

Blantyre	...	Luchenza	...	
Ngumbe	..	Chigumula	...	
Lunsu	...	Malabvi	...	
Chiradzulu	...	Soche	..	
Nsoni	...			Blantyre District.
Zomba	.	Domasi	...	
Ulumba	...	Kumsondole	...	
Matiti		Kasonga		
Nankumba	...	Chiuta	...	Zomba District.
Mlanje	.	Kambenje	...	
Chimwabvi	...	Chiopsya	...	
Mitembe	...	Machemba	...	
Chikuli	...	Matawa	...	
Chingoli	...	Chiringa	...	
Bona	...			Mlanje District.
Nthumbi		. .		Upper Shire District.

BAPTIST INDUSTRIAL MISSION CHURCH AT

Gowa	...	Upper Shire District.

146/1913,—30th June.

BAPTIST INDUSTRIAL MISSION CHURCH AT

Dzunje ... Upper Shire District.

UNITED FREE CHURCH OF SCOTLAND MISSION CHURCHES AT

Livingstonia	...	Karonga
Deep Bay	...	Mlowe
Chiweta	...	North Nyasa District.
Bandawe	...	Chifira
Kasangazi	...	Mlole
Mbamba	...	Usisya
Chihani	...	Mwambazi
Chituka	...	West Nyasa District.
Ekwendeni	...	Enukweni
Njuju	...	Enkondhlweni Mombera District.

SOUTH AFRICA GENERAL MISSION CHURCHES AT

Chididi	...	
Lulwe	...	Lower Shire District.

177/1913.—31st July.

ZAMBESI INDUSTRIAL MISSION CHURCHES AT

Muluma	...	
Dombole	...	
Ntonda	...	Upper Shire District.
Mpemba	...	Blantyre District.
Likongwe	...	West Shire District.

SEVENTH DAY ADVENTIST MISSION CHURCH AT

Malamulo ... Ruo District.

UNITED FREE CHURCH OF SCOTLAND MISSION CHURCHES AT

Loudon	...	
Hoho	...	
Entini	...	Mombera District.
Kasungu	...	
Sawara	...	Marimba District,

201/1913,—30th August.

DUTCH REFORMED MISSION CHURCHES AT

Malembo	.	
Livelezi	...	
Cape Maclear School	...	South Nyasa District.
Mphunzi	...	
Chitipi School	...	Dedza District.
Mlanda	...	Upper Shire District.
Mphoma	..	
Mvera	...	
Kongwe School	...	Lilongwe District.
Mtsala do.	...	
Malowa do.	...	
Mchinji do.	...	
Malingunde do.		
Mdanda do.	...	Lilongwe District.
Nchisi School	...	Marimba District.

235/1913,—31st October.

UNITED FREE CHURCH OF SCOTLAND MISSION CHURCH AT

Iwanda   ...   North Nyasa District.

31/1914,—20th February.

CHURCH OF SCOTLAND MISSION CHURCHES AT

Nchisi	...	
Chembeta	...	Zomba District.

166/1914,—31st August.

UNIVERSITIES MISSION TO CENTRAL AFRICA.

Universities Mission Cathe-
    dral, Likoma Island   ...   Marimba District.

228/1914,—18th November.

Church of All Saints, Kota-Kota.
Church of St. Martin, Malindi.
Church of St. Peter and St. Paul, Mpondas.
Church of Ascension, Likwenu.

Licensed Ministers.

Under Section 2.

The following have received licenses to celebrate marriages under the above Ordinance.

85/1913,—17th April.

ZAMBESI INDUSTRIAL MISSION.

Alexander Hamilton.
James Oswald.
John Chorley.

NYASA INDUSTRIAL MISSION.

J. A. Day.

116/1913,—17th May.

CHURCH OF SCOTLAND MISSION.

Rev. Alexander Hetherwick, D.D.
Rev. John Archibald Smith.
Rev. A. Melville Anderson, M.A.
Rev. James F. Alexander, M.A.
Rev. R. H. Napier, B.D.
Rev. Ernest D. Bowman, B.D.

BAPTIST INDUSTRIAL MISSION.

Alexander Smith.

147/1913,—30th June.

BAPTIST INDUSTRIAL MISSION.

Rev. William Charles Muisey.

UNITED FREE CHURCH OF SCOTLAND MISSION.

Rev. Robert Laws, M.A., M.D., D.D.
Rev. F. A. Innes, M.A., M.B.
Rev. W. Y. Turner, M.A., M.B.
Rev. Walter Angus Elmslie, M.B.
Rev. A. G. MacAlpine.
Rev. W. P. Young, M.A.
Rev. Duncan Ross Mackenzie.

SOUTH AFRICA GENERAL MISSION.

Edwin Price.

178/1913.—31st July.

SEVENTH DAY ADVENTIST MISSION.

Christopher Robinson.

UNITED FREE CHURCH OF SCOTLAND MISSION.

Rev. George Prentice, L.R.C.P. and S., L.M.
Rev. Donald Fraser.

200/1913,—30th August.

DUTCH REFORMED CHURCH MISSION.

Rev. J. J. Ferreira.
Rev. A. L. Hofmeyr.
Rev. J. W. L. Hofmeyr.
Rev. G. de C. Murray.
Rev. J. S. Murray.
Rev. L. J. Murray.
Rev. W. H. Murray.
Rev. P. A. Hens.
Rev. J. A. Retief.
Rev. A. P. Rousseau.
Rev. S. Strijdom.

ZAMBESI INDUSTRIAL MISSION.

Herbert E. Osborn.
John S. Ferguson.
Frank Gardner.

63/1914,—31st March.

ZAMBESI INDUSTRIAL MISSION.

John J. Holmes.
Hugh B. Morton.

101/1914,—10th May.

UNITED FREE CHURCH OF SCOTLAND MISSION.

Rev. Charles Stuart.
Dr. Hubert Wilson.

ZAMBESI INDUSTRIAL MISSION.

Alfred Ellis.

136/1914,—31st July.

NYASA INDUSTRIAL MISSION.

W. G. Jones.

165/1914,—31st August.

UNIVERSITIES MISSION TO CENTRAL AFRICA.

Venerable Archdeacon Glossop.

183/1914,—30th September.

UNITED FREE CHURCH OF SCOTLAND MISSION.

Rev. T. T. Alexander, M.A.
Rev. Alexander Macdonald.

ZAMBESI INDUSTRIAL MISSION.

William Twist.

201/1914,—31st October.

UNIVERSITIES MISSION TO CENTRAL AFRICA.

The Rt. Rev. The Bishop of Nyasaland.

229/1914,—26th November

UNIVERSITIES MISSION TO CENTRAL AFRICA.

Rev. H. A. M. Cox.
Rev. D. Victor.
Rev. F. Winspear.
Rev. A. Matthew.
Rev. A. R. Russell.
Rev. G. H. Wilson.
Rev. A. C. Churchward.
Rev. A. M. Jenkin.
Rev. P. Opperman.
Rev. E. Horner.

DUTCH REFORMED CHURCH MISSION.

Rev. C. J. H. Van Wyk.
Rev. H. L. Webb.
Rev. J. J. Van Heerden.

No. 2 of 1904.

REGISTRATION OF BIRTHS & DEATHS.

Rules.

Under Sections 13, 16 and 20.   *30th June, 1904.*

1. The Registrar-General of Marriages at Blantyre is hereby appointed Registrar-General of Births and Deaths under this Ordinance. *Appointment of Registrar-General.*

2. Errors in any Register being errors of fact or substance shall be rectified by means of a statutory declaration pursuant to the provisions of 37 and 38 Vict. C. 88 Section 86. Forms in accordance therewith will be supplied gratis by the Registrar. *Correction of errors.*

3.* The place in each District at which Births and Deaths may be registered and Registers inspected shall be the Office of the District Resident at the Chief Station in each District, and the hours at which such registration and inspection may be effected shall be the ordinary office hours on such days as the District Resident is in attendance. *Registrars' offices.* *Hours of attendance.*

4. Births and Deaths may be registered under this Ordinance, without personal attendance, by letter addressed to the District Resident of the district in which the birth or death takes place. Forms of registration will be supplied gratis by the District Resident. The prescribed fee shall, in every case, be paid in advance. *Registration without personal attendance.*

5. All Registers, Returns and other documents required for the purposes of this Ordinance shall be in such form as the Governor may from time to time direct. *Forms.*

6. Any Register, Return or Index in the custody of the Registrar shall be open to inspection subject to the consent of the Registrar, or failing such consent by order of a Judge of the High Court. *Inspection of Registers etc.*

7. The following fees shall be charged, viz :— *Fees.*

		s.	*d.*
(a).	On registration of a Birth or Death	2	6
(b).	On a certified copy of an entry in the Register of Births or Deaths	2	6
(c).	On inspection of Register, Return or Index	2	6
(d).	On registration of name under Section 8 of this Ordinance	2	6

* Rule amended by Notice (No. 119/1914) of June 30th 1914.

The Registrar may in any case, if he thinks fit, on account of the poverty of a party or for any other reason, dispense in whole or in part with the payment of any of the above fees.

Registration of Births and Deaths on board ships.   8. Births and Deaths on board ships while within the territorial waters of the Protectorate shall be registered at the next port of call.

121/1914,—12th June.

Appointment of Registrar-General.

Under Section 2 (c).

The Officer for the time being holding the post of Attorney-General was appointed to act as Registrar-General for the purposes of the Ordinance.

No. 18 of 1912.

CROWN LANDS.

278/1913,—4th December.

Notice.

Under Section 21.

FORM OF YEARLY TENANCY AGREEMENT.

AGREEMENT made this   day of   19
between   for and on behalf of
His Excellency the Governor and Commander-in-Chief of the Nyasaland
Protectorate (hereinafter called the Landlord) of the one part, and
                                    (hereinafter called the Tenant) of the other part :—

WITNESSETH

The Landlord agrees to let and the Tenant to take all those lands situate
at   containing   acres more or less, and bounded as follows :—

from the   day of   19 , to the   day of   19 ,
and thereafter until terminated as hereinafter provided at the yearly rental
of   clear of all deductions payable half yearly in advance on the
first day of April and the first day of October of each year in sums
of   to the Resident of the   District.

The Tenant further agrees to pay the said rent on the days and in
manner aforesaid, and to observe the special conditions and covenants
hereinafter expressed and also the conditions and covenants implied herein
by virtue of the provisions of "The Crown Lands Ordinance, 1912," except
the condition and covenant contained in Section 10 (*p*) thereof.

SPECIAL CONDITIONS AND COVENANTS.

1.   That this Agreement shall be determined by the bankruptcy of the
Tenant.

2.   That this Agreement may be determined on the 31st of March or
the 30th of September in any year by either party giving to the other six
months previous notice in writing of their intention so to do.

3.   Notices etc. shall be deemed to have been received by the Tenant if
they shall have been delivered at the Tenant's last known postal address
within the Protectorate.

4.   And the Landlord covenants with the Tenant that he, paying the
said yearly rent and performing and observing the conditions of this
Agreement, shall quietly hold and enjoy the said premises without any
interruption from or by the Landlord or any person rightfully claiming
under him.

SIGNED by the within named for and
on behalf of His Excellency the
Governor and Commander-in Chief in
my presence this
day of   19 .

SIGNED by the within named in
my presence this
day of   19 .

2/1914,—6th January.

Rule.

I. Every applicant for a Yearly Tenancy shall at the time of making his application deposit with the Lands Officer the sum of Four Pounds sterling and such sum shall be dealt with in the manner following :—

(*a*). If the application be refused the sum deposited shall be refunded to the applicant.

(*b*). If the application be granted the sum shall be placed to the credit of the applicant on account of drawing and registration fees, stamp duty, and rent.

(*c*). If the applicant withdraw his application or refuse or neglect to execute the Yearly Tenancy Agreement when called upon to do so, the sum specified in the Schedule hereto, according to the circumstances of the case, shall be forfeited to the Crown and applied to the revenues of the Protectorate, and the balance, if any, of the above mentioned deposit of Four Pounds shall be refunded to the applicant.

SCHEDULE.

		Amount to be forfeited.
1. If the Agreement has been prepared		£4.
2. If the application has been granted but the Agreement has not been prepared		£2.
3. If the ground has been examined but the application has not been submitted for the Governor's approval		£1.

No. 8 of 1912.

LAND SURVEYORS.

105/1912,—10th June.

Notice.

Under Section 8.

NOTIFIED that the following fees may be charged in respect of all surveys of land made by registered Land Surveyors from and after the date of publication hereof.

FURTHER NOTIFIED that the same scale of fees will be applicable in the case of Surveys made by Government Surveyors.

REVISED SCALE.

						Aproximate rate per acre.	Fees Payable.		
						s. d.	£	s.	d.
2 acres up to 125	acres but not including			125	acres.	—	7	0	0
125 ,,	150	,,	,,	,,	150	,,	1/2¾	8	10	0
150 ,,	175	,,	,,	,,	175	,,	1/2½	9	15	0
175 ,,	200	,,	,,	,,	200	,,	1/2¼	11	0	0
200 ,,	225	,,	,,	,,	225	,,	1/2	12	10	0
225 ,,	250	,,	,,	,,	250	,,	1/1¾	13	10	0
250 ,,	275	,,	,,	,,	275	,,	1/1½	14	15	0
275 ,,	300	,,	,,	,,	300	,,	1/1¼	15	15	0
300 ,,	350	,,	,,	,,	350	,,	1/1	17	10	0
350 ,,	400	,,	,,	,,	400	,,	1/0½	19	10	0
400 ,,	450	,,	,,	,,	450	,,	1/-	21	15	0
450 ,,	500	,,	,,	,,	500	,,	11½	22	15	0
500 ,,	550	,,	,,	,,	550	,,	11	24	10	0
550 ,,	600	,,	,,	,,	600	,,	10½	25	0	0
600 ,,	650	,,	,,	,,	650	,,	10	26	0	0
650 ,,	700	,,	,,	,,	700	,,	9¾	27	10	0
700 ,,	750	,,	,,	,,	750	,,	9½	28	15	0
750 ,,	800	,,	,,	,,	800	,,	9¼	30	0	0
800 ,,	850	,,	,,	,,	850	,,	9	31	0	0
850 ,,	900	,,	,,	,,	900	,,	8¾	32	0	0
900 ,,	950	,,	,,	,,	950	,,	8½	32	15	0
950 ,,	1,000	,,	,,	,,	1,000	,,	8¼	33	10	0

Revised Scale—*Continued.*

	Aproximate rate per acre.	Fees Payable.		
	d.	£	s.	d.
1,000 acres up to 1,100 acres but not including 1,100 acres.	$7\frac{3}{4}$	34	0	0
1,100 „ 1,200 „ „ „ 1,200 „	$7\frac{1}{2}$	36	0	0
1,200 „ 1,300 „ „ „ 1,300 „	$7\frac{1}{4}$	37	15	0
1,300 „ 1,400 „ „ „ 1,400 „	7	39	10	0
1,400 „ 1,500 „ „ „ 1,500 „	$6\frac{3}{4}$	40	15	0
1,500 „ 1,600 „ „ „ 1,600 „	$6\frac{1}{2}$	42	0	0
1,600 „ 1,700 „ „ „ 1,700 „	$6\frac{1}{4}$	43	0	0
1,700 „ 1,800 „ „ „ 1,800 „	6	43	15	0
1,900 „ 2,000 „ „ „ 2,000 „	$5\frac{1}{2}$	44	15	0
2,000 „ 2,250 „ „ „ 2,250 „	$5\frac{1}{4}$	46	0	0
2,250 „ 2,500 „ „ „ 2,500 „	$4\frac{3}{4}$	47	0	0
2,500 „ 2,750 „ „ „ 2,750 „	$4\frac{1}{4}$	48	0	0
2,750 „ 3,000 „ „ „ 3,000 „	4	50	0	0
3,000 „ 3,250 „ „ „ 3,250 „		53	0	0
3,250 „ 3,500 „ „ „ 3,500 „		56	0	0
3,500 „ 3,750 „ „ „ 3,750 „		59	0	0
3,750 „ 4,000 „ „ „ 4,000 „	$3\frac{3}{4}$	62	0	0
4,000 „ 4,250 „ „ „ 4,250 „		64	15	0
4,250 „ 4,500 „ „ „ 4,500 „		67	10	0
4,500 „ 4,750 „ „ „ 4,750 „		70	5	0
4,750 „ 5,000 „ „ „ 5,000 „	$3\frac{1}{2}$	73	0	0
5,000 „ 5,250 „ „ „ 5,250 „		75	0	0
5,250 „ 5,500 „ „ „ 5,500 „		77	0	0
5,500 „ 5,750 „ „ „ 5,750 „		79	0	0
5,750 „ 6,000 „ „ „ 6,000 „	$3\frac{1}{4}$	81	0	0
6,000 „ 6,250 „ „ „ 6,250 „		82	10	0
6,250 „ 6,500 „ „ „ 6,500 „		84	0	0
6,500 „ 6,750 „ „ „ 6,750 „		85	10	0
6,750 „ 7,000 „ „ „ 7,000 „	3	87	0	0
7,000 „ 7,250 „ „ „ 7,250 „		88	5	0
7,250 „ 7,500 „ „ „ 7,500 „		89	10	0
7,500 „ 7,750 „ „ „ 7,750 „		90	15	0
7,750 „ 8,000 „ „ „ 8,000 „	$2\frac{3}{4}$	92	0	0
8,000 „ 8,250 „ „ „ 8,250 „		92	10	0
8,250 „ 8,500 „ „ „ 8,500 „		93	0	0
8,500 „ 8,750 „ „ „ 8,750 „		93	10	0
8,750 „ 9,000 „ „ „ 9,000 „	$2\frac{1}{2}$	94	0	0
9,000 „ 9,500 „ „ „ 9,500 „		95	0	0
9,500 „ 10,000 „ „ „ 10,000 „	$2\frac{5}{16}$	96	0	0

Note :—(1). A minimum charge of £7 for all areas from 2 to 124 acres, except Township Plots for which a fixed charge of £3. 3*s*. 0*d*. per plot will be made.

(2). Areas from 10,000 acres upwards to be surveyed at rates to be mutually arranged.

(3). The above rates are inclusive of preparing and forwarding fair plan; making endorsement on 3 copies of Deeds, and all surveying expenses excepting travelling to and from the estate and cost of erecting brick and cement beacons.

(4). Travelling to and from estates will be charged for at the rate of 1/- per mile.

(5). 50% of the Survey Fees as set out above to be paid on the day of the sale of the lease and the balance on completion of the survey.

No. 7 of 1907.

RAILWAYS.

180/1912,—31st October.

Under Section 52.

Shire Highlands Railway, Nyasaland, Limited.

RULES AND REGULATIONS.

PRELIMINARY.

Definitions.

1. In these Rules the following terms shall, unless the context otherwise requires, have the meaning set against them respectively that is to say :—

"Company." The Shire Highlands Railway Company, Nyasaland, Limited.

"General Manager." The authorized Representative of the Company in Nyasaland.

"Engineer." The Chief of the Engineering Department.

"Traffic Superintendent." The Chief of the Traffic Department.

"Loco Superintendent." The Chief of the Locomotive Department.

"Station Master." The Clerk in charge of the Station.

"Railway Servant." Any person in the employ of the Company.

"Head Office." The Head Office and Management at Limbe.

"Train." Whenever this term is used it shall be understood to include light engines (engines without trains), motor trollies or any other vehicle that requires more than four men to remove it from the rail.

"Ballast Train." A train intended for the carriage of ballast, stone, water, material or fuel when picked up or put down either between stations or in station yards.

"Driver." The person in charge for the time being of a working locomotive engine.

"Guard." A brakesman and any other railway servant who may for the time being be performing the duties of guard.

"Banner Flags." Flags stretched across the line or rails and held by upright supports fixed in the ground.

"Ganger." The Railway Servant in charge of a gang of platelayers or other workmen employed on the permanent way by whatever designation he may be known.

"Special Instructions" means orders subsidiary to these Rules issued from time to time by the Manager or some person authorized by him which may be written, telegraphic or oral.

2. The Railway time shall be local mean time at Blantyre and clocks shall be regulated every day by telegraph.

Time.

3. Every railway servant shall assist in carrying out the rules and immediately report to his superior officer any infringement thereof or any occurrence which may come under his notice affecting the safe and proper working of the Railway. Any railway servant failing to report an irregularity which may incidentally or otherwise come to his knowledge shall incur the same responsibility as if he were the person at fault.

Liability of railway servant for not reporting irregularity.

WORKING OF TRAINS GENERALLY.

4. All trains until further notice, shall be worked on the Line Clear system, no two trains being permitted at the same time to enter the section between two adjacent Stations.

Line clear system.

5. The Driver shall not move any train out of a Station until he has received a "Line Clear" certificate from the Station Master or Guard.

Driver to possess Line Clear certificate.

6. Any exception to the above shall only be by order of the General Manager by writing or telegram.

Exception.

7. The time of arrival and departure of every train shall be duly booked at the Station.

Booking of arrival and departure.

8. All "Line Clear" certificates shall be signed in ink by the Station Master on duty.

Signature of "Line Clear" certificate.

9. On handing over a "Line Clear" certificate to the Guard of a train or Driver of a light engine the signature of Guard or Driver shall be obtained on the counterfoil in the "Line Clear" certificate Book, and pens and ink shall be kept in readiness to save delay to trains.

Handing over of "Line Clear" certificate.

10. When one Station Master takes over from another the former shall at once acquaint himself as to the movements of trains and ascertain if "Line Clear" has been given or asked for in either direction.

Procedure on taking over from Station Master.

11. In the event of a derailment or other accident occurring in a Station Yard at a time when another train is due to leave the next Station, if such occurrence is likely to block, delay or cause risk to the approaching train, the facts shall

Accident in station yard.

be at once wired to the Station Master at the next Station and the latter shall issue a "Caution" order stating on same the reason for such "Caution" order.

Two trains crossing Station.

12. When two trains are timed to cross a Station, the "Line Clear" certificate for the departure of the first train shall not be handed to the Guard until the other train has been brought to a stand in the Station Yard.

General duties of Guard.

13. The Guard in charge shall satisfy himself, before the train is due to start, and during the journey, that the vehicles composing the train are properly loaded, marshalled, coupled and greased, that they are in good working order and that the train is in a state of efficiency for travelling. He shall also examine the loading of any vehicles he may attach on the journey, and, if any vehicle becomes unsafe from the shifting or derangement of the load he shall at once have the load re-adjusted or the vehicle detached from the train. All irregularities shall be recorded in his journal.

SIGNALS.

Signals.

14. During daylight flags shall be used to signal all trains. After sunset, during dusk or darkness, lighted lamps shall be used to signal all trains.

Green, whether flag or lamp, shall denote proceed with caution. Red, whether flag or lamp, shall denote danger, and the Driver shall immediately stop and not proceed until the signal is removed. Any imperfect signal shall be regarded as "danger," and the train brought to a stand.

Detonating signals.

15. Detonators shall also be regarded as a danger signal, and the Driver shall immediately stop the train on hearing the explosion.

Accident to train.

16. Should any accident occur preventing a train from proceeding the Guard shall at once protect his train by sending Flagmen in opposite directions with danger signals and they shall proceed 800 paces and there remain, showing danger signals until such time as they shall be re-called.

TRAIN LIGHTS.

Train lights.

17. All trains running after sunset and before sunrise and in thick, foggy or tempestuous weather shall have the head, tail and other lamps properly lighted and every train shall carry :—

1 Head lamp burning brightly in front of the funnel.

1 Red lamp on the right side of the van.

1 Tail lamp (red) affixed at the end of the last vehicle; if a light engine, it shall be affixed to the tender.

SIGNALS FOR SHUNTING.

18. Shunting operations shall be controlled by hand signals.

19. While shunting operations are in progress, which are liable to block the main line, "Line Clear" shall not be given for any train without previously arranging for a signalman with flags by day and lamp by night to be stationed well clear of the shunting operations in order to signal or stop any expected train.

20. A white light shall never be used as a signal in any shunting.

21. A red light shall be a signal to come to a stand in whichever direction the train is going.

22. Green lights shall be used at night to start the train when shunting. The waving of the light from side to side shall indicate that the train may keep in motion at a speed not exceeding five miles an hour. The moving of the green light up and down shall indicate the train shall slow down.

23. When two engines or vehicles are approaching the same pair of points from two different lines, or, where there is a likelihood of this occurring, both shall be brought to a stand by "danger" signals and when this has been done, and not before, the person in charge of the engine or vehicle, which it is intended to allow first over the points, shall be told verbally as well as signalled to move forward, while a danger signal and a verbal order not to move shall be given to the other.

24. No engine or vehicle of any kind, either by day or by night, shall be moved from one line to another until signalled to do so by the Pointsman, *i.e.*, waved over by a green flag or light.

25. A stationary light (a lamp set on the ground) shall not be taken as a signal.

26. When shunting at night, if the shunting engine lights cannot be seen, a "danger" signal shall be exhibited on the leading vehicle by suspending a lamp on the side chain hook thrown across the buffer or by any other means.

INSTRUCTIONS TO INSPECTORS, GANGERS, PLATELAYERS OR OTHER WORKMEN EMPLOYED ON THE PERMANENT WAY.

27. Except in case of emergency, Platelayers or other workmen employed on the Permanent Way shall work under the protection of special signals. Such special signals shall be red and green hand flags, banner flags, red and green lights and detonators and shall be used as prescribed by special instructions.

Signals for shunting.

Shunting liable to block main line.

White light not to be used.

Meaning of red light.

Use of green light.

Two engines approaching same points.

Moving engine from one line to another.

Stationary light.

Shunting at night.

Special signals.

Train running between sunset and sunrise.

28. Whenever any train shall be timed to run or expected to run on any portion of the line between sunset and sunrise all the necessary lamps for signalling shall be lighted at sunset or at such earlier time as shall be prescribed by the authorized officer. The lamps shall not be put out until the train or trains shall have passed, except in accordance with special instructions.

Signals in foggy weather.

29. Notwithstanding anything contained in the last two paragraphs the signalling lamps shall always be lighted and kept burning during thick, foggy or tempestuous weather.

Signals to be in order before Line Clear given.

30. Whenever signals have to be used in accordance with these rules, the Station Master or other Railway servant shall not give " Line Clear " for a train to proceed to his Station until the necessary lamps have been lighted and the Signalmen are on duty.

Arrival of two trains at Station.

31. At Stations where two trains are timed to cross, they shall not be signalled into the Station at the same time. One train shall first be brought to a stand inside the points. The Station Master shall then satisfy himself that the points are correctly set for the other train and shall then give the signal for it to come into the Station. The second train shall then run slowly through the Station and beyond the points at the opposite end of the Yard and shall be backed by hand signal on to the Station road at the rear of the first train.

Speed over line protected by " proceed " signal.

32. When the " proceed " signal is shown by the Platelayers or others employed on the Permanent Way, the speed of the train over the line protected by such signal shall not exceed five miles per hour or such lower rate as may be prescribed by special instructions.

Driver and danger signal.

33. When a danger signal is shown the Driver shall stop his train before reaching it, and then, if so signalled, shall draw in cautiously until his train is protected.

Obstruction on line.

34. If owing to any obstruction on the line the Driver is unable to bring his whole train within the signal shown, he shall inform the Guard, who shall go or send a man back, with signals to protect the train.

Points.

Responsibility of Station Master.

35. The Station Master shall examine the Station points at his Station at least once every day and always within one half-hour of the arrival of a passenger train.

Inspection in stormy and wet weather.

36. During stormy and wet weather the points shall be inspected more frequently. He shall see they are properly cleaned and kept lubricated. He shall also satisfy himself that they are in working order by trying and using the levers and seeing that the switch of the points fits properly and truly to the stock rail.

37. All facing points on main line shall be secured by a padlock or other locking device. **Locking of facing points.**

38. The Driver shall bring the train to a stand in front of all facing points unless signalled forward. **Driver and facing points.**

39. The Station Master shall be responsible that all facing points over which a train will pass are correctly set and locked and trailing points correctly set. **Station Master and facing points.**

40. No Driver shall take an engine upon or across the main line without being signalled by the person in charge of the points. **Driver and signal of Pointsman.**

41. Drivers shall exercise great care in passing over facing points and shall see that they are properly set. **Driver passing facing points.**

42. Every Pointsman whilst on duty shall have with him flags by day and hand signal lamps after sunset. **Signals of Pointsman.**

43. The condition of the hand signal and of other lamps and flags in the possession of the Station Staff shall receive the careful attention of the Station Master, who shall be held responsible for seeing that lamps are kept clean and well trimmed. All defective lamps and discoloured flags shall be forwarded without delay to the Storekeeper for repairs or replacing. **Condition of lamps and flags.**

44. Should there be any obstruction on the line within sight or knowledge of any Pointsman he shall show the "danger" signal and shall continue to show such signal to any trains approaching in the direction of the obstruction until the obstruction has been removed and the line made clear and safe, and shall as soon as practicable take steps to report the obstruction to the Station Master. **Danger signal in case of obstruction.**

45. Every Pointsman observing anything wrong or unusual in a passing train shall report the circumstances to the Station Master and, if the occurrence is of such a nature as to involve danger to the train or to the public, he shall show a "danger" signal to the Guard and Driver. **Pointsman observing anything wrong in a passing train.**

Rules for Drivers.

46. Drivers and Firemen shall be at their engines at least forty-five minutes before starting time in order to see that their engines are in good order and that there is a sufficient supply of fuel, water, oil and other necessary stores. **Attendance of drivers and firemen.**

47. The Driver shall attach his engine to the train at least fifteen minutes before the time for starting in order to satisfy himself that the vacuum brake is in good working order. **Driver to attach engine.**

Driver to sound whistle before moving engine.	**48.** The Driver shall always sound the engine whistle before putting the engine in motion.
Other occasions on which whistle to be sounded.	**49.** The engine whistle shall also be sounded when— Approaching or passing through a Station. Entering a curve in cutting. Approaching a bridge round a curve in cutting. Approaching a permanent way gang at work.
Driver and engine lamps.	**50.** The Driver shall satisfy himself that— The engine carries lamps as provided. That such lamps are in good order. That such lamps are properly trimmed and are lighted and burning brightly between sunset and sunrise or in thick, foggy or tempestuous weather.
Management of train.	**51.** The Driver shall start, run, and stop his train steadily and without a jerk.
Driver to observe state of weather.	**52.** In stopping a train the Driver shall, in order to determine when to shut off steam, give particular attention to the state of weather, the condition of the rails and the length of the train.
Control of train.	**53.** Drivers shall be solely responsible for having their trains under proper control and pulling up at the place required.
Assistance of guard's brake.	**54.** Should the Driver require the assistance of all the brake power on the train he shall notify the Guard by giving three short whistles, on hearing which, the Guard shall at once apply all the brake power at his disposal.
Skidding.	**55.** Drivers are cautioned against "skidding" their engines and tender wheels when applying their brakes.
Speed over facing points.	**56.** Speed over facing points shall not exceed five miles per hour.
Driver to keep look out.	**57.** The Driver shall keep a good look out, frequently looking back during the journey and shall see that the whole of the train is following in a safe and proper manner.
Part of train becoming detached.	**58.** Should any part of the train become detached while in motion on a down grade care 'shall be taken that the front portion is not stopped until the rear part has been brought to stand.
Firemen to keep looking out.	**59.** Every Fireman shall when not otherwise engaged, keep a good look out while the engine is in motion and should he see anything requiring attention, which owing to a curve the Driver cannot see, he shall immediately call the attention of the Driver thereto.

60. Drivers and Firemen are cautioned that in leaning over to watch the working of their engines they shall always be careful to see that there is no water column or other thing likely to touch them. After taking water at a tank or water column, the Driver of the engine shall see that the hose or water crane is left clear of the line and properly secured.

Drivers and Firemen leaning over.

61. The Firemen shall obey the orders of the Driver in all particulars.

Firemen to obey Driver.

62. No engine shall be put in motion outside station limits unless the Driver and Firemen are upon it.

Engine in motion outside Station limits.

63. Firemen are strictly prohibited from moving engines unless under instructions to do so.

Firemen not to move engine.

64. Any person authorized by special licence in accordance with the provisions of the Ordinance to travel on an engine may do so, but on no account shall he be permitted to touch the regulator or in any way interfere with the work of the Driver, Firemen or engine crew. Should any interference be persisted in after a remonstrance on the part of the Driver he shall stop the train and request the offender to leave the engine, and, if necessary, he shall call in the assistance of the Guard.

Interference with work of Driver &c.

65. When an engine has been attached to a train, and until the end of the journey, the Driver shall obey all orders of the Station Master when within the Station limits and he shall obey the orders of the Guard in charge of train in all matters affecting the stopping or moving of the train and shall promptly obey all other orders given and all signals shown to him whether by the Guard in charge of the train or by the Station Master, so far as the safe and proper working of the train will permit.

Driver to obey Guard and Station Master.

66. The Driver shall take notice of all signals displayed on the line and on no account shall he pass a red flag by day or a red light by night except as provided in the rules and he shall not pass a green flag at more than five miles per hour.

Driver to take notice of signals

67. Any improper display of signals shall at once be reported to the Locomotive Superintendent.

Improper display of signal.

68. Imperfect signals shall be treated as danger signals.

Imperfect signals.

69. Any violent waving of a light of whatever colour or of a man's arms towards the Driver shall be taken as indicating danger.

Danger signal.

70. The Driver shall see that the proper equipment of tools (as per list in engine tool box) is on the engine. Any loss or breakage shall be at once reported to the Locomotive Superintendent.

Equipment of tools &c.

Other articles to be carried by driver.

71. The following articles shall be carried on the engine or tender :—

A complete set of lamps viz :—

1 Head Lamp.	1 Bucket.
1 Tail Lamp.	2 Screw Jacks.
1 Gauge Glass Lamp.	2 Spare Coupling Links.
1 Hand Lamp.	1 Complete Set of Fire-irons,
1 Red Flag.	

and such other tools as the Locomotive Superintendent may order from time to time.

Driver to examine Notices.

72. Drivers shall examine all notices posted for their guidance before leaving the Running Shed in order to ascertain if there is anything requiring special attention on any part of the line.

Driver to report defect in road.

73. Drivers shall report any defect in the road, works, telegraph posts, wires or signals at the first Station and shall in addition note any such defect in their journal.

Driver to report state of engine.

74. Every Driver shall report the state of his engine and tender at the end of the journey in writing in a book kept apart for that purpose.

Driver not to leave engine.

75. A Driver when on duty shall not leave his engine unless it is absolutely necessary for him to do so; and under no circumstances shall he leave it without a competent man being left in charge of it and before ensuring that the reversing lever is in the centre position and the tender brake is hard on.

Driver to regulate running of trains.

76. The Driver shall run his train on each section of the line within the limits of speed prescribed by the Time Table and the speed boards fixed along the line.

Making up time.

77. The Driver shall not attempt to make up lost time by exceeding these limits.

Coupling between engine and train.

78. The Driver shall satisfy himself that the coupling between engine and train or between tender and train is properly made, the safety chains hooked on and the vacuum hose pipe properly connected.

Prescribed signals for starting.

79. No engine with vehicles attached shall be started from a Station until the Guard in charge of the train has given the prescribed signals for starting to the Driver.

Guards to give starting signals.

80. Guards shall in all cases give the starting signal for trains by a whistle during the day and by a green light at night waved horizontally above the head.

81. When two or more engines are attached to a train the Driver of the leading engine shall be responsible for the proper observation of signals, and the Driver or Drivers of the other engine or engines shall watch and take signals from the leading Driver.

82. Drivers shall not trust entirely to signals but shall always be vigilant and cautious.

83. Should the Driver over-run the Station or place where a train may be timed or ordered to stop at, he shall on no account set back his train until signalled to do so.

84. Such signal shall be a waving green flag by day and a green light by night in the direction required.

85. No engine shall pass the Station limits, either with or without vehicles attached, until the Driver thereof has a " Line Clear " certificate in his possession.

86. Drivers shall be especially vigilant on approaching Chiromo Bridge to see that the red counter-weights of the lifting span are up. If these weights are not in the hoisted position the train shall be immediately brought to a stand.

ENGINE NOT TO PUSH TRAINS.

87. Except as shown below, no engine shall push a train upon any line but shall draw it :

Exceptions :—

(a). When within Station limits during daylight or where especially authorized by the Chief Engineer or Traffic Superintendent.

(b). In special circumstances when assisting up inclines.

(c). In the case of the hauling engine being disabled, a following engine may push the train slowly to the next Station.

(d). When the line is blocked and trains are being worked to the point of obstruction on both sides, an engine may push but only from or to the Station nearest the point of obstruction.

(e). Ballast trains working in a section of the line.

CHIROMO BRIDGE.

88. During such months as the River is navigable for steamers above Chiromo the lifting span of the Chiromo Bridge shall be raised on written application to the Station Master at Chiromo within one hour of such notice, provided that no train be due within that hour to cross the Bridge.

Ganger in charge to raise or lower span.

89. No person other than the Ganger in charge shall be allowed to raise or lower the lifting span unless the Permanent Way Inspector be present.

Duty of Station Master.

90. On the Station Master at Chiromo receiving notice of the passing of a steamer as provided in Rule 88 he shall at once notify the Bridge Ganger and the Permanent Way Inspector, stating the time at which the lifting span will be raised. At the same time the line between Port Herald and Chiromo shall be absolutely blocked and remain so until the Bridge Ganger or the Permanent Way Inspector shall notify the Station Master at Chiromo that the lifting span has been lowered to rail level.

Record of applications.

91. A record of all applications from Shipowners or Agents for the lifting of the Bridge shall be kept at Chiromo Station in accordance with the instructions to the Chiromo Station Master.

RULES FOR WORKING BALLAST TRAINS.

Order to run necessary.

92. No ballast train shall be run on any line without orders from the General Manager.

Guard to accompany train.

93. A Guard shall accompany each ballast train running on the line.

Times of running.

94. The Guard in charge of a ballast train shall carry out the instructions of the Station Master as to the times between which the train may run.

Labourers on train.

95. The Guard of a ballast train shall, before giving the starting signal, see that all labourers working on the train are safely seated.

Ballast train treated as special train.

96. If a ballast train is proceeding direct to the nearest Station without stopping it shall be treated as a special train and shall run under ordinary rules, but it shall not be allowed to start until it is certain to reach the nearest Station before any other train is due at either end of the section.

Procedure of booked trains.

97. Booked trains shall always take precedence of ballast trains, except in cases of accident or of extreme emergency.

Line Clear procedure to apply.

98. If a ballast train has to work between two Stations, the procedure as regards "Line Clear" certificate shall be strictly adhered to.

Assistance in case of emergency.

99. Every person employed on the permanent way or works shall be bound, on the request of the Guard, to assist him in case of emergency.

TROLLIES.

Working of trollies.

100. Trollies shall not be put upon the line unless they are in charge of a person who is properly authorized to work them.

101. When a trolly is placed on the line, it shall be protected, in front and rear, for a distance of at least 800 yards, by a man showing a danger signal.

Protection of trolly by danger signal.

102. The speed of trollies shall not exceed 10 miles an hour.

Speed of trollies.

103. No trolly shall be attached to a train.

Attachment to train.

104. No trolly shall be run if it can be avoided except during daylight, and when the weather is sufficiently clear for a signal to be distinctly seen at a distance of half a mile.

Time of running.

105. All trollies when not in use, shall be taken off the rails and placed well clear of the line, and the wheels shall be secured with chain and padlock.

Trollies not in use.

106. No trolly shall be brought into use, unless accompanied by sufficient men to ensure its prompt removal in the case of a train approaching.

Number of men to accompany trolly in use.

107. To control the running of trollies, a Trolly Book shall be kept at each Station in which shall be recorded :—

Record in Trolly Book.

> The name of railway servant in charge of trolly.
> The number of Natives accompanying trolly.
> The place and mileage of destination.
> The time of departure from Station.
> The date and hour of anticipated arrival at destination.
> The signature of railway servant in charge of trolly.

108. Station Masters shall assure themselves as to the identity of the person in charge of trolly, and shall inspect his card giving him permission to be in charge of same. A list of persons in charge of trollies shall be sent to all Stations.

Identity of person in charge of trolly.

109. Every person in charge of a trolly shall examine it before starting with a view to ascertaining whether—

Examination of trolly.

> The brake blocks act properly.
> Brake sticks are carried, so that they can be used in case of the failure of the attached brake.
> The wheels, axles and working parts are sound.
> The bearings are properly greased.
> The trolly is booked at each Station,

and shall further ascertain from the Station Master when any train is expected and that the line is clear.

CARRIAGE OF PASSENGERS.

110. Tickets issued to passengers shall be available for a direct journey on the date of issue.

Passengers' tickets.

111. The Company reserves the right to issue passenger tickets in accordance with the accommodation or class of vehicle on each train. The seating accommodation of each vehicle or compartment shall be indicated thereon.

Right of Company.

Insufficient room.

112. If there is not sufficient room in any carriage, the Company shall allow a passenger to travel in a superior class to that for which he may have purchased a ticket.

Revision of tickets.

113. Passengers shall examine their tickets and any change prior to leaving the Booking Office window, as any claim for error shall not afterwards be entertained.

Provision for children.

114. Children under three years of age shall travel free when accompanied by an adult and those from three to twelve years at half fares.

Refund.

115. Any passenger leaving the train voluntarily, previous to the Station for which the ticket held may be valid, shall not be entitled to any refund for the remainder of the journey.

Lighted lamps &c.

116. Passengers shall not use any lighted lamps or stoves or carry any loaded firearms on the Company's trains.

Dogs accompanying passengers.

117. Dogs shall not be permitted to accompany passengers in a first class coach. They shall however be carried in a third class coach if muzzled and in custody of an attendant on payment of the published rates.

Inspection of tickets.

118. Passengers shall, on request of any Railway servant, produce their tickets but Guards, Station Masters or Ticket Inspectors after once satisfying themselves that a passenger has a ticket shall refrain from unduly molesting passengers.

Correction of receipt.

119. If any charge shall be entered incorrectly in any receipt or if any excess ticket shall be given to a passenger, the Company shall correct the entry.

Passenger changing to superior class.

120. Any passenger may change from an inferior to a superior class of carriage on payment of the difference in fare. The Guard in charge of the train shall collect such difference and issue an excess fare ticket to the passenger.

Lady passengers.

121. When ladies are travelling alone, the Guard shall pay every attention to their comfort, and in placing them in the train, shall, if so requested, endeavour to select a carriage or compartment according to the class of the tickets held, in which other ladies are travelling.

Prisoners and insane persons.

122. Prisoners and insane persons shall not be allowed in the same compartment or coach as other passengers but shall, upon reserved accommodation being engaged, be placed with escort of attendance in a separate compartment.

PASSENGERS SUFFERING FROM INFECTIOUS DISEASES.

Infectious or contagious diseases.

123. The following shall be deemed to be infectious diseases :—

Plague, Cholera, Small-Pox, Typhus, Typhoid or Enteric Fever, Scarlet Fever, Membranous Croup, Relapsing Fever, Yellow Fever, Scarlatina, Puerperal Fever, Measles, Erysipelas, Epidemic Cerebro-Spinal Meningitis, Sleeping Sickness, Leprosy, Beri-Beri, Yaws, Diptheria, Whooping Cough or other communicable disease which the Governor in Council may consider it desirable, in the public interest, to attempt to control.

124. (1). No person suffering from an infectious disease as defined in the preceding Rule, shall be allowed in any train, unless a reserved vehicle has been engaged for him and his attendants.

Conditions on which passengers allowed to travel.

(2). All necessary arrangements have been made for the separation of the passenger and his attendants during the whole time that they remain upon the Railway from other persons being or travelling in the train.

DISINFECTION OF CARRIAGES.

125. When any carriage or compartment thereof has been used by persons suffering from an infectious disease, such carriage or compartment shall be disinfected in accordance with the instructions given below immediately after it has arrived at its destination.

Disinfection of carriages.

126. If at any time a passenger suffering from an infectious disease shall alight from a train, the carriage from which he alighted shall be fumigated at destination.

Fumigation of carriages.

127. Should such passenger leave the train previous to its destination, the carriage in which he travelled shall not be occupied by other passengers until after being disinfected.

Carriage not to be occupied till disinfected.

128. The following instructions are laid down for disinfecting carriages. The carriage or compartment to be disinfected shall first of all be rendered as far as possible airtight with tow or waste packing around windows and doors and pieces of sacking stuffed into lamp holes. When this has been done, about 6 ℔s. of red hot coal on iron pan or sheet shall be prepared and on the top of this sulphur shall be spread.

Instructions for disinfecting.

If a compartment is to be disinfected—1 ℔. sulphur. If a truck or coach is to be disinfected—4℔s. sulphur. The door shall be closed up at once and the sulphur allowed to burn itself out. The door shall not be opened for three hours afterwards. As soon as the door is opened the pan or sheet shall be removed and the atmosphere allowed to clear. The carriage or compartment shall then be washed down with a solution of disinfectant. Half a pint of disinfectant to four gallons of water shall be used.

Luggage defined.

129. The term "luggage" is intended to cover such articles as may be for the passenger's own domestic use. Articles of furniture, crockery, bicycles and the like shall not be carried as luggage under the free allowance made to passengers. Such articles shall be booked and freight paid thereon.

Carriage of specie.

130. Specie may be carried as luggage at owner's risk, provided it is within the free allowance of weight according to ticket held.

Specie in parcels.

131. Specie in parcels or consignments carried by passengers, the total weight of which is greater than the free allowance of weight, shall be charged for at the Specie rate and no free allowance shall be made.

Personal luggage.

132. Passengers may take into a carriage only such small articles of personal luggage under the free allowance granted as are required for their own use during the journey and can be placed in the carriage without inconvenience to other passengers or reducing the available accommodation in the carriage.

Loss &c. of luggage taken in carriage.

133. The Company shall not be responsible for the loss, destruction or deterioration of any luggage taken into a carriage by or at the direction of a passenger.

Delivery of luggage.

134. Luggage shall be delivered at a Station at least 15 minutes before the fixed time for departure of the train by which the passenger intends to travel.

Luggage delivered late.

135. Luggage delivered later than 15 minutes before the fixed time of departure of the train shall either be taken at owner's risk or left to follow by the next train.

Quantity allowed free.

136. Each passenger holding a full ordinary ticket shall be allowed the undermentioned quantity of luggage conveyed free of charge and at his own risk in the train by which he travels, if the accommodation will permit :—

1st class	...	...	112lbs.
2nd class	...	...	56lbs.
3rd class	...	...	28lbs.

Small articles not reckoned in weight.

137. In computing the weight of luggage to be conveyed free of charge, an umbrella, walking stick or other small articles likely to be required on the journey such as wraps, pillows, small hand-bags, dressing cases or small luncheon baskets, which can be placed in the compartment without inconvenience to other passengers, will not be reckoned. Such items shall not be included in the Company's receipt for the luggage of any passenger.

138. No responsibility or liability shall be accepted by the Company in respect of any passenger's luggage unless the following conditions are complied with :—

Each package shall be securely fastened or locked and shall have attached to it a label fully and legibly describing the passenger's name and destination.

139. Passengers desirous of insuring their luggage may do so on making a declaration as to the value of the same to the Station Master at the dispatching Station. The insurance premium shall be 1% of the declared value, with a minimum of 2/-.

140. The Company shall not accept liability for luggage handed to the care of a Porter or other Railway Servant, except for the purpose of booking or for the purpose of being conveyed forthwith to or from the train.

141. In the event of a passenger on arrival at destination being unable to produce his luggage ticket, the packages of which he claims to be the owner shall only be handed to him if he can prove ownership by stating the contents of the same, producing the keys or proving to the satisfaction of the Station Master that the luggage belongs to him.

142. The Company reserves the right to convey luggage in the case of lack of space by a train later than that by which the passenger may have taken his ticket. The passenger may, however under such circumstances, free of cost, change his ticket for another available by the train by which his luggage is conveyed.

143. Luggage or parcels may be left at the station for safe custody on payment of the Company's published rates.

144. Parcels tied together shall be charged for separately.

145. A receipt for the number of parcels will be issued at the Station and this receipt shall be produced when claiming the packages.

146. Articles left for safe custody at any station for a period exceeding one month shall be removed to the Company's Unclaimed Goods Depôt at owner's risk and expense.

147. The Company reserves the right to refuse any dangerous or offensive packages for safe custody and shall not be responsible for the value in excess of £2-0-0 of any parcel deposited for safe custody unless insured.

148. Any articles of a perishable nature likely to putrefy or become a nuisance shall be removed from the Company's premises without compensation.

Sale of luggage. **149.** Any luggage or parcel not claimed within six months shall be sold by the Company.

PARCELS.

Parcels for dispatch by passenger train. **150.** Parcels for dispatch by passenger trains shall be delivered at the Stations at least thirty minutes before the departure of the train by which they are intended to go forward.

Packing and addressing of parcels. **151.** All parcels shall be securely packed and the Consignee's name and address stated plainly thereon.

Rejection of parcels traffic. **152.** The Company may reject as parcels traffic any packages the weight of which shall exceed 112 lbs. or the measurement of which shall exceed 10 cubic feet.

Contents of parcels. **153.** The contents of parcels containing :—
   (1) Articles carried at special rates,
   (2) Articles of special value,
   (3) Articles of a perishable nature,
shall be declared at the time of dispatch but the contents of ordinary parcels need not be declared.

Removal of parcels. **154.** Parcels shall be removed from the Company's premises at destination within 48 hours of the arrival of the train. After that period they shall become liable to storage charges, unless booked for safe custody.

Rejection of offensive goods. **155.** The Company may reject as parcel traffic any packages suspected to contain offensive or decayed matter, carcases, bones or manure.

Carriage of explosives. **156.** No explosives shall be conveyed as parcels by passenger train except of the kinds and in the manner specified hereafter. The Company however reserve the right to reject any explosives for dispatch by passenger trains.

Exceptions (a). Safety cartridges and percussion caps and safety fuse (for blasting) also fog signals for railway use shall be conveyed in ordinary wagons or carriages.

(b). Dynamite may be carried in the form of cartridges up to the limit of 5 lbs., provided that no detonators are carried in the same vehicle.

(c). Detonators may be carried up to the number of 200, provided that no other explosives be in the same vehicle.

(d). Sporting gunpowder or non-safety cartridges packed in double cases shall be carried, provided that the gunpowder is contained in tin canisters or in metal-lined cases and that no case shall contain more than 25 lbs. of gunpowder, and that the total consignment of gunpowder or non-safety cartridges as parcels traffic by any passenger train shall not exceed 80 lbs.

(*e*). Nothing in this Rule shall apply to the consignment of small arms ammunition despatched in Army-service pattern boxes.

157. The passenger fares and parcel and baggage rates shall be as set forth in Schedule " A " hereto.

Passenger Fares, Parcel and Baggage Rates.

GOODS AND PRODUCE TRAFFIC.

158. The Company's Goods Sheds shall be open daily excepting Sundays, Good Friday and Christmas Day for receiving and delivering goods and produce from 7 a.m. till 6 p m. and on Saturdays from 7 a.m. till 12-30 p.m.

Goods Sheds when open.

159. Goods and produce shall be conveyed according to the Company's published rates exhibited at Stations.

Conveyance at published rates.

160. Subject to the provisions of the Ordinance the Company reserves the right to alter the rates from time to time. Any such alterations of rates shall be notified one month previous to their operation. All alterations of rates shall be notified to the public on the Notice Boards at Stations.

Alteration of rates.

161. The Company does not guarantee the dispatch of goods or produce by any given train nor the date and time of arrival at destination.

Dispatch.

162. All consignments for dispatch shall be accompanied by the Company's Goods Consignment Note duly completed.

Consignment Note to accompany goods.

163. The Consignment Note shall contain a declaration of the description and weight of the goods or produce delivered for dispatch and the Consignor shall be held liable for any incorrect declaration.

Declaration of goods and produce.

164. Consignors shall satisfy themselves that all goods or produce for dispatch are properly packed and that each package bears a distinguishing mark, as the Company accepts no responsibility for inaccuracies in regard to same.

Packing of goods and produce.

165. Consignment Note Forms may be had on application at any Station.

Application for forms.

166. Packages presented for dispatch of which the contents are not declared or described shall be charged at the highest rate. The Company may also refuse to receive for dispatch any package the contents of which are not declared.

Packages contents of which not declared.

167. The Company shall not be responsible for any loss which may be caused by detention or examination of incorrectly declared goods.

Incorrect declaration.

168. Any package containing goods of various classes shall be charged at the rate corresponding to the highest of these classes, and the same regulation shall apply when a consignment consists of various packages containing goods of different classes, unless the contents of each package shall be declared at the time of dispatch.

Package containing goods of various classes.

Duration of liability.	**169.** The Company shall only be responsible for insured goods from the time the goods are placed in their custody to the time at which they arrive at the Station of destination. On arrival at the Station of destination, they shall be held at owner's risk.
Carriage of live stock.	**170.** Live stock shall be carried at owner's risk and freight on same shall be prepaid at the dispatching Station.
Printed receipt.	**171.** The Company shall not be responsible for loss, injury or damage to goods or produce on railway premises unless such goods shall have been accepted for dispatch and a printed receipt form issued.
Issue of receipt.	**172.** Receipts shall not be issued until the conditions attached to each consignment are fulfilled.
Delivery of goods.	**173.** The Company shall only deliver goods or produce at destination on obtaining a receipt, and no delivery shall be made to Native Carriers without an order to that effect from the Consignee.
Notification of consignees.	**174.** The Company does not undertake to notify Consignees or Agents as to arrival of goods and the non-receipt of such advice shall not exempt Consignees from demurrage charges. The Company shall endeavour when practicable to advise the arrival of goods to Consignees or Agents.
Freight to be prepaid.	**175.** The Company may decline to dispatch any consignment freight to pay at destination and the freight on all goods of a perishable nature shall be prepaid.
Detention of consignment.	**176.** Any consignment may be detained by the Company until freight and charges thereon have been paid.
Verification at destination.	**177.** The Company shall accept all weights and measurements declared in Consignment Notes as an estimate for freight charges and all weights, measurements and freight charges shall be subject to verification and correction at destination.
Test of weights.	**178.** The Company shall only accept weights as ascertained on its own weighbridges or weighing machines.
Claim as to shortage &c.	**179.** Any claim as to shortages, damage, difference in weight or measurement shall be preferred before the goods or packages are removed from the Company's premises.
Cheques.	**180.** Cheques shall not be accepted in payment of freights, unless arranged for with the Company at Limbe.
Minimum weight charge.	**181.** The minimum weight of consignments for dispatch as goods traffic shall be as provided for under the separate rates. In such cases, as when the consignment does not reach the minimum weight, the freight corresponding to the minimum charge provided shall be applied.

182. In applying the Company's rates, fractions of a mile shall be reckoned as a mile.

Fraction of mile.

183. The Company's rates shall include loading and unloading by Railway, excepting that for "C" class produce.

What rates include.

184. All traffic carried at "C" class rates shall be loaded by the Consignor, and, on arrival at destination, shall be unloaded by the Consignee at such time and place as the Company may direct. The Company may undertake the loading and unloading of "C" class traffic at such rates as shall be agreed between the Company and the Consignee or Consignor.

Loading &c. of dangerous goods.

185. Goods or produce left on Railway premises at destination more than 48 hours after midnight of the day of arrival shall be subject to a charge of storage or demurrage in accordance with the Company's demurrage rates.

Demurrage.

186. Goods or produce brought on to the Company's premises and remaining unbooked for dispatch for more than 48 hours after midnight on the day of arrival of the first portion of the consignment shall be subject to demurrage or storage charges in accordance with the Company's rates as fixed under this Ordinance.

Demurrage on unbooked goods.

187. The minimum charge shall be as for one day.

Minimum charge.

188. When more than one truck shall be required for conveyance of any goods or material whose lengths require that same occupy an additional wagon or wagons, freight shall be charged on the consignment at published rates plus a charge as for three tons for each additional two axles at the same rate of freight.

Goods of exceptional length.

CRANE CHARGES.

189. For packages or material lifted at Port Herald by the Company's Crane a charge shall be made as follows :—

Crane charges.

Any lift up to and including 2 tons	5/- per ton.
Lifts over 2 tons	7/6 „
Minimum charge	5/-.

OFFENSIVE GOODS.

190. The following shall be deemed offensive goods :—
  (a). Decayed vegetable matter, fish, meat and other articles in a decayed condition.
  (b). Dead bodies (corpses).
  (c). Carcases.
  (d). Bones and manure.

Offensive goods.

191. Dead bodies shall be conveyed in a separate compartment of van or in a separate wagon or carriage and charged for as for 1,120 ℔s. at parcels rate.

Carriage of corpses.

Accumulation on Railway premises.	**192.** No offensive consignments shall be allowed to accumulate on railway premises. Each consignment shall be arranged for in anticipation and loaded direct into wagons by Consignor.
To be kept separate.	**193.** All offensive goods shall be kept separate from other traffic. At destination they shall be taken delivery of and unloaded by Consignee on arrival of train. No offensive goods shall be allowed in the Company's Sheds.
Freight to be prepaid.	**194.** Freight shall be prepaid on all offensive goods.
Offensive goods not provided for.	**195.** Offensive goods not provided for in the Rules shall not be accepted, unless by previous arrangement with the Traffic Superintendent.

DANGEROUS GOODS.

Dangerous goods.	**196.** For the purpose of Section 47 of the Ordinance the following shall be deemed to be dangerous goods. They are classed from " A " to " F " for the purpose of regulating the conditions under which same are carried by rail :—

Acids mineral and other	B.	Fireworks	C.
Alcohol absolute ...	D.	Fog Signals	C.
Ammonia solution ...	B.	Fulminate of Mercury	C.
Acetyloid	A.	Fuse	C.
Ammunition	C.	Fusel Oil	A.
Aqua fortis	B.	Gas compressed ...	F.
Asphaline	C.	Gasoline	E.
Benzine or Bensol ...	E.	Gun Cotton	C.
Bisulphate of Carbon	D.	Gun Powder	C.
Blasting Powder and		Hydrogen compressed	F.
Charges	C.	Iodide of Nitrogen ...	C.
Bromine	B.	Incandescent Oil (as	
Calcium Carbide ...	A.	Methylated Spirit)	D.
Carbonite	C.	Kerosine	A.
Carbolic Acid ...	A.	Matches	C.
Cartridges	C.	Motor car Spirit ...	B.
Chlorates generally ...	C.	Methylated Spirit ...	D.
Chlorides	C.	Naptha	D.
Chloroform	B.	Napthaline	A.
Collodian	D.	Nitrates	C.
Coloured Fires ...	C.	Nitro-glycerine ...	C.
Cordite	C.	Oil of Vitriol	B.
Combustibles ...	C.	Paraffin	A.
Cotton Powder ...	C.	Percussion Caps ...	C.
Crackers	C.	Petrol	E.
Detonators	C.	Petroleum	A.
Dynamite	C.	Potash Chloride ...	C.
Ether	D.	Potassium	D.
Explosives generally	C.	Spirits of Turpentine	D.

Spirits of Wine	...	D.	Tubes for firing Explo-			
Spirit Nitric ...	...	D.	sives	...	...	C.
Spirits Wood	...	D.	War Rockets		..	C.
Torpedos	...	...	C.			

MODE OF CONVEYANCE.

197. No explosives shall be conveyed on the Railway, unless securely packed to the satisfaction of the Company.

Packing of explosives.

198. There shall not be conveyed in any wagon which is being used for the conveyance of an explosive any explosive of a different class, unless it be sufficiently separated therefrom to prevent any fire or explosion, which may take place by one such explosive being communicated to another.

Explosives of different classes.

199. Except in the case of small consignments carried by the Railway which may be unloaded at any time, explosives shall be loaded or unloaded only between sunrise and sunset. For the purpose of this rule no consigment of more than one half-wagon load booked to one Station shall be deemed to be a small consignment.

Time for loading &c.

200. (1). Whilst any explosive is being loaded on or unloaded out of any carriage no fire or artificial light nor any article which is liable to cause or communicate fire or explosion (such as charcoal, lucifer matches, articles for striking a light, petroleum or any spirit or oil or substance that gives forth an inflammable vapour) shall be or shall be allowed to be brought had or used near to such carriage and no smoking shall be allowed in or near to the same.

Special Rules for loading and unloading explosives.

(2). Provided that when the use of a light, for the purpose of such loading or unloading is unavoidable, a lamp of such construction, position or character as not to cause any danger from fire or explosion shall be used, and no person while handling any explosive shall wear boots or shoes with iron or steel nails, heels or tips.

(3). In loading or unloading any explosive the cask and package containing the same shall be passed from hand to hand and not rolled upon the ground; they shall not be thrown or dropped down but shall be carefully deposited and stowed.

201. Explosives shall be conveyed in covered wagons, or, if loaded in open wagons, shall be completely covered with painted cloth, tarpaulin or other suitable material so as to effectually protect it against communication of fire.

Conveyance of explosives.

Notice of sending explosives.

202. No person shall send for carriage upon the Railway any consignment of an explosive nature unless he has given notice to the Station Master of his intention to send such consignment and has stated the true name, description, quantity and mode of packing of the explosive proposed to be conveyed, and his own name and address, and also the name and address of the proposed Consignee, and unless he has had an intimation in writing from the Company that such consignment will be received.

Explosives which Company refuse to accept.

203. No explosives which the Company shall by any notice or Rules for the time being in force notify that they will not receive, shall be brought, sent or forwarded to or upon the railway.

Time for receiving explosives.

204. Consignments of explosives shall be sent to the forwarding Stations and shall be received by the Railway servants only at such time, between sunrise and sunset, as the Company may appoint, and every package containing any explosive proposed to be conveyed on any Railway shall immediately on arrival at the Station be unloaded and placed in a safe place under the personal direction of the Station Master.

Explosives to be removed by Consignee.

205. All explosives shall be removed by the Consignee from the receiving Station within the first twelve hours of daylight after arrival. If this condition is not strictly complied with, the Company may return the consignment to the Consignor at his own risk and expense and such shall, in the meanwhile, be kept as far from the Station building as possible in the wagon they were conveyed in, or, if unloaded, shall be completely covered with tarpaulins or other suitable material and, if necessary, shall be protected by an adequate guard.

Explosives sent in contravention of Rules.

206. The Company may refuse to receive any packages which they suspect to contain any explosive packed or sent in contravention of these Rules. And in case any package which the Company suspect shall be upon the Railway, they may open or require to be opened any such package to ascertain the fact at the risk and expense of the Consignor, and may return the explosive contained in the package to the Consignor at his risk and expense, keeping the packages pending such return in the manner prescribed in the preceding rule.

Separation of explosives from matches &c.

207. There shall not be conveyed in the same vehicle with any explosive the following : matches, fuses, pipelights, acids, naptha, paraffin or any other volatile spirit or substance liable to give off an inflammable vapour liable to spontaneous ignition or to cause or communicate fire or explosion.

208. Packages containing explosives shall be stowed and secured so as to prevent movement during transit.

209. Wagons used for the carriage of explosives shall be cleaned out before they are loaded. Haircloth, hides or other suitable material shall be spread on the floor of the wagon and between each layer of packages except when the packages are covered with gunny or felt, or contain small arms ammunition packed in tin-lined service pattern boxes.

210. Wagons containing explosives shall be loaded and unloaded as far distant as possible from the Station buildings.

211. More than three layers of packages containing explosives shall never be packed one above another except in the case of small arms ammunition packed in tin-lined service pattern boxes.

212. When a train is being marshalled, wagons loaded with explosives may be shunted by a locomotive, provided that they are separated from the engine by not less than three vehicles containing no explosives nor inflammable substance. The speed of these movements will be restricted to five miles an hour. Flying shunts are strictly prohibited.

213. Wagons shall in every case be locked immediately the loading of explosives has been completed.

214. The Company shall publish and exhibit at Stations from time to time a list of such articles as will be carried as Dangerous Goods.

215. (a). Dangerous goods marked " A " shall be securely packed in strong tins or bottles corked or sealed enclosed in wooden cases. In the case of Kerosine or Paraffin the Consignor shall certify that it does not flash below 76° fahrenheit.

Carbide of Calcium shall be contained in hermetically sealed tins or drums packed in cases of wood not less than 5/8 inch thick and bound with hoop iron so that the package will resist the wear and tear of transport and prevent the contents becoming affected by air or moisture. Packages containing Carbide of Calcium shall be free from copper and no package shall contain more than 225 lbs.

(b). Dangerous goods marked "B" shall be in stoneware jars or glass stoppered bottles well secured and standing upright in case. Fluoric Acid shall be in leaden or gutta percha bottles. Solution of Ammonia shall be in metal bottles with soldered caps. Bottles containing Aqua Fortis, Bromine, Muriatic and Nitric Acids and Solution of Ammonia shall be only three-quarters filled to allow for expansion vapour.

Only one description of the articles marked "B" shall be packed in each case and the case shall be marked distinctly with the name of the contents. The weight of each case shall not exceed 280 ℔s.

(c). Dangerous goods marked "C" shall be packed in strong cases the nails of which shall be brass or copper. No iron shall be used. Matches shall be in metal-lined cases. Detonators and explosive powder shall not be dispatched together. Chlorate Mixture, Coloured Fires and Fireworks shall be packed in hermetically sealed metallic cases enclosed in wood. All packages of Dangerous Goods marked "C" shall have the contents indicated on them.

(d). Dangerous goods marked "D" shall be packed as indicated for those marked "B." Metal vessels of tin or copper, provided with screw stoppers or corks with metal caps soldered on, may however be employed.

(e). Dangerous goods marked "E" shall be in drums or receptacles of not more than 10 gallons each. The drums or receptacles shall be made of tin or galvanized sheet iron or lead plate. The drums or receptacles shall be fitted with screw plugs or screw caps with air-tight under-cap. They shall be gas-tight. The packages shall be marked "highly inflammable" and also indicate contents. Drums in a damaged condition shall not be accepted, as the chief danger is from leakage.

(f). Dangerous goods marked "F" (gas) shall be received for conveyance in cylinders of wrought iron or steel. They shall not exceed 8 feet in length and 10 inches in diameter and shall be packed separately in wooden cases or covered with hemp or coir. The maximum weight of each package shall not exceed 280 ℔s., and the cylinders shall not be charged to a greater pressure than 1,800 ℔s. per square inch.

Goods and produce Rates.   **216.** The Company's rates for goods and produce shall be as set forth in Schedule "B" hereto.

BREACH OF RULES.

Penalty.   **217.** Any person who wilfully does any act which is forbidden or neglects to do any act which is required by the provisions of these Rules, and for which no penalty is provided by the Ordinance, shall be liable on conviction to a fine not exceeding £5.

Schedule "A"

THE SHIRE HIGHLANDS RAILWAY, NYASALAND, LIMITED.

Passenger Fares, Parcel and Baggage Rates.

PASSENGER FARES.

First Class.

From PORT HERALD TO	From Chiromo	From Mlanje Road	From Luchenza	From Mikalongwe	From Limbe
Chiromo	0 10 0				
Mlanje Road	1 1 0	0 11 0			
Luchenza	1 6 8	0 16 8	0 5 8		
Mikalongwe	1 11 0	1 1 0	0 10 0	0 4 4	
Limbe	1 15 8	1 5 8	0 14 8	0 9 0	0 4 8	
Blantyre	1 17 8	1 7 8	0 16 8	0 11 0	0 6 8	0 2 0

Second Class.

	From Chiromo	From Mlanje Road	From Luchenza	From Mikalongwe	From Limbe
Chiromo	0 3 9				
Mlanje Road	0 7 9	0 4 0			
Luchenza	0 10 0	0 6 3	0 2 3		
Mikalongwe	0 11 8	0 7 11	0 3 11	0 1 8	
Limbe	0 13 5	0 9 8	0 5 8	0 3 5	0 1 9	
Blantyre	0 14 2	0 10 5	0 6 5	0 4 2	0 2 6	0 0 9

Third Class.

	From Chiromo	From Mlanje Road	From Luchenza	From Mikalongwe	From Limbe
Chiromo	0 1 3				
Mlanje Road	0 2 8	0 1 5			
Luchenza	0 3 4	0 2 1	0 0 9		
Mikalongwe	0 3 11	0 2 8	0 1 3	0 0 7	
Limbe	0 4 6	0 3 3	0 1 10	0 1 2	0 0 7	
Blantyre	0 4 9	0 3 6	0 2 1	0 1 5	0 0 10	0 0 3

PARCELS AND BAGGAGE.

STATION from or to	Distance in Miles	Blantyre	Limbe	Mikalongwe	Luchenza	Mlanje Road	Chiromo	Port Herald
Blantyre	—	—	2d.	2d.	3d.	4d.	5d.	6d
Limbe	6	2d.	—	2d.	3d.	4d.	5d.	6d.
Mikalongwe	20	2d.	2d.	—	2d.	3d.	4d.	5d.
Luchenza	33	3d.	3d.	2d.	—	2d.	3d.	4d.
Mlanje Road	51	4d.	4d.	3d.	2d.	—	2d.	3d.
Chiromo	83	5d.	5d.	4d.	3d.	2d.	—	2d.
Port Herald	113	6d.	6d.	5d.	4d.	3d.	2d.	—

The above Rates are applicable per 7 lbs. or fraction.

Minimum charge for Parcels, One Shilling.

The Company will not be responsible for any Parcel or Package dispatched under the above mentioned Rates beyond the value of £2 sterling, unless a higher value be declared and insurance paid thereon at the Dispatching Station at the rate of 20/- per cent. Minimum premium 2/-.

SPECIAL RATES FOR BICYCLES, MOTOR CYCLES, RICKSHAS & MACHILLAS.

The following Rates will be charged for the above when dispatched by a Passenger travelling on the same train :—

> Bicycles ... 2/6 each for any distance.
> Motor Cycles 3/6 „ „
> Rickshas ... As for 1 ton, Class " C" traffic. Minimum charge, 10/-
> Machillas .. „ 10 cwt., „ „ „ „ „ 5/-

These Rates are not applicable to Bicycles, Motor Cycles, and Rickshas *imported at and dispatched from* Chiromo or Port Herald, *although accompanied by Passengers.*

The Company does not guarantee the dispatch of Rickshas or Machillas by any given train. Intending Passengers should give notice of their intention to dispatch.

The Company will not be responsible for any Bicycle, Motor Cycle, or Ricksha dispatched under these Rates beyond the value of £2, unless a higher value be declared and insurance paid thereon, at the Dispatching Station at the rate of 20/- per cent. Minimum premium. 2/-.

SPECIAL PARCEL RATES FOR FRESH VEGETABLES, MEAT, FRUIT, FISH & BUTTER.

Fresh Vegetables, Meat, Fruit, Fish, and Butter will be dispatched, as under :—

> In Baskets up to 21 lbs. .. .. 1/- each ⎱
> „ „ 35 lbs. . .. .. 1/6 „ ⎰ To or from any Station
> „ „ 56 lbs. ... ... 2/- „ at Owner's risk.

Schedule "B"

THE SHIRE HIGHLANDS RAILWAY, NYASALAND, LIMITED.

Goods Rates.

CLASS "A"

IMPORTED GOODS AND GENERAL MERCHANDISE, ALSO MICA FOR EXPORT.

Station From or to	Blantyre	Limbe	Mikalo-ngwe	Luche-nza	Mlanje Road	Chiromo	Port Herald
Blantyre ..	—	9 6	17/8	25/3	35/2	48/5	63/5
Limbe ...	9/6	—	14/2	21/9	31/8	44/11	59/11
Mikalongwe ...	17/8	14/2	—	13/7	23/6	36/9	51/9
Luchenza ...	25 3	21/9	13/7	—	15/11	29/2	44/2
Mlanje Road ...	35/2	31/8	23/6	15/11	—	19/3	34/3
Chiromo ...	48/5	44/11	36/9	29/2	19/3	—	15/0
Port Herald ...	63/5	59/11	51/9	44/2	34/3	15/0	—

The above Rates are applicable by weight or measurement at Company's option, and are divisible in fractions of 28 lbs. Minimum charge, One Cwt. Minimum freight, One Shilling.

CLASS "B."

COTTON IN BALES, CHILLIES, COFFEE BEANS, FIBRE, TEA, WAX, TOBACCO IN BALES FOR EXPORT.

Station From or to	Blantyre	Limbe	Mikalo-ngwe	Luche-nza	Mlanje Road	Chiromo	Port Herald
Blantyre	—	8/2	13/1	17/8	24/1	35/5	41/8
Limbe	8/2	—	11/0	15/7	21/11	33/3	39/6
Mikalongwe	13/1	11/0	—	10/7	17 0	28/4	34/7
Luchenza	17/8	15/7	10/7	—	12/5	23/9	30/0
Mlanje Road	24/1	21/11	17/0	12 5	—	17/4	23,7
Chiromo	35/5	33/3	28/4	23/9	17/4	—	12/3
Port Herald	41/8	39/6	34/7	30/0	23/7	12/3	—

The above Rates are per ton weight of 2,240 lbs., divisible in fractions of 28 lbs. Minimum charge, One Cwt. Minimum freight, One Shilling. Cotton must be pressed to a density of 20 lbs. per cubic foot.

SPECIAL RATES FOR TOBACCO IN CASKS TO PORT HERALD.

From Blantyre	From Limbe	From Mikalongwe	From Luchenza	From Mlanje Road	From Chiromo
45/8	43/8	39/0	34,8	29/0	18/0

The above Rates are per ton weight of 2,240 lbs., divisible in fractions of 28 lbs. Minimum charge, One Cwt. Minimum freight, One Shilling.

CLASS "C."

MAIZE, MAIZE FLOUR, MAPIRA GRAIN (LOCAL), GROUND NUTS, OIL SEED, SEED COTTON, KOTA-KOTA RICE.

Station From or to	Blantyre	Limbe	Mikalo-ngwe	Luche-nza	Mlanje Road	Chiromo	Port Herald
Blantyre	—	4/1	6/8	9/0	12 3	13/10	14/9
Limbe	4/1	—	5/7	7/11	11 2	13/10	14/9
Mikalongwe	6/8	5/7	—	5/4	8/8	12 3	13/8
Luchenza	9/0	7/11	5/4	—	6,3	12 1	13/5
Mlanje Road	12/3	11/2	8 8	6/3	—	10/0	11/4
Chiromo	13/10	13 10	12/3	12/1	10/0	—	8/0
Port Herald	14/9	14/9	13/8	13/5	11/4	8 0	—

The above Rates are per ton weight of 2,240 lbs., divisible in fractions of 28 lbs. Minimum charge, One Ton; otherwise " B " Rates.

Salt in Bags and Native Hoes.

Minimum 5 Tons.

Station from or to	Blantyre	Limbe	Mikalongwe	Luchenza	Mlanje Road	Chiromo	Port Herald
Blantyre	—	8/0	12/8	17/0	22/8	33/8	43/8
Limbe ..	8/0	—	10/8	15/0	20/8	31/8	41/8
Mikalongwe	12/8	10/8	—	10/4	16/0	27/0	37/0
Luchenza	17/0	15/0	10/4	—	11/8	22/8	32/8
Mlanje Road	22.8	20,8	16/0	11/8	—	17/0	27/0
Chiromo	33/8	31/8	27/0	22/8	17/0	—	15/0
Port Herald	43/8	41/8	37/0	32/8	27/0	15/0	—

The above Rates are per ton weight of 2,240 lbs., divisible in fractions of 28 lbs.

Hoes and Salt in Consignments under 5 Tons are Charged at Class "A."

Agricultural Implements and Machinery.

Class "A."

but charged on dead weight only.

Live Stock.

Horses, Mules, Donkeys, & Cattle.	*Pigs, Sheep, Goats, & Calves.* *Loose or in Crates.*
Number of Head. Rate. 1 ... 3d. per 2-axle wagon per mile. 2 ... 5d. „ „ 3 ... 7d. „ „ 4 ... 9d. „ „ For Calves with Cows 1½d. per head For 2-axle wagon loads (*i.e.*, 10 animals) for slaughter 1/3 per wagon per mile. Minimum Rate as for 30 miles.	Up to and including 4 animals 1¾d. per mile. „ „ 8 „ ... 2¼d. „ „ „ 12 „ ... 3¼d. „ „ „ 20 „ ... 4¼d. „ For each 5 animals or fraction thereof above 20 in same consignment at the rate of 1d. per mile extra.

Turkeys & Poultry for Breeding.

For each 7 lbs., or fraction. Minimum 28 lbs. ... ... up to 30 miles 6d.

„ „ „ „ „ ... ... „ 80 „ 7d.

„ „ „ „ „ ... ... „ 113 „ 8d.

Aerated or Mineral Waters, Local Manufacture.

At Class "A" Rates, but reckoned by weight only.

Empties, Cases and Bottles, if returned by Original Consignee to Consignor at Station where Traffic originated, will be carried for half Rates at Owner's risk.

RUBBER, NOT MANUFACTURED. FOR EXPORT.

Station to	From Blantyre	From Limbe	From Mikalo-ngwe	From Luche-nza	From Mlanje Road	From Chiromo	From Port Herald
Chiromo	49/3	46/2	38/9	32/0	22/8	—	21/8
Port Herald	64/10	61/9	54/5	47/8	38/4	21/8	—

The above Rates are per Ton weight of 2,240 ℔s., divisible in fractions of 28 ℔s. Minimum charge, One Cwt. Minimum freight, One Shilling..

IVORY.	STROPHANTHUS.
One Shilling per Ton per mile.	7d. per Ton per mile.

The above Rates are per Ton weight of 2,240 ℔s., divisible in fractions of 28 ℔s. Minimum charge, One Cwt. Minimum freight One Shilling.

PARAFFIN.	RICKSHAS.	USED EMPTY BAGS.
In minimum consignments of 100 cases, Class, "A" by weight. Under 100 cases, Class "A," by measurement.	Rickshas other than those provided for under Parcel Rates will be carried at "A" Rates as for One Ton.	Used Empty Bags will be carried by the Company at "A" Rate by weight.

Rules.

Accidents.

181/1912,—31st October.

Under Section 7.

1. The Notice referred to in Section 41 of The Railway Ordinance 1907 shall contain the following particulars namely :—mileage or station, or both, at which the accident occurred ; time and date of the accident ; number and description of the train or trains ; nature of the accident, number of people killed or injured as far as known ; cause of the accident as far as known ; probable detention to traffic.

Particulars to be furnished.

2. In the case of the following accidents namely :—

(*a*). Accidents attended with loss of human life, or with grievous hurt or with serious injury to property ; or

(*b*). Collisions between trains, one of which is a train carrying passengers ; or

Accidents of which telegraphic notice is required.

(c). Derailment of any train carrying passengers, or of any part of such a train; such notice shall be sent, by telegraph, immediately after the accident has occurred by the Station Master of one or other of the stations between, or of the Station at, or where there is no Station Master, by the railway servant in charge of the section of the railway on which the accident has occurred.

DUTIES OF RAILWAY SERVANTS.

Railway servants to report accidents coming to their notice.   **3.** Every railway servant shall report, with as little delay as possible, every accident occurring in the course of working the railway on which he is employed which may come to his notice: Such reports shall be made to the nearest Station Master, or, where there is no Station Master, to the railway servant in charge of the section of railway on which the accident has occurred.

General Manager to cause enquiry to be held.   **4.** (1). Whenever an accident such as is described in Section 41 of The Railway Ordinance, 1907, has occurred in the course of working a railway the General Manager shall cause an enquiry to be promptly made by a Committee of Railway Officers (to be called a "Joint Enquiry") for the thorough investigation of the causes which led to the accident: Provided that such enquiry may be dispensed with —

(a). If the accident has not been attended with loss of human life or with serious injury to person or property, or

(b). If there is no reasonable doubt as to the cause of the accident.

(2). Where such enquiry is dispensed with it shall be the duty of the Head of the Department of the railway responsible for the accident to make such enquiry (to be called a "Departmental Enquiry") as he may consider necessary, and if his staff or the system of working is at fault to adopt or suggest such measures as he may consider expedient for preventing a recurrence of similar accidents.

Notice of Enquiry to be given to Magistrate.   **5.** (1). Whenever a Joint Enquiry is to be made, the General Manager shall cause notice of the date and hour at which the enquiry will commence to be given to the District Magistrate having jurisdiction over that section of the line in which the accident occurred, or to such other Magistrate as may be appointed by the Governor in that behalf.

(2). The date and hour at which the enquiry will commence shall be fixed so as to allow the officer referred to in Sub-Rule (1) sufficient time to reach the place where the enquiry is to be held.

6. (1). As soon as the Joint or Departmental Enquiry has been completed, the President of the Committee or the Head of the Department, as the case may be, shall send to the General Manager a report which in the case of all accidents of the nature described in Rule 15 shall be submitted in the form prescribed by that Rule.

General Manager to receive report of Joint or Departmental Enquiry and to transmit same to Magistrate.

(2). The General Manager shall forward, with his remarks as to the action it is intended to take in regard to the staff responsible for the accident, or for the revision of the Rules or system of working, a copy of such report to the District Magistrate having jurisdiction over that section of the line in which the accident occurred or to such other Magistrate as may be appointed by the Governor in that behalf.

(3). Such copy shall be a ccompanied by a statement of the person, if any, whom the General Manager desires to prosecute, and a copy of the evidence taken at the enquiry.

7. (1). Whenever any accident has occurred in the course of working a railway, the General Manager shall give all reasonable aid to the District Magistrate or to the Magistrate appointed by the Governor in that behalf and to the Medical Officer and others concerned, and shall assist those authorities in making enquiries and in obtaining evidence as to the cause of the accident.

General Manager to give reasonable aid to authorities.

(2). When any magisterial enquiry under Rule 9 is being made the General Manager shall arrange for the attendance, for as long as may be necessary, at the office or place of enquiry of all railway servants whose evidence is likely to be required.

8. Whenever any accident occurring in the course of working a railway has been attended with serious personal injury, it shall be the duty of the General Manager to afford prompt medical aid to the sufferers and to see that they are properly and carefully attended to, until they are removed to their homes or handed over to the care of their relatives or friends. In any case involving loss of human life or serious personal injury the nearest Medical Officer shall be summoned.

Duty of General Manager to summon medical aid.

DUTIES OF MAGISTRATES.

9. Whenever an accident, such as is described in Section 41 of the Railway Ordinance 1907 has occurred in the course of working a railway, the District Magistrate having jurisdiction in the District in which the accident occurred, or any other Magistrate appointed by the Governor in that behalf may either —

Steps to be taken by Magistrate on occurrence of accident.

(a). Himself make an enquiry into the causes which led to the accident : or (b). May accept a report on the accident from the General Manager :

Provided always that action shall not be taken by a Magistrate under clause (a) of this Rule until the Joint Enquiry referred to in Rule 4 has been held, unless for reasons, to be specially recorded by him, which reasons shall be at once communicated by him to the General Manager, he considers it necessary to take such action in the interests of justice.

Notice to be given by Magistrate to Railway Administration.

10.   Whenever it is decided to make a magisterial enquiry under Rule 9 clause (a) the District Magistrate or other Magistrate appointed as aforesaid as the case may be shall proceed to the scene of the accident and conduct the enquiry there, and shall at once advise the General Manager and the Traffic Superintendent by telegraph of the date and hour at which the enquiry will commence, so as to enable the Railway Administration to summon the requisite expert evidence.

Conduct of magisterial enquiry.

11.   A Magistrate holding an enquiry under Rule 9 may summon any railway servant and any other person whose presence he may think necessary, and after taking evidence and completing the enquiry shall, if he considers that there are sufficient grounds for a judicial enquiry, take the requisite steps for bringing to trial any person whom he may consider to be criminally liable for the accident. Whenever technical points are involved the Magistrate should be careful to call for, and take, the opinions of professional persons.

General Manager to be notified of result.

12.   The result of every magisterial enquiry held under Rule 9 shall be communicated by the Magistrate to the General Manager.

Assistance of General Manager and attendances of railway servant at Judicial Enquiry.

13.   If in the course of any judicial enquiry into an accident occurring in the course of working a railway the Magistrate desires the assistance of the General Manager or the attendance of any railway servant to explain any matter relating to railway supervision, management or working, he shall issue a requisition to such railway servant through the Head of his Department to attend the Court stating at the time the nature of the assistance required. In summoning railway servants the Magistrate shall take care not to summon so large a number of the railway servants, especially of one class, on the same day, as to cause inconvenience to the working of the railway. In the case of very serious accident it will generally be advisable for the Magistrate to receive either the evidence of or a report from the General Manager before concluding the judicial enquiry.

14. On the conclusion of any such judicial enquiry the Magistrate shall send a copy of his decision to the General Manager and shall report the result of the enquiry to the Governor.

15. In the case of all accidents to a train (whether carrying passengers or not) which is attended with loss of human life or serious injury to person or property, the report referred to in Rule 6 shall contain :—

(1). A brief description of the accident;

(2). A description of the locality of the accident;

(3). A detailed statement of the evidence taken;

(4). The conclusions arrived at the Joint or Departmental Enquiry;

(5). A statement of the damage done;

(6). A sketch illustrative of the accident.

No. 9 of 1913.
CENTRAL AFRICA RAILWAY (Construction).*

R u l e s.

80/1914,—29th April.

1. The recruitment and engagement of natives of Nyasaland by the contractor for service on the construction of the Railway shall be subject to these Rules which shall be read as implied terms and conditions of any licence to recruit granted to the contractor and, where applicable, of every agreement of service entered into between him and any native for such employment.

2. Every agreement between the contractor and a native for service on the construction of the Railway shall be in the form set forth in Schedule I. hereto and shall be entered into before the Magistrate of the District in which the native has been recruited.

3. The contractor shall not recruit a larger number of natives than the number specified in his licence.

4. If any native of Nyasaland shall apply to the contractor for employment, the contractor shall send him to Port Herald to enter into an agreement before the Magistrate there.

5. Every native engaged by the contractor shall have his agreement countersigned at Port Herald by the Superintendent of Native Affairs or an officer deputed by him. The contractor shall not employ any native whose agreement has not been so countersigned.

6. The employee shall proceed direct from Port Herald to the place of employment and shall there work on the construction of the Railway for the number of months specified in his agreement in such place and manner as the contractor may direct.

7. The period of service, which shall not exceed six months, shall be reckoned from the day on ·which his agreement was countersigned by the Superintendent of Native Affairs and shall include that day.

8. The contractor shall pay to the employee wages at the rate of not less than seven shillings per month reckoned as 26 working days. Any employment during a calendar month in excess of the said 26 working days shall be outside the terms of the contract and shall be a matter of arrangement between the contractor and the employee.

9. If the employee has not paid his hut tax for the current year at the date of the agreement it shall be paid by the contractor to the Magistrate of the District in which the employee is recruited, before the Magistrate approves of the agreement. The sum so paid may be regarded as an advance of pay and may be deducted by the contractor from the deferred pay of the

---

* And the Employment of Natives Ordinance 1909. § 27.

employee. The proviso to Section 3 of the Native Hut Tax Ordinance shall apply to service upon the Railway under the terms of these Rules.

10. Wages shall be paid as follows :—Two shillings shall be paid to the employee at the place of employment at the end of each month. The balance, less any deduction made under the preceding Rule, shall be sent by the contractor to the Superintendent of Native Affairs at Port Herald for payment to the employee at the expiry of his term of service.

11. As soon as the agreement is entered into the contractor shall issue free to the employee one blanket.

12. The contractor shall, where a steamer or a railway is available, provide the employee with a free pass by rail and steamer from his home to the place of employment and on the completion of the service from the place of employment to his home.

13. The contractor shall supply every native recruited or employed by him with food, as prescribed by The Employment of Natives Ordinance, during the period of service and also for the time necessarily occupied on the journeys between his home and the place of employment and *vice versa* : Provided that in the case of natives who may travel on the railway there may be substituted, as regards that part of the journey which lies between the native's home and the station at which he is required to entrain, conduct money at a rate of not less than one penny for each ten miles of such journey with a minimum of threepence.

14. In the case of the death of an employee the contractor shall remit any balance of pay due which is in his hands and any sums and effects in the possession of the employee together with a report of the cause of death and a statement of the wages due to the Superintendent of Native Affairs.

15. The contractor shall provide qualified medical attendance, medicine and hospital accommodation free for all employees to the satisfaction of the Governor.

16. The contractor shall provide quarters for each employee to the satisfaction of the Governor.

17. No deductions on account of absence shall be made from the wages of an employee if absent from work on account of illness for a period not exceeding two days in each month.

18. The contractor shall at his own expense send any employee who, by reason of illness is unable to complete his period of service, to his home provided that a certificate is obtained from a medical practitioner that the employee is fit to travel. Every certificate of unfitness to work and of fitness to travel shall be sent to the Superintendent of Native Affairs with a statement of the pay due.

19. If an employee is injured in the course of his employment the contractor shall pay to him through the Superintendent of Native Affairs compensation at the following rates :—

For partial disablement—Three pounds.

For total disablement—Five pounds.

Provided that any question arising out of this Rule may be tried by the Magistrate at Port Herald who may order the payment of such compensation not exceeding ten pounds as he may consider just.

20. If an employee is killed in the course of his employment or dies in consequence of the employment, the sum of five pounds shall be paid by the contractor to the Superintendent of Native Affairs for distribution among the heirs of the deceased.

21. A report of every accident involving the death or disablement of any employee shall be forwarded to the Superintendent of Native Affairs.

22. The Provisions of Section 16, 17, 18 and 19 of " The Employment of Natives Ordinance, 1909," shall apply to agreements of service under these Rules. For the purposes of this Rule the service shall be deemed to be service within the Lower Shire District of the Protectorate.

23. Where no other penalty is provided by " The Employment of Natives Ordinance, 1909," or any other law or Ordinance any person contravening any of these Rules shall be liable on summary conviction—

(*a*). If a native, to a fine not exceeding one pound or to imprisonment with or without hard labour for a term not exceeding three months, with or without the option of a fine or to both such fine and imprisonment.

(*b*). If a non-native, to a fine not exceeding twenty-five pounds or to imprisonment with or without hard labour for a term not exceeding three months, with or without the option of a fine, or to both such fine and imprisonment.

Schedule I.

No

NYASALAND PROTECTORATE

CERTIFICATE OF AGREEMENT

FOR SERVICE WITH MESSRS. PAULING AND COMPANY LIMITED ON THE CONSTRUCTION OF THE RAILWAY FROM PORT HERALD TO THE ZAMBESI RIVER.

I HEREBY CERTIFY that the undermentioned Native has appeared before me, and has satisfied me that he has voluntarily agreed to work for   months for Messrs. Pauling and Company, Limited on the construction of the Railway from Port Herald to the Zambesi River, on the conditions endorsed hereon, and that he thoroughly understands the nature and terms of the contract he has entered into.

The said native having complied with Section 19 (1) of " The Employment of Natives Ordinance, 1909," is hereby permitted to proceed to the place appointed by Messrs. Pauling and Company, Limited, for the above service.

Name
Tribe
Village
District

And that he desires in case of death that all sums due him or found in his possession together with his effects be handed to the undermentioned relative for distribution :—

Name
Tribe
Village
District

£   s.   d.

Wages advanced
 Hut Tax @   for the year 191

Date
Station Stamp   Magistrate.

Examined
Port Herald
Date   Superintendent of Native Affairs.

No. 6 of 1909.
EMPLOYMENT OF NATIVES.

Rules.

79/1914,—29th April.

Under Section 27.

1. Every employer shall provide every native labourer employed by him, otherwise than on transport, tenga-tenga, domestic or personal service who is required by the nature of his work to sleep at or near his place of work or is unable to return to his own village at least once a week, with rations of good quality free of charge as specified in the Schedule to these Rules or with cash in lieu of rations as specified in sub-sections (1) and (2)—

(1). Native labourers who usually reside in the Blantyre, Zomba or Mlanje Districts and whose work is done in one of these districts and native labourers of other districts whose work is done in the districts in which they usually reside shall at their option be given a cash allowance in lieu of rations. Such cash allowance shall not be less than threepence per week.

(2). During the period from 1st May to 31st October inclusive all native labourers not referred to in sub-section (1) shall at their option be given food as specified in the Schedule hereto or cash which shall not be less than threepence per week in lieu thereof. During the period from 1st November to 30th April inclusive they shall be given food as specified without any option of cash in lieu thereof.

2. All labourers' contracts for service made before a Magistrate shall have endorsed thereon particulars of the food agreed on between employer and employee, or the amount of cash in lieu thereof.

3. Employers may, in agreement with the native, make variations in the specified rations, provided always that such variations do not reduce the nutritive value of the diet.

4. No employer shall supply or cause to be supplied to any native labourer for consumption by him, any article of food which is diseased, unsound or unwholesome, or otherwise unfit for consumption.

5. Rations shall be issued raw, to be cooked by the native labourers themselves: Provided that any employer may erect and maintain a proper kitchen for the cooking of native food under proper supervision.

6. Every employer shall supply his native labourers with an adequate supply of firewood for cooking purposes free of charge.

7. Nothing in these Rules contained shall prevent any Magistrate from giving directions as provided in Section 12 (a) of "The Employment of Natives Ordinance, 1909."

8. Any person who contravenes any of the these Rules shall for each offence be liable on conviction to a fine not exceeding £25 or to imprisonment for a term not exceeding three months.

9. These Rules shall come into force as from the 1st day of June, 1914, and from that date the Rules published under Government Notice No. 182 of the 31st October, 1912, are repealed.

Schedule.

SCALE OF RATIONS.

Minimum Ration Scale.

(1). 12 ℔s. of Maize Meal, Millet Meal, Cassava Meal or Meal made from other grain, or Hulled Rice, per week. Not less than 18 ℔s. of shelled Maize may be issued in lieu of 12 ℔s. of Meal at the option of the native : and

(2). 2 ℔s. of Beans, Ground Nuts, Pea Nuts or the like, per week : and

(3). 6 ounces of Salt per week, or 2 ounces of Salt and 2 ℔s. of fresh green food such as Tubers, Pumpkins, Gourds, Bananas and the like.

No. 13 of 1911.

NATIVE HUT TAX.

Proclamation fixing rate of Hut Tax.

152/1911,—26th September.

Under Sections 3 and 4.

By the Governor in Council :—

Fixing hut
tax at 8/-.

WHEREAS it has been made to appear to me both just and expedient that subject to the provisions contained in Sections 6, 7 and 8 of the above Ordinance every native being the owner or occupier of a hut in any district of the Protectorate should pay to the revenue of the Protectorate a tax at the rate of 8/- for each year in respect of each hut owned or occupied by him during any portion of that year :

NOW THEREFORE by virtue of the powers in me as Governor in Council vested I DO HEREBY proclaim and declare that subject to the provisions hereinbefore recited from and after the 1st day of April, 1912, every native being the owner or occupier of a hut in any district of the Protectorate shall pay to the revenue of the Protectorate a tax at the rate of 8/- for each year in respect of each hut owned or occupied by him during any portion of that year.

30/1914,—12th February.

Under Section 6.

Whereas it is provided that the Governor in Council may by Proclamation in the *Gazette* order that in any district the Resident may accept in lieu of a labour certificate a certificate from an European or other person approved by such Resident that a native presenting such certificate has cultivated in that district and sold to such European or other person as aforesaid economic produce of such kind and in such quantity as may be specified in such order :

AND WHEREAS it has been made to appear to me both just and expedient that certificates as aforesaid should be accepted from natives in respect of certain kinds and quantities of economic produce.

NOW THEREFORE by virtue of the powers in me as Governor in Council vested as aforesaid I DO HEREBY proclaim and order that from and after the 1st day of April, 1914, such certificates shall be accepted from natives subject to the following provisions :—

(1). Every native producing a certificate as aforesaid that he has cultivated and sold as aforesaid 120 ℔. of rice or 100 ℔ of tobacco.

(2). Every native in the following districts producing a certificate as aforesaid that he has cultivated and sold as aforesaid 56 ℔. of cotton :—

ZOMBA.   MARIMBA.   NORTH NYASA.   DOWA.

No. 10 of 1912.

PURCHASE OF CATTLE FROM NATIVES.

183/1912,—31st October.

R u l e s.

Under Section 7.*

Form of permit.

1. The form of permits to be issued under this Ordinance shall be as set forth in the Schedule hereto.

Sale of two cattle.

2. In any case where cattle removed under Section 6 of the Ordinance do not exceed two in number the District Resident of the district into which they are removed for purposes of sale therein shall, on the owner of such cattle delivering up the permit referred to in the aforesaid section, authorize the sale of such cattle by endorsing the permit to the effect that the owner is authorized to sell the said cattle.

Endorsed permit, authority for purchase.

3. The permit so endorsed shall be deemed to authorize a person to purchase from the holder of the permit the cattle referred to therein, notwithstanding that such person has not obtained a permit in accordance with the provisions of Section 3 of the Ordinance.

Export prohibited.

4. No cattle purchased under Rule 3 hereof shall be exported from the Protectorate.

Procedure on completion of sale.

5. On the completion of a sale under Rules 2 and 3 hereof the vendor shall re-deliver the permit to the District Resident of the district in which the sale took place for transmission to the District Resident of the district from which the cattle were brought.

Schedule.

The Purchase of Cattle from Natives Ordinance, 1912.

PERMIT TO PURCHASE CATTLE.

IN PURSUANCE of the provisions of Section 3 of "The Purchase of Cattle from Natives Ordinance, 1912" I DO HEREBY authorize   to purchase   cattle from   of the   village in the   section of the   District. Subject to the conditions endorsed on the back hereof.

Nyasaland

191 .   *District Resident*

* And under the Interpretation and General Clauses Ordinance 1911. Section 9.

The Purchase of Cattle from Natives Ordinance, 1912.

PERMIT TO REMOVE CATTLE.

IN PURSUANCE of the provisions of Section 6 of "The Purchase of Cattle from Natives Ordinance, 1912," I DO HEREBY authorize
                                of the   village in the
        section of the   District to remove
cattle the property of   from the said District.
Subject to the conditions endorsed on the back hereof.

        Nyasaland
        191 .   *District Resident.*

No. 1 of 1909.

POLITICAL REMOVAL AND DETENTION OF NATIVES.

Rules.

71/1909,—1st May.

Under Section 8.

Treatment
of natives
detained.

1. Politically detained Natives shall not be placed in any prison or lock-up, but shall be provided with suitable accommodation. They shall not be handcuffed or placed in irons nor shall they be subjected to any other bodily restraint, unless such restraint is necessary for their safe custody.

Wives, &c., to
have access.

2. The wives, children, relations, followers and friends of Politically detained Natives may in the discretion of the Resident be permitted to remain with or have access to such natives.

Supply of food.

3. When necessary food shall be supplied to Politically detained Natives and to such of their wives, children and followers as are permitted to remain with them.

Native to be
permitted to
work.

4. All Politically detained Natives shall be permitted to work or engage themselves for labour in the place in which they are detained. They shall report themselves in person to the Resident at least once a week or oftener if required so to do.

Monthly report
of natives
detained.

5. Residents shall state in their Monthly Reports the names of any Natives who are politically detained in their districts.

Medical
supervision.

6. Politically detained Natives shall be subject to such medical supervision as may be deemed necessary.

No. 2 of 1912.

NATIVE FOODSTUFFS.

Proclamations.

102/1912,—25th June.

Under Section 3.

PROCLAIMED that from the date of publication hereof the purchase and barter of native foodstuffs generally from natives in the following districts for the purpose of re-sale in or export from any of the said districts shall be and is hereby prohibited unless the written permission of the District Resident be first had and obtained :—

LOWER SHIRE	MLANJE
RUO	ZOMBA
WEST SHIRE	UPPER SHIRE
BLANTYRE	SOUTH NYASA.

112/1913,— 31st May.

Proclaimed that the restrictions imposed by the above Proclamation on the purchase and barter of Native Foodstuffs are HEREBY removed in so far as they affect the following Districts :—

LOWER SHIRE, RUO, WEST SHIRE, BLANTYRE, ZOMBA, SOUTH NYASA, and as regards Ground Nuts are removed also in the MLANJE and UPPER SHIRE Districts.

No. 13 of 1912.

DISTRICT ADMINISTRATION (Native).

Proclamations.

Under Section 2 (1).

Districts to which the Ordinance shall apply.

110/1913,—31st May.

The Lower Shire District.
The West Shire District.
The Ncheu Division of the Upper Shire District.
The Lilongwe Division of the Lilongwe District.
The Kota Kota Division of the Marimba District.
The North Nyasa District.

133/1914,—20th July.

The Liwonde Sub-Division of the Upper Shire District.

193/1914,—23rd October.

The Fort Manning Sub-Division of the Lilongwe District.

Division of Districts into Administrative Sections.

142/1913,—30th June.

Under Section 4 (1).

* The Lower Shire District into 7 Administrative Sections.
* The West Shire District into 12 Administrative Sections.
* The Ncheu Division of the Upper Shire District into 8 Administrative Sections.
* The Kota Kota Division of the Marimba District into 3 Administrative Sections.

172/1913,—31st July.

* The Lilongwe Division of the Lilongwe District into 5 Administrative Sections.

249/1913,—3rd November.

* The North Nyasa District into 8 Administrative Sections.

* N. B. Official plans of the above Administrative Sections have been deposited in the Office of the Registrar of Documents at Blantyre.

The Liwonde Sub-Division of the Upper Shire District, into four Administrative Sections, bounded as follows :—

Section No. 1.

Bounded on the North by the South Nyasa-Upper Shire inter-district boundary; on the East by the Zomba-Upper Shire inter-district boundary; on the South by the Liwonde-Zomba road and on the West by the Shire river.

Section No. 2.

Bounded on the North by the South Nyasa-Upper Shire inter-district boundary; on the East by the Shire River; on the South by the Liwonde-Ncheu road and on the West by the boundary between the Liwonde and Ncheu Divisions.

Section No. 3.

Bounded on the North by the Liwonde-Ncheu road; on the East by the Shire River; on the South by the Upper Shire-West Shire inter-district boundary and on the West by the boundary between the Liwonde and Ncheu Divisions.

Section No. 4.

Bounded on the North by the Liwonde-Zomba road; on the East by the Zomba-Upper Shire inter-district boundary; on the South by the Blantyre-Upper Shire inter-district boundary and on the West by the Shire River,

and as appears in the official plans deposited in the Office of the Registrar of Documents in Blantyre.

The Fort Manning Sub-Division of the Lilongwe District, into two Administrative Sections, bounded as follows :—

Section No. 1.

Starting from a point on the Northern Rhodesian border where the African Transcontinental Telegraph Line intersects it, the boundary shall follow the telegraph line to the Bua River; thence it shall follow the Bua River upstream to a point opposite Fort Manning station; thence it shall be carried in a straight line to the nearest point of the said Rhodesian border; thence it shall be carried along the said border to the point of commencement;

Section No. 2.

Starting from a point on the Bua River opposite Fort Manning station the boundary shall follow the Bua River downstream to its junction with the Namitete River; thence it shall follow the Namitete River upstream to its source on the Anglo-Portuguese border; thence it shall be carried along the said Anglo-Portuguese and Rhodesian borders to the nearest point opposite Fort Manning station; thence it shall be carried in a straight line to the point of commencement,

and as appears in the official plan deposited in the Office of the Registrar of Documents in Blantyre.

Notices.

Appointment of Principal Headmen.

145/1913,—14th June.

District or Area Proclaimed.	Section.	Name of Principal Headman.
LOWER SHIRE DISTRICT ...	1	Tengani
	2	Chataika
	3	Chipwembwe
	4	Ngabu
	5	Chimombo
	6	Nachikadza
	7	Ndamera
WEST SHIRE DISTRICT	1	Simon Likongwe
	2	Cheku Cheku Apiri
	3	Dambe Achanza
	4	Chikalema Aliwambabi
	5	Lekani Abanda
	6	Kanduku Amaseko
	7	Ntachi Ngondo
	8	William Angwena
	9	Dzintenga Amputi
	10	Bell Abanda
	11	Katunga Apiri
	12	John Apiri
NCHEU DIVISION OF UPPER SHIRE DISTRICT	1	Chakumbira
	2	Njeromole
	3	Njovualema
	4	Kamwamba
	5	Yohane Champiti
	6	Pfuko
	7	Kwataine
	8	Makwangwala
KOTA-KOTA DIVISION OF MARIMBA DISTRICT	1	Mwadzama
	2	Kalumo
	3	Msusa

176/1913,—31st July.

LILONGWE DIVISION OF LILONGWE DISTRICT	1	Chimdidi
	2	Matanda
	3	Kalolo
	4	Masula
	5	Mazengela

Notices.

Appoinment of Principal Headmen,—*Continued.*

District or Area Proclaimed.	Section.	Name of Principal Headman.
		253/1913,—3rd November.
NORTH NYASA DISTRICT	1	Kameme
	2	Mwenimisuku
	3	Kirupula
	4	Chungu
	5	Mweniwenya
	6	Ntalire
	7	Chikulamayembe
	8	Mwafulirwa
		226/1914,—10th November.
FORT MANNING SUB-DIVISION OF LILONGWE DISTRICT	1	Zulu
	2	Mlonyeni
		227/1914,—18th November.
LIWONDE SUB-DIVISION OF UPPER SHIRE DISTRICT	1	Namputu
	2	Chingwalungwalu
	3	Kungwalu
	4	Mpilisi

103/1913,—31st May.

Rule.

1. The District Resident of any district to which this Ordinance is applied may take such steps and issue such orders as he shall consider necessary for the concentration of native huts, the establishment and grouping of villages and generally for the better carrying into effect of the sanitary, administrative and other purposes of the said Ordinance.

Power of District Resident to order the concentration of huts.

No. 4 of 1894.

POSTAL.*

180/1914,—30th September.

R u l e s.

Money Order
Offices.

1. Inland Money Order business shall be transacted at the following Post Offices :—

Blantyre	Fort Johnston	Mzimba
Chinteche	Karonga	Ncheu
Chiromo	Kota-Kota	Neno
Dedza	Lilongwe	Port Herald
Dowa	Mlanje	Zomba

At Post Offices where Money Order business is not transacted Postmasters shall assist in obtaining the issue of Money Orders from the nearest Money Order Office provided that facilities exist for the sending of a remittance to such Money Order Office otherwise than by the transmission of cash.

Rates of
Commission.

2. The following charges shall be made on the issue of Inland Money Orders :—

For sums not exceeding	£2	...	...	6d.
,, ,, ,, ,,	£5	...	...	1s. 0d.
,, ,, ,, ,,	£7	...	...	1s. 6d.
,, ,, ,, ,,	£10	...	...	2s. 0d.

and at the same rate to the maximum allowed.

A Money Order shall not be issued for a sum exceeding £40, and shall not contain a fractional part of 1d.

Remittances of over £40 may be made by means of a number of Money Orders; but no remitter shall send more than four Orders at £40 each on the same day.

Mode of
application.

3. Every application for a Money Order shall be made upon the form supplied at all Money Order Offices and shall state as fully as possible the name, title and designation, as the case may be, of the payee and the name and address of the remitter.

The surname and initial of one other name of both remitter and payee shall be given, provided that, in the case of a native having only one name, that name shall be given. The ordinary title of a Peer or Bishop, the official designation of an Officer of the Government, and the name of a business firm or company or of a corporation or society may be given.

---

* And under the Interpretation Ordinance 1911, Section 9.

4. A Money Order when issued shall be handed by the Postmaster to the remitter to be transmitted by him to the payee, and an advice shall be sent from the Issuing Office to the Paying Office, containing information as to the amount and as to the name of the payee and of the remitter. Unless the Order be presented through a Bank, the person presenting it for payment shall furnish the remitter's name for comparison with the advice.

5. Payment of a Money Order shall be subject to the possession by the Postmaster of the Paying Office of sufficient funds, and no claim shall be made or entertained by reason of any delay arising therefrom.

Payment of an Order shall not be demanded on the same day as that on which the Order was issued.

Money Orders do not require a receipt stamp.

6. If a Money Order, when presented for payment (otherwise than through a Bank), is properly receipted, and the name of the remitter, as furnished by the applicant, is in agreement with the advice, it shall be paid, unless the Postmaster has reason to suppose that the applicant is neither the payee nor his agent.

In the case of a Money Order payable to any company, corporation or society, the name of the payee shall be stamped or written in the receipt space, and where it is written the person presenting the Order shall also sign his own name, and state his office in the company, corporation or society.

If payment of an Order be refused in consequence of the remitter's name not being furnished correctly, or in consequence of the signature on the Order not corresponding with the entry on the advice, the applicant for payment should communicate with the remitter, and request him to apply to the issuing Postmaster.

7. If the payee of a Money Order is unable to write or sign his name in English characters, he shall make his mark in the space provided on the Order for the signature of the payee, and this mark shall be witnessed by some person known to the Paying Officer.

The witness shall sign his name and write his address in the presence of the Paying Officer, but the latter shall, in no circumstances, act as witness.

8. The remitter may at the time of issue request that the Order be crossed like a cheque thus, " ——— & Co. ", or may himself so cross the Order. An Order so crossed shall only be payable through a Bank.

Payment through a Bank.

9. The holder of a Money Order payable in Nyasaland may, by crossing it, direct that the Order be paid through a Bank, even though its payment was not originally so restricted.

When an Order is presented through a Bank, duly crossed with the name of that Bank, by a person known to be in its employment, the formalities observed on presentation in the ordinary way shall be dispensed with.

Orders unpaid for one month.

10. If a Money Order shall remain unpaid for one month, the remitter shall be advised of non-payment.

Advice of payment.

11. The remitter of an Inland Money Order, who desires to be informed when the Order has been paid, shall apply at the Office of issue, either at the time of issue of the Order, or subsequently. Upon payment of a fee of 3d. for each Order, an advice of payment shall be sent to the remitter in due course.

Repayment to remitter.

12. The Postmaster-General has power to refund to the remitter the amount of a Money Order, and thereupon no claim shall be made or entertained in respect thereof.

Alteration of name.

13. If any alteration in the name of the remitter or payee of a Money Order be required, application accompanied by the payment of a second commission of 3d. shall be made by the remitter to the Postmaster of the Office at which the Order was issued.

Transfer of payment.

Repayment.

Persons desiring to transfer payment of an Inland Order from one Office to another in Nyasaland, or the re-payment of the amount of an Order, shall make an application therefor on the printed form to be obtained at any Money Order Office and enclosing the Order to the Postmaster at whose Office the Order is payable. The Postmaster will transmit, in exchange, a new Order payable at the place desired, deducting the amount of a second commission.

Where such transfer or repayment is necessitated by reason of a mistake on the part of an Officer of the Post Office, the charge shall be remitted.

Loss.

14. In case of the miscarriage, or loss, of an Inland Money Order, a duplicate shall be granted on a written application, with the necessary particulars, being forwarded to the Controller, Money Order Department, General Post Office, Zomba, together with an additional commission in postage stamps of one shilling for each Order not exceeding £40.

If the original Order shall have been lost during transmission through the post, the Postmaster-General may authorize the refund of the second commission paid.

A Postmaster is required to give advice as to the procedure for obtaining a duplicate Order, etc., and to supply the prescribed form of application.

15. At the end of twelve months from the month in which it was issued, a Money Order, if still unpaid, shall become void, but the Postmaster-General may, if satisfied that good reason exists for the delay in presenting it, authorize the issue of a new Order on payment of a fee of one shilling. *Lapsed Orders.*

16. Payment of mutilated or defaced Orders shall be refused, but the Postmaster-General may either authorize payment without charge or cause a duplicate Order to be issued on payment of a fee of one shilling. *Spoilt Orders.*

17. If it be desired to stop payment of an Inland Order, a notice, accompanied by a fee of 3*d.*, shall be sent to the Office where the Order is payable. *Stoppage of payment.*

18. After once paying a Money Order, by whomsoever presented, the Postmaster-General shall not be liable to any further claim, and shall not be liable to pay compensation for loss or injury arising out of any other irregularity in connection with the Order. *Non-liability of Postmaster-General.*

No. 2 of 1906.

MINING.

Proclamations.

20/1911,—1st February.

Appointment of Director of Mines.

Under Section 4.

THE FOLLOWING officer has been appointed Director of Mines under the above Ordinance with effect from the 28th February 1906 :—

The Director of Public Works.

Fixing Royalties.

114/1911,—28th July.

Under Section 28 (iii).

(a) ASBESTOS.

Proclaimed that a royalty of 5 per cent on the actual sale price shall be paid on all asbestos found and extracted from lands subject to the provisions of the above Ordinance.

130/1911,—5th August.

(b) MICA AND PLUMBAGO.

Proclaimed that a royalty of 10 per cent on the actual sale price shall be paid on all mica found and extracted from lands subject to the provisions of the above Ordinance· and further that a royalty of 5 per cent on the actual sale price shall be paid on all plumbago similarly found and extracted.

Rules.

31st March, 1906.

SAFE MINING RULES.

Under Section 32 (c).

Ventilation.   1. An adequate amount of ventilation shall be produced in every mine, so as to render every part of that mine in which working is taking place fit for working and passing therein.

2. Safety lamps shall be used in every coal mine in which inflammable gas has been found to exist within the preceding twelve months.

Use of safety lamps.

3. In every coal mine in which inflammable gas has been found to exist within the preceding twelve months, then once in every twenty-four hours the manager of the mine, or a competent person appointed by him, shall before the work is commenced in any part of the mine, inspect with a safety lamp that part of the mine, and shall make a true report of the conditions thereof in a book to be kept for the purpose, which report shall be signed by the person making the inspection.

Inflammable gas.

Such book shall at all times be open to inspection by the Director of Mines or other officer appointed by the Governor for the purpose.

4. All entrances to any place not in actual course of working and extension shall be properly fenced across the whole width of such entrances, so as to prevent persons inadvertently entering the same.

Disused workings to be fenced.

5. No person except the Inspector of Mines shall enter any mine unless authorized to do so by the manager or competent person deputed by him.

Unauthorized persons prohibited from entering mines.

6. If at any time it is found by the person for the time being in charge of the mine or any part thereof, that by reason of noxious gases prevailing in such mine or such part thereof, or from any cause whatever, that the mine or the said part is dangerous, every workman shall be withdrawn from the mine or of such part thereof as is so found dangerous, and a competent person, who shall be appointed for the purpose shall inspect the mine or such part thereof as is so found dangerous, and, if the danger arises from inflammable gas, shall inspect the same with a locked safety lamp, and in every case shall make a true report of the condition of such mine or part thereof, and the workmen shall not, except in so far as is necessary for inquiring into the cause of the danger, or for the removal thereof, or for exploration, be re-admitted into the mine or such part thereof as was so found dangerous, until the same is stated in such report not to be dangerous.

Precautions to be taken in case of discovery of gas.

Every such report shall be recorded in a book, which shall be kept at the mine for the purpose, and shall be signed by the person making the same.

7. In every coal mine where safety lamps have to be employed, a competent person shall be appointed by the

Examination of safety lamps.

Mining.

person in charge of the mine, whose duty it shall be to see and examine every lamp taken into the mine. He shall see that it is secure and securely locked. No person shall, unless appointed for the purpose, have in his possession any key or contrivance for opening the lock of any such lamp, or lucifer match, or any kind of apparatus for striking a light. Wherever safety lamps are required or directed to be used, no person shall use any open lamp.

Explosives, proper use of.

8. Gunpowder or other explosive or inflammable substance shall only be used in the mine underground as follows :—

(*a*). It shall not be stored in the mine.

(*b*). It shall not be taken into the mine except in a case or canister containing not more than 4 ℔s.

(*c*). A workman shall not have in use at one time, in any one place, more than one of such cases or canisters.

(*d*). In charging holes for blasting, an iron or steel pricker shall not be used, and a person shall not have in his possession in the mine underground, any iron or steel pricker, and an iron or steel tamping rod or stemmer shall not be used for ramming either the wadding or the first part of the tamping or stemming on the powder.

(*e*). A charge of powder which has missed fire shall not be unrammed.

(*f*). It shall not be taken into, or be in the possession of any person in any mine except in cartridges, and shall not be used except in accordance with the following Rules, during three months after any inflammable gas has been found in any such mine, viz :—

(1). A competent person who shall be appointed for the purpose, shall immediately before firing the shot, examine the place where it is to be used, and the place contiguous thereto, and shall not allow the shot to be fired unless he finds it safe to do so, and a shot shall not be fired except by or under the direction of a competent person who shall be appointed for the purpose.

(2). If the said inflammable gas issued so freely that it showed a blue cap on the flame of the safety lamp it shall only be used,

(*a*). Either in those cases of stone drifts, stone work, and sinking of shafts in which the ventilation is so managed that the return air from the place where the powder is used passes into the main return air course without passing any place in actual course of working ; or (*b*). When the persons ordinarily employed in the mine come out of the mine or out of the part of the mine where it is used.

(*c*). Where a mine is divided into separate panels in such manner that each panel has an independent intake and return airway from the main air course, and the main return air course, the provisions of this rule with respect to gunpowder or other explosive inflammable substance, shall apply to each such panel in like manner as if it were a separate mine.

9. Where a place is likely to contain a dangerous accumulation of water, the working approaching such place shall not exceed 8 feet in width, and there shall be constantly kept at a sufficient distance, not being less than 5 yards in advance, at least one borehole near the centre of the working and sufficient flank boreholes on each side.

Precautions to be taken to ascertain if dangerous accumulation of water in workings.

10. Every underground plane on which persons travel, which is self-acting, or worked by an engine, windlass, or gin shall be provided (if exceeding 30 yards in length) with some proper means of signalling between the stopping places and at the end of the plane, and shall be provided in every case, at intervals of not more than 20 yards, with sufficient manholes for places of refuge.

Signalling in levels, places of refuge.

11. Every road on which persons travel underground where the load is drawn by a horse or other animal, shall be provided, at intervals of not more than 50 yards, with sufficient manholes, or with a space for a place of refuge, which space shall be a sufficient length and of at least 3 feet in width between the wagons running on the tramroad and the side of such road.

Places of refuge on horse roads.

12. Every manhole and space for a place of refuge, shall be constantly kept clear, and no person shall place anything in a manhole or such place, so as to prevent access thereto.

Places of refuge to be kept clear.

13. The top of every shaft which for the time being is out of use, or used only as an air shaft, shall be securely fenced.

Disused shafts to be covered in.

14. The top of all entrances between the top and bottom of every working or pumping shaft, shall be properly fenced but this shall not be taken to forbid the temporary removal of the fence for the purpose of repairs, or other operations if proper precautions are used.

Entrances to shafts to be fenced.

15. Where the natural strata are not safe, every working or pumping shaft shall be securely cased, lined, or otherwise made secure.

Shafts, security of.

Underground workings, security of roof, &c.

16. The roofs and sides of every travelling road and working place shall be made secure, and a person shall not, unless appointed for the purpose of exploring or repairing, travel or work in any such travelling road or working place which is not so made secure.

Winding engine, competent person to be in charge of

17. A competent person shall be stationed at the mouth of every shaft, for the purpose of working the machinery which may be employed in raising or lowering persons therein, during the whole time any person is below ground.

Single-linked chain not to be used for winding gear.
Winding gear.

18. A single linked chain shall not be used for lowering or raising persons, in any working shafts or place, except for the short coupling chain attached to the cage of the load.

19. There shall be on the drum of every machine used for lowering or raising persons, such flanges or horns and also, if the drum is conical, such other appliances as may be sufficient to prevent the rope from slipping.

Brake.

20. There shall be attached to every machine worked by steam, water, or mechanical power, and used for lowering or raising persons, an adequate brake, and also a proper indicator (in addition to any mark on the rope) which shows to the person who works the machine the position of cage or load in the shaft.

Exposed machinery to be fenced.

21. Every flywheel, and all exposed and dangerous parts of the machinery used in or about the mine shall be, and shall be kept, securely fenced.

Boilers.

22. Every steam-boiler shall be provided with a proper steam-gauge and water-gauge, to show respectively the pressure of steam and the height of water in the boiler with a proper safety-valve.

23. After dangerous gas has been found in any mine, a barometer or thermometer shall be placed above the ground in a conspicuous position near the entrance to the mine.

24. No person shall wilfully damage or, without proper authority, remove or render useless any fence, fencing, casing, lining, guide, means of signalling, signal, over-chain, flange, horn, brake, indicator, steam-gauge, water-gauge, safety-valve or other appliance or thing provided in any mine with a view to compliance with these Rules.

Inspection of machinery &c.

25. Once in every week a competent person appointed for the purpose, shall examine the state of the machinery, headgear, shafts, working place, levels, planes, ropes, chains and other works of the mine, which are in actual use, and shall make a true report of the result of such examination; such report shall be recorded in a book kept for the purpose, and shall be open always for inspection by the Director of Mines or other officer deputed by him.

26. Any accident occurring in or about any mine, resulting in injury to the life or limb of any person, shall be at once reported to the Director of Mines and a report shall be forwarded, setting forth how the accident occurred, within twenty-four hours.

Accidents in mines.

27. Steam engines may not be placed in charge of any person under 18 years of age.

Charge of steam engines.

28. Every mine must be under the control and daily supervision of a thoroughly competent manager.

Competent manager to be employed.

29. The owner, agent, or manager of a mine is required to furnish in triplicate to the Director of Mines, or his duly authorized deputy, all such returns and statistics of, and relating to the workings and operations of the said mine, verified on oath, if required, at such times and in accordance with such forms as the Director of Mines may prescribe.

Returns to be furnished to Director of Mines.

30. A correct plan of an abandoned mine must be sent to the Director of Mines.

Plan of abandoned mines.

31. The registered owners of all mining and mineral leases and prospecting areas or ground held for mining purposes under any other form of holding, upon which development work, exceeding in the aggregate 500 feet of shafts, winzes, levels, and cross-cuts has been carried out, may be called upon by the Director of Mines to employ a surveyor, duly admitted and licensed to practise in the Protectorate, once every six months, or oftener if necessary, who shall prepare in triplicate (two copies may be cloth tracings), in accordance with technical instructions issued by the Director of Public Works, the following plans and sections of the workings up to date, viz :—

Working plans.

(1). General plan.

(2). Working plan.

(3). Vertical, longitudinal projections of the workings on each reef, or mineral deposit, where the average inclination is more than 45 degrees.

(4). Longitudinal section on the plane of each reef, or mineral deposit stoped, where the average inclination is more than 45 degrees.

(5). Transverse section at right angles to the longitudinal projection.

The original to be kept on the mine, and the tracings to be supplied to the Director of Mines, who shall forward one of them to the Director of Public Works for verification in the usual way.

In the event of returns of tonnage of ore or coal extracted, and of ore or coal in reserve, which may appear inaccurate to the Director of Mines, the owners of all mining properties may be called upon to tender a statement prepared by the surveyor employed, as to the said tonnage, based upon the survey of the mine, at the expense of the owner, to the satisfaction of the Director of Mines.

The surveyor is to report opposite to each instruction whether he has carried it out or not, and if he has not carried it out to give his reasons.

Notice of new workings or discontinuance of workings to be furnished to the Director of Mines.

32. In any of the following cases, namely :—

(*a*). Where any working is commenced for the purpose of opening a new mine, or a new shaft, or a seam of any mine ;

(*b*). Where a shaft or seam of any mine is abandoned or the working thereof discontinued ;

(*c*). Where the working of shaft or a seam of any mine is recommenced after any abandonment, or discontinuance for a period exceeding two months ; or

(*d*). Where any change occurs in the name of any mine or in the name of the owner, agent, or manager of any mine, or the principal officers of any incorporated company which is the owner of a mine ; the owner, agent, or manager of the mine shall give notice thereof in writing to the Director of Mines, within two months after the commencement, abandonment, discontinuance, recommencement or change : and if such notice is not given, the owner, agent, and manager shall be liable for failing to give such notice.

Power of inspection of Director of Mines or other officer.

33. The Director of Mines or other officer appointed as Inspector for the purpose, shall have power to do all or any of the following things namely :—

(*a*). To make, or cause to be made, such inquiry and examination as he may consider necessary to ascertain whether the provisions of these Rules are duly complied with.

(*b*). To enter, inspect, and examine any mine, and every part thereof and any fence, fencing, casing, lining, guide, means of signalling, signal, cover, chain, flange, horn, brake, indicator, steam-gauge, water-gauge, safety-valve, or other appliance or things provided in any mine, or any machinery or plant used in connection with such mine, and any mining area, at all reasonable times by day and night, but so as not to impede or obstruct the working of the mine.

(*c*). To examine into, and make inquiry respecting the state and condition of any mine, or any part thereof, and the ventilation of the mine, and the sufficiency of the special rules for the time being in force in the mine, and all matters and things connected with or relating to the safety of persons employed in or about the mine, or any mine contiguous thereto, or in any mining area, or the care and treatment of the horses and other animals employed in the mine or mining area.

(*d*). To exercise such other powers as may be necessary for carrying these Rules into effect.

34. Every person who wilfully obstructs the Director of Mines, or other officer appointed as an Inspector, in the execution of his duty under these Rules, and every owner, agent and manager of a mine who refuses or neglects to furnish to the Inspector the means and assistance necessary for making an entry, inspection, examination, or inquiry under these Rules in relation to the mine or mining area, shall be guilty of an offence against these Rules.

Offences against Rules.

35. If in any respect (which is not provided against by any express provision of these Rules, or by any special rule) the Inspector finds any mine or any part thereof, or any fence, fencing, casing, lining, guide, means of signalling, signal, cover, chain, flange, horn, brake, indicator, steam-gauge, water-gauge, safety-valve, or other appliance or thing provided in any mine, or any matter, thing, or practice, in or connected with any such mine or mining area, or with the control, management or direction thereof, by the manager to be dangerous or defective, so as, in his opinion, to threaten or tend to the bodily injury of any person, he may give notice in writing thereof, to the owner, agent or manager of the mine, and shall state in the notice the particulars in which he may consider the mine, or any part thereof, or any matter, thing, or practice, to be dangerous, and require the same to be remedied forthwith, and it shall be the duty of the owner, agent, or manager to carry out such orders, but such notice shall not absolve such owner, agent or manager from liability to prosecution for contravening any of these Rules.

Liability of owners, agents managers, &c.

36. No person shall be precluded by any agreement from doing, or be liable under any contract to any penalty or forfeiture for doing, such acts as may be necessary in order to comply with the provisions of these Rules.

Contractors not exempt from provisions of these Rules.

37. The powers of the Director of Mines or other officer appointed as Inspector shall extend over the whole of the mining area of the digging or mine to which he may be appointed, in so far only as the general safety of life and limb is concerned.

Jurisdiction of Director of Mines or other officer.

38. Any person found guilty of contravening any of these Rules shall be liable on conviction thereof to pay a penalty not exceeding 50*l*.

Rules.

92/1911,—28th June.

Under Section 32.

Prospecting areas and claims to be beaconed off.

1. Every prospecting area and every claim must be properly beaconed off at the four corners with pegs not less than three inches in diameter and standing not less than three feet above the ground. On each peg shall be legibly inscribed the date on which the area or claim was pegged off and by whom.

Working of prospecting areas and claims.

2. Every prospecting area and claim shall be worked by at least one European and two natives during at least seven days out of every calendar month.

When prospecting area or claim may be beaconed off.

3. No prospecting area or claim shall be beaconed off as aforesaid before the prospector shall have obtained from the Director of Mines an exclusive licence to prospect within such area in the form in the Schedule hereto.

Mode of application for exclusive licence.

4. (1). Every application for such exclusive licence shall be made in the first instance to the District Resident and shall be accompanied by a sketch plan and a description of the boundaries sufficient in the opinion of the District Resident for the identification of the prospecting area or claim.

Issue of licence by Director of Mines.

(2). The District Resident on being satisfied that particulars sufficient for the identification of the prospecting area or claim have been furnished shall forward the application with sketch plan and description of boundaries to the Director of Mines.

Registration of licence.

(3). Every such licence shall be registered in the office of the Director of Mines.

Miner's Right.

5. For every Miner's Right there shall be payable to the Director of Mines twenty shillings each month or portion of a month.

Rent on mining and mineral leases.

6. * Rent will be charged in respect of mining and mineral leases at such rate as may be agreed upon between the Governor and the lessee. Such rent shall in the case of mining leases in no case exceed the sum of one pound per acre nor shall it be at a lower rate than one shilling per acre. In the case of mineral leases it shall not exceed five shillings per acre nor be less than sixpence per acre. Any fractional part of an acre will be considered as a full acre and any fractional part of a month will be considered as a full month and charged for accordingly; and such rent shall be computed and paid up to the 1st day of January, April, July, and October next following the date of the lease and shall thereafter

---

* This rule replaces original Rule 6 (*Gazette* No. 131/1911).

be made payable quarterly in advance during the whole term of the lease, provided that one half of the amonnt received by the Governor on account of rents for mining or mineral leases granted over any private land, will be paid to the owner of such land on application.

7. The fee chargeable on a licence to deal in precious metals or precious stones shall be for each place of business in which such dealing is carried on, Ten Pounds.

Duty on licence to deal in precious metals or stones.

SCHEDULE.

The Mining Ordinance, 1906.

EXCLUSIVE LICENCE TO PROSPECT, No. . . . .

Subject to the provisions of the Mining Ordinance, 1906, and any Rules from time to time made thereunder, the sole and exclusive right is hereby granted to (*insert name and address of Licensee*) to prospect for (*state kind of mineral or minerals*) during a term of six months from (*state date*) within the lands (*state boundaries, area, district &c..*) delineated on the plan attached hereto and thereon coloured (*insert colour*).

This   day of   19

Director of Mines.

Rules Governing Mineral Leases.

116/1911,—21st July.

1. In the event of the holder of a licence to prospect finding any mineral or minerals within or under the lands named in his licence and being desirous of obtaining a lease for any such mineral or minerals, he shall forthwith mark off the area or areas of the lands within or under which he desires to obtain the right to mine any mineral or minerals aforesaid, and apply in writing to the Director of Mines for a lease or leases of such area or areas.

Marking off of areas and application for lease.

2. For the purpose of Rule 1 the boundaries may be marked off by placing on trees or posts of hard wood at the limits of the lands at intervals of not more than 400 yards and at every alteration in the direction of the boundary the initials of the holder of the licence and the number of his licence.

Method of marking.

The posts shall not be less than six inches square, or if round seven inches in diameter, and five feet long and not less than three feet in the ground.

Particulars to be stated.

3. Every application shall contain the following particulars :—

(*a*). If the applicant is an individual, his full name, nationality, description and address; if a firm or syndicate, the full name, nationality, description and address of each partner; and, if a limited company, the same particulars of each director and the amount of the subscribed capital of such company ;

(*b*). The boundaries, extent and situation of the area of the lands within or under which it is desired to obtain a lease to mine any mineral or minerals ;

(*c*). The dates at which the marking off of the area was commenced and completed ;

(*d*). The names of the owner or owners of such lands ;

(*e*). The length of term desired ;

(*f*). The mineral or minerals of which a lease is required;

(*g*). An address in the Protectorate for service of notices ;

(*h*). If the applicant is a limited company, a copy of the memorandum and articles of association shall be attached to the application.

With every application the person applying for a lease shall send to the Director of Mines specimens of the mineral or minerals found in the area referred to in the application.

Separate application for each area.

4. A separate application shall be made in respect of each area within or under which the right to mine any mineral or minerals is required.

Power of Governor to direct survey.

5. The Governor may at any time in any case where he shall deem it necessary require that the boundaries of any area marked off as aforesaid shall be surveyed by a Surveyor or approved by the Director of Mines and the costs of such survey shall be paid by the applicant for the lease.

Priority.

6. Subject to Rule 7 the holder of a licence who first marks off an area, and applies within thirty days of such marking off for the grant of a lease of any mineral or minerals named in his application within or under such area shall have the prior right to the grant of a lease of such mineral or minerals.

Power of Governor to refuse lease.

7. The Governor may in the exercise of his discretion refuse to grant a lease without giving any reason for such refusal.

Form of lease.

8. Leases granted by the Governor shall be in the form in the Schedule to these Rules or to the like effect.

9. A Lessee shall have the following rights for the *Rights of lessee.*
purposes of mining :—

(*a*). To enter upon any lands named in his lease;

(*b*). To mine such mineral or minerals as is or are named
in his lease and for that purpose to make all necessary
pits and shafts;

(*c*). To erect, construct and maintain houses and buildings for the use of his agents and workmen;

(*d*). To erect, construct and maintain such engines,
machinery, buildings and workshops and other erections as
may be necessary or convenient;

(*e*). To deposit rubbish produced in mining;

(*f*). To make watercourses and ponds, dams and
reservoirs, and to divert and use any water on or flowing
through the land named in the lease subject to the provisions
of Rule 33.

(*g*). To cut such trees as may be necessary for the
purpose of obtaining wood for carrying on mining and for
domestic purposes provided that none of the reserved trees
enumerated in Schedule I of the Forests Ordinance 1911 may
be cut or removed under this Rule;

(*h*). To construct and maintain all such railways, tramways, roads, communications and conveniences as may be
necessary.

10. If for the exercise of any of the rights conferred by *Entry upon land under cultivation.*
Rule 9 a lessee shall require to enter upon any lands under
cultivation, he shall before entering thereon give not less than
one month's previous notice to the District
Resident and to the occupiers and owners of such land and
shall pay such compensation as may be agreed upon or in case
of dispute assessed by the Court.

11. Every lessee shall begin to mine within six months *Time for com-mencement of work.*
after the date of his lease or within such extended time as the
Governor may allow and shall not without the consent of the
Governor discontinue work for any periods together exceed- *Continuance of work.*
ing six months in any one year or for any continuous period
exceeding one year during the term of his lease.

12. Every lessee shall make and maintain sufficient *Pits, &c. to be fenced off.*
fences for the protection of man and beast round every open
pit and shaft which shall be made on the lands comprised in
his lease.

13. Every lessee shall at all times during the continuance *Number of men to be employed.*
of his lease employ for the purposes of mining such number
of men as the Director of Mines shall from time to time by

notice in writing determine to be the number necessary in his opinion for mining effectively the mineral or minerals.

List of men employed to be furnished.

14. Every lessee or his attorney shall during the continuance of his lease on the first day of October in every year furnish to the Director of Mines a full and true list of the names of all persons employed in mining the mineral or minerals subject to his lease.

Accounts to be kept and verified if required.

15. Every lessee shall keep at his principal office within the Protectorate to the satisfaction of the Director of Mines accurate and regular accounts of all minerals raised or got within or under the lands comprised in his lease, and of the sales thereof, and of the times of the removal of the same from such lands, together with all such particulars of weights, quantities, sales, and other facts and circumstances as may be necessary to enable the quality and value of such minerals to be estimated.

Plans to be kept.

16. (1). Every lessee shall at all times during the continuance of his lease keep at his principal office in the Protectorate true and correct plans and sections of all mines worked under his lease, and all the workings thereof, and of all veins, seams or lodes which shall have been discovered therein, upon which the extent, position and actual condition of the works shall on the first day of January and first day of July in every year be accurately set forth and delineated.

(2). Such plans and sections shall be made on the scale 1 in 792 on the horizontal or ground plane, and of 1 in 120 on the vertical plane.

Inspection of accounts, mines &c.

17. The Director of Mines or any person authorized by him may at all reasonable times have access to, inspect and take copies of and extracts from all accounts, plans and sections directed by these Rules to be kept and may at all such times enter into and upon and inspect the mines, buildings, machinery and works on and within the lands comprised in the lease and every lessee and his attorney, agents and workmen shall give facilities for the purposes aforesaid.

Lessee to appoint attorney in Protectorate.

18. Every lessee if absent from the Protectorate shall appoint an attorney ordinarily resident in the Protectorate to represent him in all matters relating to his lease and any power of attorney creating such appointment or effecting a change in such appointment shall be registered in the Registry of Documents.

Annual statement of profit.

19. (1). Every lessee or his attorney on or before the first day of May in every year shall prepare and deliver to the

Director of Mines a true and correct statement of all profits made and of the minerals raised or gotten and exported and sold with the details of sales during the twelve months ending the 31st March preceding. No appropriation or distribution shall be made until such statement has been made and accepted by the Governor as a true and correct statement of such profits.

(2). "Profits" shall mean the gross profits less the actual cost of working, and less interest at the rate of 10 per cent on the capital actually expended on the equipment works for the development of the mines.

20. The Director of Mines may require every lessee or his attorney, and his clerk or accountant, to produce to him or any person duly authorized by him all accounts, vouchers and papers required for supporting the statement aforesaid, and may also require every lessee or his attorney, and his clerk or accountant or either of them, so far as their or his knowledge goes, to verify such statement by affidavit.

Production of books of account &c.

21. Upon receipt of such statement the Director of Mines or any person appointed by him shall assess the royalties prescribed under Section 28 (iii) of the Mining Ordinance 1906 on the actual sale price of the minerals sold during the year.

Assessment of royalty.

22. Where any person makes default in delivering a true and correct statement of accounts as required by these Rules, or if the Governor shall not be satisfied with such statement, the Director of Mines or any person authorized by him, shall assess the royalty on such sum as according to the best of his judgment ought to be charged under these Rules, and shall add thereto the amount of any costs which he may have incurred for the purpose of assessing such royalty. The amount of royalty and costs so fixed shall be deemed in every case to be the amount of the royalty payable by the lessee, and shall, subject to appeal to the High Court, be final and conclusive.

Assessment where statement not delivered or unsatisfactory.

23. * As soon as the amount of the royalty has been assessed under Rule 21 or Rule 22, the Director of Mines shall give notice thereof in writing to the Lessee by whom the amount is payable, or if such lessee is not resident in the Protectorate, to the attorney in the Protectorate of such lessee, and such amount shall be paid within fourteen days after the date of such notice, if no appeal is lodged, or where an appeal has been lodged, within fourteen days or such time after the decision of the Court as the Court may direct.

Payment of royalty.

This Rule replaces the original Rule (*Gazette* 60/1912).

Where an appeal has been lodged and afterwards discontinued, payment shall become due immediately upon such discontinuance.

Revocation of lease on breach of Rules.

24. In case of the breach by a lessee of any of these Rules relating to leases, the Governor may, by notice in writing, summarily determine his lease, and thereupon all rights conferred thereby or enjoyed thereunder shall cease as from a date mentioned in such notice.

Determination of lease on exhaustion of minerals.

25. If the minerals comprised in a lease be wholly exhausted before the expiration of the term of the lease, the lease shall thereupon cease and determine, as if the same had expired by effluxion of time.

Surrender.

26· A lessee may surrender his lease or any of the rights conferred thereby on such terms as the Governor may in his discretion think fit.

Liability when lease determined.

27. Notwithstanding the revocation, determination or surrender of his lease under Rules 24, 25 or 26, the lessee shall remain liable for any breach of any of these Rules committed prior to such revocation, determination or surrender.

Transfer or assignment of lease.

28. A lessee may transfer or assign or sublet his lease or any of the rights conferred thereby, provided the consent of the Governor in writing be first had and obtained.

Publication of grant, &c., of leases.

29. The grant, issue, revocation, determination, surrender, transfer and assignment of every lease shall be advertised in the *Gazette.*

Power of Director of Mines to order security to be given.

30. The Director of Mines may at any time require any person applying for a lease or any lessee to give security for due payment of any costs of survey, fees and royalty or any of them, payable under these Rules, in such sum as he may direct, either by depositing the same in the Treasury or by a bond with two sureties approved by him.

Damages to houses, &c. forbidden.

31. In the exercise of the rights conferred by these Rules a lessee shall not do or permit any damage to any house, building or erection or to any land under cultivation, excepting land entered into under the provisions of Rule 9; and to avoid such damage he shall not exercise any of the rights conferred upon him by these Rules within 100 yards from any such house, building, erection or land under cultivation without the consent of the District Resident and the occupier and owner thereof.

Interference with public road, &c., forbidden.

32. In the exercise of the rights conferred by these Rules a lessee shall not disturb or interfere with or permit any disturbance or interference with any railway, public road or pathway, or with any public building or works, or any burial ground or land appropriated to any public purpose.

33. In the exercise of the rights conferred by these Rules a lessee shall not without the consent of the District Resident pollute or permit to be polluted any water on or flowing through the land subject to his lease so as to render the same unfit for domestic or farming purposes or divert or permit to be diverted any such flowing water.

Pollution and diverting of water forbidden.

34. The lessee shall not interfere with or disturb any native village, settlement, plantation or pasture land.

Native rights.

35. The lessee shall be liable for all damage caused to the surface by his workings except for such damage as may be necessarily caused under Rule 9.

Surface damage.

36. Any person who contravenes any of the aforesaid Rules shall for each offence be liable on conviction to a fine not exceeding £25 or to imprisonment with or without hard labour for any term not exceeding three months.

Penalty.

Schedule.

Form of Lease.

THIS INDENTURE made the   day of   19 , Between   Governor of the Nyasaland Protectorate for and on behalf of the Government thereof, hereinafter called the Government, of the one part and   hereinafter called the lessee (which expression shall include the lessee and his successors in the title) of the other part WITNESSETH that the Government does hereby grant and demise unto the Lessee all [*here insert "minerals" or specify the mineral leased, e.g. "mica"*] within or under the lands, delineated on the plan attached hereto and thereon coloured   together with all the rights conferred by the Mining Ordinance 1906 and the Rules from time to time made thereunder TO HOLD USE AND ENJOY the same unto the Lessee from the   day of 19 , to the   day of   19 at an annual rental of   sterling, payable the first instalment on the   day of 19 and thereafter on the   day of   and the   day of   in each year.

IN WITNESS WHEREOF the Governor has hereunto set his hand and the seal of the Protectorate has been affixed and the Lessee has set his hand and seal, the Governor this   day of   19 , at   and the Lessee this   day of   19 , at

SIGNED SEALED AND DELIVERED by the }
above named
in my presence this   day of   19 .

SIGNED SEALED AND DELIVERED by the }
above named
in my presence this   day of   19 .

Rules.*

118/1914—2nd June.

Under Section 3.

   1. Every application for the issue of a Permit for the extraction from Crown lands of any substance specified in the Ordinance shall be made at the Boma of the District or Sub-District in which the lands are situate.

   2. Every such Permit shall be in the form in the Schedule hereto or as near thereto as the circumstances of the case shall require and shall be issued by the Resident or Assistant Resident of the District or Sub-District.

   3. The following conditions shall apply to every Permit issued under these Rules :—

   (*a*). It shall not be transferable.

   (*b*). It shall be carried by the grantee while working, and shall be produced on demand to any District Officer.

   (*c*). It shall remain in force for such period not exceeding 12 months as the Resident or Assistant Resident shall determine, and shall expire on the date specified in it.

   4. No substances shall be removed until the prescribed fee has been paid and the second part of the Permit has been endorsed by the District Resident or Assistant Resident.

   5. All openings in the surface of the land made in the extraction of the substance shall be filled in where possible to the satisfaction of the Resident or Assistant Resident, but where this is impracticable the Resident or Assistant Resident may require the opening to be properly drained and fenced. If the person to whom the Permit is issued fails to comply with any direction given by the Resident or Assistant Resident in pursuance of these Rules, the work may be executed by the Resident or Assistant Resident and the cost thereof shall be recoverable from the person aforesaid.

   6. The following fees shall be payable in respect of Permits issued under these Rules:—

To excavate clay or earth and burn bricks ...	1/- per 1,000 bricks.
To excavate raw limestone ...	2/- per ton.
In respect of lime excavated and burnt	2/9 per ton.
To excavate sand or other like substance ...	6*d.* per ton.
To excavate building stone	6*d.* per ton.

   In calculating the number of bricks in a kiln the cubic area of the kiln (less the fire holes) shall be measured and 14 bricks of the standard size of 9″ × 4½″ × 3″ shall be allowed for each cubic foot.

---

* These Rules are made under the Mining (Amendment) Ordinance, 1914.

Schedule.

COUNTERFOIL.	NYASALAND PROTECTORATE

The Mining (Amendment) Ordinance 1914.

The Mining (Amendment) Ordinance. 1914.

No.   [1].

PERMIT.

Under the provisions of the above Ordinance and the Rules made under it this permit is issued to

No.
Issued to
of
to extract
for
Expires
Date

Fees paid

of   for the extraction
from Crown Lands situate at or near
in the District of   of the
following substance
for the purpose of
    The quantity to be extracted is
    This permit shall expire on the
    Issued at
(Date)   District Resident.

[2].

AUTHORITY FOR REMOVAL.

Date

The above named person having paid the sum of
is authorised to remove from Crown Land:—

District Resident.

Such removal to be effected before the (*date*)
    District Resident.

No. 5 of 1910.

MINING REGULATION (OIL).

171/1910,—12th November.

R u l e s.

Under Section 11.

Deposits.

1. (*a*). The following deposits shall be paid :—

Every person applying for a licence to drill for and work mineral oils under this Ordinance, and every person applying for a lease of mineral oils under this Ordinance, shall at the same time deposit with the Director of Mines to whom such applications shall be made an amount which shall from time to time be fixed by the Governor, but not exceeding £1,000 in respect of each such licence or lease.

(*b*). This amount shall be returned on the applicant commencing to drill in accordance with the Rules made under Section 20 of this Ordinance, but in the event of drilling not being carried out as provided by such Rules, the amount of the deposit shall be entirely forfeited to the Government.

Rents.

2. The following rents shall be paid :—

(*a*). By every holder of a licence, £1 per annum for every square mile or part thereof of the lands named in his licence.

(*b*). By every lessee, £15 per annum for every quarter of a square mile or part thereof subject to the lease.

(*c*). By every holder of a licence or lessee, £15 per annum for every hole drilled by him and producing oil.

Fees.

3. The following fees shall be paid :—

(*a*). By every holder of a licence or lessee, the sum of £10 in respect of every hole drilled by him.

(*b*). By every assignee or transferee of a licence or of any of the rights thereunder on assent of the Governor, £20.

(*c*). By every assignee or transferee on assignment or transfer of lease or of any of the rights thereunder on assent of the Governor, £1 for every quarter of a square mile or part thereof subject to the assigned or transferred lease.

Royalties.

4. The following royalties shall be paid :—

(*a*). A royalty of 5 per cent on the value of all oil raised, won, or gotten under any licence or licences to drill for or work mineral oils or under any lease or leases of mineral oils which may be granted to the holder of such licence or licences. Such lease or leases shall not exceed a total area of 10 square miles selected from the total area of the lands subject to such licence or licences.

(*b*). Subject to the provisions of the preceding paragraph a minimum royalty of 7½ per cent shall be paid on the value of all oil raised, won or gotten from any lands the subject of a lease of mineral oils.

(*c*). If any part of the lands subject to any such lease shall be situate further than 300 yards and not more than 2,000 yards from an oil producing hole, a minimum royalty of 10 per cent shall be paid on the value of all oil raised, won or gotten from lands subject to such lease.

(*d*). If any part of the lands subject to such lease shall be situate 300 yards or less from an oil producing hole, a minimum royalty of 12½ per cent shall be paid on the value of all oil raised, won or gotten from lands subject to such lease.

(*e*). All oil used by the holder of a licence or a lessee for fuel for driving machinery, for winning oil, and for the usual and customary purposes of the oil holes, and for domestic consumption in the houses and offices of agents and workers for the time being employed in and about the said oil holes and premises shall be free from royalty.

5. The Governor may appoint any person or persons for the purpose of inspecting and checking the amount of oil produced and ascertaining the royalty payable thereon. *Checking amount of oil raised.*

Such person or persons shall at all reasonable times have access to all books, accounts, vouchers and other documents kept by the holder of a licence or by a lessee in connexion therewith.

6. (1). In addition to or in lieu of the provisions contained in the last preceding Rule the Governor may require that every holder of a licence or every lessee on or before the 1st day of July in every year, shall prepare and deliver to the proper officer a true and correct statement, verified by affidavit, of all mineral oil raised, won or gotten by such holder of a licence or lessee during the twelve months ended the 31st March preceding. *Annual statement of oil gotten.*

(2). For the verification of such statement the Governor may require the production to the proper officer of all books, accounts, vouchers and other documents from which such statement has been prepared.

Penalty.

7. Any person who prevents or obstructs the proper officer from inspecting or checking the amount of mineral oil raised, won or gotten by him or who fails or neglects to deliver any statement or who wilfully delivers a false statement or neglects or refuses to produce any books, accounts, vouchers or other documents when required so to do or who refuses or neglects to verify any statement as aforesaid by affidavit when so required, shall be liable on conviction to a fine not exceeding £50 or to imprisonment with or without hard labour for any period not exceeding six months or to both fine and imprisonment.

Assessment of royalty.

8. Upon the receipt of such statement the Governor or any person appointed by him shall assess the royalty due thereon.

Oil, how valued.

9. For the purposes of assessing the royalty the value of the oil shall be either agreed upon or shall be taken to be the current market value.

Assessment where statement not delivered or unsatisfactory.

10. Where any person makes default in delivering a true and correct statement of mineral oils raised, won or gotten as required by these Rules, or if the Governor shall not be satisfied with such statement, the Governor, or any person authorized by him, shall assess the royalties to be charged and shall add thereto the amount of any costs which he may have incurred for the purpose of assessing such royalties. The amount of royalties and costs so fixed shall be deemed in every case to be the amount of the royalties payable by the holder of a licence or the lessee, and shall, subject to appeal to the High Court of the Protectorate, be final and conclusive:

Provided that in the event of its being shewn subsequently to the satisfaction of the Governor that the statement delivered was true and correct, the amount of the costs which may have been paid shall be refunded by the Government.

Payment of royalty.

11. As soon as the amount of the royalties has been assessed as hereinbefore provided, the Chief Secretary shall give notice thereof in writing to the holder of a licence or the lessee by whom the amount is payable, or if such holder of a licence or lessee is not resident within the Protectorate, to the agent or representative of such holder of a licence or lessee then being within the Protectorate, and such amount shall be paid within fourteen days after the date of the delivery of such notice, if no appeal has been lodged, or, where an appeal has been lodged, then within fourteen days after the date of the decision of the High Court or such other time as the said Court may order.

171/1910,—22nd November.

Rules.

Under Section 20.

LICENCES.

1. Every person desiring to obtain a licence to drill for and work mineral oils shall apply in writing to the Director of Mines and shall give the following particulars :— Application for Licences. How made.

(*a*). If an individual, his full name, nationality, description and address. If a firm or syndicate, the full name, nationality, description and address of each partner, and if a limited company the same particulars of each director.

(*b*). The boundaries and the extent and situation of the area to be named in the licence.

(*c*). An address in the Protectorate for service of notices, and

(*d*). If the applicant is a limited company, a copy of the memorandum and articles of association of the company shall be attached.

2. All such applications shall be submitted to the Governor who may in the exercise of his discretion refuse to grant any licence without assigning any reason for his refusal. Power to refuse application.

3. Every licence may be granted for any period not exceeding four years from the date thereof, and shall be in the Form A annexed hereto and subject to all the provisions of the Ordinance and any Rules made thereunder. Form of licence.

4. All licences shall be issued by the Director of Mines and countersigned by the Governor. A record of all such licences shall be registered in the Land Register at Blantyre. Issue and registration.

5. Subject to the provisions of the Ordinance and these Rules or any Rules made in addition thereto or in substitution therefor the holder of every licence upon the issue thereof shall have the following rights :— Rights under licences.

(*a*). To enter upon any lands named in his licence ;

(*b*). To drill for and work mineral oils on any such lands and to dredge any stream or pool so far as may be required for the purposes of such drilling and working ;

(*c*). To construct his camp on any unoccupied land ;

(*d*). To take firewood from any forest land for domestic purposes ; and

(*e*). To take water from any stream, spring, pool or well not private property for domestic use or for the purposes of drilling for and working mineral oil :

Provided that the foregoing rights shall be exercised subject to the laws of the Protectorate and in such manner and on payment of such rates as the Director of Mines shall deem fair and reasonable or as shall be prescribed by any Rules made under the Ordinance.

Transfer of assignment of licence.

6. The holder of a licence may transfer or assign such licence or any of the rights conferred thereby, provided the consent in writing of the Governor be first had and obtained.

Surrender of licences.

7. The holder of a licence may surrender the same or any of the rights conferred thereby on such terms as the Governor may in his discretion think fit.

Revocation of licences : effect.

8. In case of the breach by the holder of a licence of any of the provisions of the Ordinance, or of these or any other Rules relating to licences, the Governor may by notice in writing summarily revoke such licence and thereupon all rights conferred thereby or enjoyed thereunder shall cease as from the date mentioned in such notice.

Liability when licence revoked, etc.

9. Notwithstanding the revocation or surrender of his licence, the holder thereof shall be liable for any breach of the Ordinance or of any of these Rules committed prior to such revocation or surrender.

Production of licences.

10. Every person drilling for or working mineral oils shall produce his licence or where the person drilling for or working mineral oils is an agent authorized by the holder of the licence, the written authority of such holder to the District Resident or any person authorized by such District Resident on demand.

Publication of grants, etc. in Gazette.

11. Every grant, issue, transfer, assignment, surrender and revocation of every licence shall be published in the *Gazette*.

Limitation clause.

12. No licence shall be granted to drill for or work mineral oil on land within 2,000 yards of any oil producing hole.

LEASES.

Application for lease how made.

13. Any person desirous of obtaining a lease under the provisions of this Ordinance shall proceed as in Rule 1 hereof.

Marking of boundaries.

14. Every area applied for under the preceding Rule shall be marked off by the applicant to the satisfaction of the Director of Mines.

Application to be confined to one area.

15. A separate application shall be made in respect of each area for which a lease is desired.

Power of Governor to direct survey.

16. The Governor may at any time in any case where he shall deem it necessary require that the boundaries of any area marked off as aforesaid shall be surveyed by a surveyor

appointed or approved by the Governor, and the costs of such survey shall be paid by the applicant for the lease.

17. The holder of a licence shall have the sole right at any time before the expiration of his licence to mark off an area or areas in accordance with these Rules and apply for the grant of a lease or leases of mineral oils in respect of such area or areas being part of the land subject to his licence.

Prior right of holder of a licence to leases.

18. The Governor may on the expiration of a licence grant to any person other than the holder of such licence a lease or leases of mineral oils in respect of any area or areas previously subject to such licence in respect of which such licence holder shall not have applied under Rules 17 or 22 for any lease or leases.

Grant of leases to other persons.

19. The Governor may in the exercise of his discretion refuse to grant a lease to any person other than the holder of a licence without giving any reason for such refusal.

Power of Governor to refuse lease.

20. Every lease may be granted for any period not exceeding 25 years, subject however to renewal for any further period not exceeding 25 years and upon such terms and conditions as may be hereafter agreed upon. Such lease shall be in Form B annexed hereto and subject to the terms and conditions stated therein or such other terms and conditions as may be from time to time prescribed by any Rules made under this Ordinance.

Duration of lease.

21. The area of lands which may be included in any one lease shall not be less than one quarter of a square mile nor more than four square miles in extent, and the aggregate extent of areas of the land which may be included in any lease held by any person in his own right or jointly with others shall not exceed 20 square miles.

Areas.

22. (1). Around every area in respect of which a lease shall be granted to the holder of a licence a zone of four times that area or of such less area as the Governor may in special circumstances determine shall be reserved : Provided that such reservation shall only be made in respect of leases to be granted to the holder of any licence or licences up to the aggregate of 10 square miles in respect of which the minimum royalty of 5 per cent shall be payable as provided by the Rules made under Section 12 of the Ordinance.

Reserved zones.

(2). A licensee to whom any lease shall have been granted as aforesaid shall have the prior right to apply at any time within 50 days from the grant of such lease for the grant of a lease or leases in respect of the whole or any portion of any zone reserved as aforesaid adjoining the area subject to his said lease. No such reserved zone shall form a part of the aggregate of 10 square miles in respect of which the minimum royalty of 5 per cent shall be payable as provided by the rules made under Section 12 of the Ordinance.

(3). Subject to the preceding paragraph, the Governor may in the exercise of his discretion grant a lease in respect of the whole or any portion of any such reserved zone to any person subject to the Rules made under Section 12 of the Ordinance, or may refuse to grant such a lease without giving any reason for such refusal.

Breach of Rules.

23. In case of the breach by a lessee of any of the provisions of the Ordinance or these Rules or any other Rules relating to leases, the Governor may by notice in writing summarily determine his lease and thereupon all rights conferred thereby or enjoyed thereunder shall cease as from the date mentioned in such notice.

Exhaustion of mineral oils.

24. If the mineral oils within or under the lands subject to a lease be wholly exhausted before the expiration of the term of the lease, the lease shall thereupon cease and determine as if it had expired by effluxion of time.

Surrender.

25. A lessee may surrender his lease or any of the rights conferred thereby on such terms as the Governor may in his discretion think fit.

Liability when lease determined.

26. Notwithstanding the determination or surrender of his lease under Rules 24 or 25 the lessee shall remain liable for any breach of any of these Rules committed prior to such determination or surrender.

Transfer or assignment of lease.

27. A lessee may transfer or assign his lease or any of the rights conferred thereby, provided the consent of the Governor in writing be first had and obtained.

Gazetting.

28. The grant, issue, transfer, assignment, surrender, and determination of every lease shall be published in the *Gazette*.

Rights of His Majesty's Government.

Rights of His Majesty's Government.

29. Every licence or lease granted shall be subject to the following conditions :—

(1). His Majesty's Government shall have the right of pre-emption of all crude oil raised, won or gotten under the provisions of the Ordinance or any Rules made thereunder, and of all products of the refining or treatment of such oil.

The holder of every licence or lease shall furnish an undertaking that he will use every endeavour within his power to afford to His Majesty's Government the means of exercising such right of pre-emption.

(2). The price to be paid by His Majesty's Government for all oil or products as aforesaid taken under the provisions of this Rule shall either be as specified in a separate agreement, or, if no such agreement has been entered into prior to the exercise of the right of pre-emption, then the price shall be the market rate ruling at the time for the particular oil or product delivered by the holder of the licence or the lessee free-on-board at Port Herald. If no such market rate has been established and publicly quoted at the time at which the right of pre-emption is exercised, then the price to be paid shall be the market price of Texas Oil or products of similar description free-on-board at Port Arthur (Texas). The right of pre-emption by H. M. Government shall extend to any oil or products which may have been already sold by the holder of the licence or lessee to other customers, but not yet dispatched from the Protectorate; and for such oil or products the price to be paid by H. M. Government shall be as expressed above, viz., either the publicly quoted market rate for the particular oil or products, or, failing such rate, then the Port Arthur (Texas) rate, or the actual contract price at which the oil or products was originally sold if such contract price is less than either the Protectorate or the Texas market rate and in addition any actual penalties or damages the holder of the licence or the lessee may prove that he has suffered owing to cancellation or alteration of charters of vessels for the conveyance of such oil or products sold to other customers provided that such penalties or damages shall only be payable on a charter actually entered into for a particular voyage, and not on any general freight agreement in respect of prospective charters.

The holder of the licence or the lessee shall furnish to the Governor for the confidential information of H. M. Government, if so desired, particulars of the quantities of oil or products sold or of charters entered into for freight, and in the event of the right of pre-emption being exercised by H. M. Government he shall also furnish particulars of contract prices for oil or products and freight, and shall exhibit to H. M. Government original or authenticated copies of contracts for oil or products and charter-parties for freight.

(3). In the event of war, the Governor on behalf of His Majesty's Government shall have power to take control of the works and plant in the area subject to the licence or lease.

(4). The Governor shall have the power to regulate the site of any refinery or place of storage of oil in the Protectorate.

WORKING.

Definition of "worker."

30. In Rules 31 to 53 inclusive, the term "Worker" shall mean the licensee or the lessee as the case may be.

Rights of worker.

31 (1). Subject to the provisions of the Ordinance and these Rules a worker shall have the following rights for the purpose of drilling for and working mineral oils :—

(*a*). To enter upon any lands named in his licence or lease;

(*b*). To drill for and work mineral oils and for that purpose to make all necessary bore-holes and wells;

(*c*). To erect, construct and maintain such houses, buildings, workshops, tanks, pipe-lines and other erections as may be necessary or convenient;

(*d*). To deposit rubbish produced in drilling for and working mineral oils;

(*e*). To make watercourses and ponds, dams and reservoirs and to divert and use any water on or flowing through the land named in the licence or lease;

(*f*). To cut such trees as may be necessary for the purpose of obtaining wood for carrying on the drilling for and working of mineral oils and for domestic purposes; and,

(*g*). To construct and maintain all such railways, tramways, roads, pipe-lines, communications and conveniences as may be necessary :

Provided that the foregoing rights shall be exercised in such manner and on payment of such rates as the Director of Mines shall deem fair and reasonable or as shall be prescribed by any Rules made under the Ordinance.

Entry upon land under cultivation.

(2). If for the exercise of any of the rights conferred by Rule 31 (1) a worker shall require to enter upon any lands under cultivation he shall before entering thereon give not less than one month's previous notice of his intention to the District Resident and to the occupiers and owners of such lands and shall pay such compensation as may be agreed on, or in case of dispute assessed by the Court.

Notice of proposed drilling.

32. Notice of the location of any proposed drilling shall be sent to the Director of Mines and no drilling shall be commenced at such location without his consent thereto.

Distances of holes.

33. No two holes may be drilled at a less distance apart than 100 yards nor shall any boring be commenced at a less distance than 50 yards from the boundary of the lands subject to any licence or lease.

Drilling operations

34 All drilling operations shall be carried out with steam-drilling machinery and shall be commenced within twelve months from the date of the licence or lease.

35. No water drilling shall be employed and all water whether from the surface or otherwise must be shut off with proper casing before the oil is reached, or in the event of oil being unexpectedly reached before the water is shut off then the water must be properly shut off before any oil is extracted.

Prohibition of water drilling and shutting off of water.

36. Should it be found from causes beyond the control of the worker impossible to shut off the water without also shutting off the oil, then the hole shall be either properly plugged or the oil and water properly cased off before the worker commences to drill for lower strata.

Plugging and casing off.

37. Holes having water in them which may be abandoned must be plugged to the satisfaction of the Director of Mines.

Abandoned holes to be plugged.

38. In the event of the conditions provided for in Rules 35, 36 and 37 not being complied with, the Director of Mines shall be at liberty to make good the default at the expense of the worker.

Default.

39. The worker shall commence drilling within three months from the date of the notice referred to in Rule 32 and shall keep one rig continuously at work subject to " force majeure," of which latter the Governor shall be sole judge, and in the event of stoppage of work, save as aforesaid, for more than thirty days, the Governor shall be at liberty to cancel the licence or lease.

Date of beginning drilling and rate of work.

40. In the event of the worker striking oil in paying quantity, he shall commence within two years therefrom to drill with at least two rigs on the area covered by the licence or lease upon which such oil was struck, and shall, subject to Rule 39, keep both such rigs continuously at work.

Increase of number of rigs on striking oil.

Should the worker fail to comply with the foregoing provision, the Governor shall be at liberty, subject to Rule 39, to cancel the licence or lease.

41. So soon as twelve holes on the area covered by any licence or lease are producing oil in paying quantities, then the number of rigs that must be kept constantly drilling shall be increased to three until there shall be nine producing holes drilled for each quarter of a square mile, when the obligation to drill further holes on the lands subject to such licence or lease shall thereupon cease.

Further increase of number of rigs.

Should the worker fail to comply with the foregoing provision, he shall forfeit all rights conferred by the licence or lease in respect of any portion or portions of the area subject to the licence or lease distant more than 100 yards from the nearest hole.

Pits, &c. to be fenced off.

42. Every worker shall make and maintain sufficient fences for the protection of man and beast round every open pit and shaft which shall be made on the lands subject to his licence or lease.

List of employees to be furnished.

43. Every worker or his attorney shall during the continuance of his licence or lease on the first day of October in every year furnish to the Governor a full and true list of the names of all persons employed by him in drilling for or working mineral oils.

Accounts to be kept and verified if required.

44. Every worker shall keep at his principal office within the Protectorate accurate and regular accounts of all mineral oils raised, won or gotten within or under the lands subject to his licence or lease, and of the sales thereof and of the times of removal of the same from such lands, together with all such particulars, facts and circumstances as may be necessary to enable the quantity and value of such mineral oils to be estimated, and shall, if required by the Governor, verify such accounts by affidavit of himself and his clerk or accountant or either of them as the Governor may direct, so far as his or their knowledge goes.

Plans, records and samples.

45. Accurate plans and records shall be kept of all the strata and the depths at which they were passed through, and if called upon to do so the worker shall supply samples of the cuttings to the Governor.

Inspection of accounts, &c.

46. The Governor or any person authorized by him may at all reasonable times have access to inspect and take copies of and extracts from all accounts, plans and records directed by these Rules to be kept, and may at all such times enter into and upon and inspect the mines, buildings, machinery and works on and within the lands, subject to the licence or lease, and every worker and his attorney, agents and workmen shall give facilities for the purposes aforesaid.

Keeping of records in default of worker.

47. In the event of the Governor not being satisfied with the method in which the records are kept, he shall have the right to appoint some person or persons to keep such records, and in that case the salary and expenses of such person or persons shall be payable half by the worker and half by the Government.

Worker to appoint attorney.

48. Every worker if absent from the Protectorate shall appoint an attorney ordinarily resident in the Protectorate to represent him in the Protectorate, in all matters relating to his licence or lease.

Power of Governor to order security to be given.

49. The Governor may at any time require any worker or any person applying for a licence or lease to give security for the due payment of any costs of survey, fees, and royalty, or any of them payable under these Rules in such sum as he may direct, either by depositing the same in the Treasury or by a bond with two sureties approved by him.

50. In the exercise of the rights conferred by these Rules, a worker shall not do or permit any damage to any house, building or erection, or to any land under cultivation, excepting land entered into under the provisions of Rule 31, and to avoid such damage he shall not exercise any of the rights conferred upon him by these Rules within 100 yards from any such house, building, erection, or land under cultivation, without the consent of the occupier and owner thereof, and in the case of Crown lands, buildings or erections without the consent of the District Resident. *Damage to house, &c. forbidden.*

51. In the exercise of the rights conferred by those Rules a worker shall not cut down or destroy or permit any timber tree, rubber or other produce-bearing tree to be cut down or destroyed on Crown land without the consent of the District Resident or on private property without the consent of the owner thereof. *Damage to timber and produce-bearing trees forbidden.*

52. In the exercise of the rights conferred by these Rules, a worker shall not disturb or interfere with or permit any disturbance or interference with any railway, public road or pathway, or with any public building or works, or any burial ground or land appropriated to any public purpose. *Interference with public roads &c., forbidden.*

53. In the exercise of the rights conferred by these Rules, a worker shall not, without the consent of the District Resident, pollute or permit to be polluted any water on or flowing through the land subject to his licence or lease so as to render the same unfit for domestic or farming purposes, or divert or permit to be diverted any such flowing water. *Pollution or diversion of water forbidden.*

54. Any person who contravenes any of the aforesaid Rules shall for each offence be liable on conviction to a fine not exceeding £25 or to imprisonment with or without hard labour for any period not exceeding three months. *Penalty.*

55. In these Rules the expression "The Ordinance" means "The Mining Regulation (Oil) Ordinance, 1910." *Definition.*

Form A.

The Mining Regulation (Oil) Ordinance, 1910.

LICENCE TO DRILL FOR AND WORK MINERAL OILS.   No.

Subject to the provisions of the Mining Regulation (Oil) Ordinance, 1910, and the Rules from time to time made thereunder, the sole and exclusive right is hereby granted to (*insert name and address of licensee,*) to drill for and work mineral oils during a period of four years from (*insert day of month and year*) within the lands (*state boundaries, area, abuttals and district*) delineated on the map attached hereto and thereon coloured (*insert colour*) for which licence he has paid in advance £——

This (*insert day of month and year*)

(Signature).

Approved:

Governor.

Director of Mines.

Form B.

The Mining Regulation (Oil) Ordinance, 1910.

No ..

FORM OF LEASE.

THIS INDENTURE made the (*insert day of month and year*) BETWEEN (*insert name of Governor*) Governor of the Nyasaland Protectorate for and on behalf of the Government of the said Protectorate hereinafter called the Government of the one part and (*insert name of lessee*) hereinafter called the lessee (*which expression shall include the lessee and his successors in title*) of the other part WITNESSETH that in consideration of the covenants hereinafter recited and of the rent   per annum hereby agreed to be paid in advance by the lessee to the Government in half-yearly instalments of   on the 1st day of April and the 1st day of October in each year respectively and of a Royalty of   per cent on all mineral oils obtained from within or under the said lands the Government doth hereby grant and demise to the lessee all mineral oils within or under the lands (*insert boundaries, area, abuttals and district*) delineated on the map attached hereto and thereon coloured (*insert colour*) together with all the rights conferred by The Mining Regulation (Oil) Ordinance, 1910, and the Rules from time to time made thereunder TO HOLD USE AND ENJOY the same unto the lessee from the (*insert day of month and year*) for a term of (*insert period*) SUBJECT nevertheless to all the provisions of the said Ordinance and the Rules from time to time made thereunder.

IN WITNESS WHEREOF the Governor has hereunto set his hand, and the Public Seal of the Protectorate has been affixed, and the lessee has set his hand and Seal the day and year first above written.

Signed, Sealed and delivered by the above named

in the presence of

Witness.

(*Signature of Governor*).

(Public Seal of Protectorate).

Signed, Sealed and delivered by the above named

(*lessee*)

in the presence of

Witness.

(*Signature of Lessee*),

Seal of Lessee.

No. 5 of 1911.

FORESTS.

142/1912,—22nd August.

RULES.

Under Section 13.

Rubber Rules.

1. The following officers are hereby authorized to issue licences in the form specified in Schedule I hereto for the collection of rubber in Crown Forests :—

Officers empowered to issue rubber licences.

(a). District Residents in their respective Districts.

(b). The Chief Forest Officer.

2. Licences to collect rubber in Crown Forests are issued subject to the following conditions :—

Conditions of licences.

(1). Licences shall not be transferable.

(2). Every licence shall be produced on demand to any District Magistrate or to the Chief Forest Officer or to the Director of Agriculture.

(3). Every licence shall expire on the 31st day of March next following the date of issue.

(4). Every licence shall contain particulars of the plant and of the part of the plant from which the licensee is permitted to extract rubber.

(5). Any licensing officer may refuse to issue a licence to any person without giving reasons for such refusal : Provided that the applicant may appeal to the Governor whose decision shall be final.

(6). All rubber shall be shewn to the District Resident of the district in which the rubber was collected and shall remain Government property until the prescribed royalty on such rubber has been paid to the District Resident as aforesaid.

(7). No rubber collected under licence shall be taken out of the district in which it was collected and no such rubber shall be sold or offered for sale without a Rubber Transit Pass in the form specified in Schedule II hereto first had and obtained from the District Resident of such district.

(8). Royalty on the quantity of rubber for which a Transit Pass is required shall be paid before a Pass is issued.

(9). The quantity of rubber on which royalty has been paid will be stated on the Transit Pass.

(10). The Transit Pass shall be delivered up to the Customs Officer at the Port of Export by the person exporting the rubber in respect of which the Pass has been granted.

3. An exclusive licence to collect rubber in a particular locality or district will only be granted by the Governor in Council.

Power of Governor in Council to grant exclusive licence.

4. Any District Resident or the Chief Forest Officer may seize any rubber collected, purchased or possessed or suspected of being collected, purchased or possessed in contravention of the Ordinance or of these Rules and may detain the same until a Court has given directions for the disposal thereof.

Seizure.

5. Nothing contained in these Rules shall be deemed to invalidate any existing agreement between Government and any person whereby such person is permitted to collect rubber.

Schedule I.

DEPARTMENT OF AGRICULTURE, FORESTRY DIVISION.
RUBBER LICENCE.

Licence subject to "The Forests Ordinance, 1911," and any Rules made thereunder in favour of

to extract rubber from the $\frac{\text{aerial stems}}{\text{root stems}}$ of

in $\frac{\text{Undemarcated}}{\text{Demarcated}}$ Forest within the area

known as   in the   Section or Sections of the   District.
  Royalty at the rate of   per ℔. to be paid on all rubber collected under this Licence.
  For period from   to
  Date of Issue   Station

Licensing Officer.

Schedule II.

DEPARTMENT OF AGRICULTURE, FORESTRY DIVISION.
RUBBER TRANSIT PASS.

Permission is hereby granted to
to remove from the   District   tons
  qrs.   lbs. of $\frac{\text{root}}{\text{vine}}$ rubber collected in the said District under

Licence No.
Royalty amounting to   has been paid this
      day of   191 , on the above mentioned quantity of rubber.
          Station

District Resident.

62/1913,—31st March.

Firewood Rules.

1. The following Officers are hereby authorized to issue licences in the form specified in the Schedule hereto for obtaining and removing firewood from Crown Forests for domestic purposes only :— *Officers empowered to issue firewood licences.*

(*a*). District Residents in their respective Districts.

(*b*). The Chief Forest Officer.

2. Licences to obtain and remove firewood from Crown Forests for domestic purposes are issued subject to the following conditions :—

(1). Licences shall not be transferable.

(2). Licences shall be returned to the Licensing Officer, if so required, at the expiration of the period for which they are issued.

(3). Every licence shall be available for one household only.

(4). A licensee shall be entitled to obtain up to 120 ℔s. weight of firewood daily.

(5). Persons employed by a licensee to obtain and remove firewood shall carry the licence with them when gathering the firewood and shall produce it on demand to any public officer or to any native forest guard or policeman for inspection.

(6). No growing trees of any kind shall be cut within thirty yards of any stream or within eight yards of any public road without the special permission in writing of the Licensing Officer.

(7). A licence required under these Rules may be refused in the discretion of the Licensing Officer without cause assigned : Provided that upon refusal by a Licensing Officer to grant a licence an appeal shall lie to the Governor whose decision shall be final.

3. Any person travelling through or over any Undemarcated Forest may cut and gather such firewood as he may need for camping or outspanning purposes within the said Undemarcated Forest, without a licence, on condition that no unnecessary damage is done in cutting and gathering such firewood. *Right of travellers to cut and gather firewood without licence.*

4. These Rules shall come into force as from the 1st July, 1913. *Commencement.*

No.   NYASALAND PROTECTORATE.

QUARTERLY LICENCE TO OBTAIN AND REMOVE FIREWOOD FOR DOMESTIC PURPOSES.

LICENCE subject to "The Forests Ordinance, 1911," and Rules made thereunder, in favour of *(name)* of *(address)* who is hereby granted permission to obtain and remove firewood for domestic purposes for one household only from any Undemarcated Forest and from certain Demarcated Forests, namely, *(name and locality of demarcated areas for which this licence is available)* for the quarter ending   19

Date of issue

Station

Licensing Officer.

No.   NYASALAND PROTECTORATE.

MONTHLY LICENCE TO OBTAIN AND REMOVE FIREWOOD FOR DOMESTIC PURPOSES.

LICENCE subject to "The Forests Ordinance, 1911," and Rules made thereunder in favour of *(name)* of *(address)* who is hereby granted permission to obtain and remove firewood for domestic purposes for one household only from any Undemarcated Forest and from certain Demarcated Forests, namely *(name and locality of demarcated areas for which this licence is available)* for the month ending   19

Date of issue

Station

Licensing Officer.

198/1913,—30th August.

Strophanthus Rules.

Officers empowered to issue licences.

1. The following officers are hereby authorized to issue licences in the form specified in Schedule I hereto for the collection of Strophanthus in Crown Forests.

(*a*). District Residents in their respective Districts.

(*b*). The Chief Forest Officer.

Conditions of licences.

2. Licences to collect Strophanthus in Crown Forests are issued subject to the following conditions :—

(1). Licences shall not be transferable.

(2). Every licence shall be produced on demand to any District Magistrate or to the Chief Forest Officer, or any forest guard or policeman acting on their behalf.

(3). Every licence shall expire on the 31st day of March next following the date of issue.

(4). Any licensing Officer may refuse to issue a licence to any person without giving reasons for such refusal: Provided that the applicant may appeal to the Governor whose decision shall be final.

(5). All Strophanthus shall be shown to the District Resident of the district in which it was collected, and shall remain Government property until the prescribed royalty on such Strophanthus has been paid to the District Resident as aforesaid.

(6). No Strophanthus collected under licences shall be taken out of the district in which it was collected, and no such Strophanthus shall be sold or offered for sale without a Strophanthus Transit Pass in the form specified in Schedule II hereto first had and obtained from the District Resident of such district.

(7). Royalty on the quantity of Strophanthus for which a Transit Pass is required shall be paid before a Pass is issued.

(8). The quantity of Strophanthus on which royalty has been paid will be stated in the Transit Pass.

(9). The Transit Pass shall be delivered up to the Customs Officer at the Port of Export by the person exporting the Strophanthus in respect of which the Pass has been granted.

3. An exclusive licence to collect Strophanthus in a particular locality or district will only be granted by the Governor. *(Power of Governor in Council to grant exclusive licences.)*

4. Any District Resident or the Chief Forest Officer may seize any Strophanthus collected, purchased or possessed or suspected of being collected, purchased or possessed in contravention of the Ordinance or of these Rules and may detain the same until a Court has given directions for the disposal thereof. *(Seizure.)*

Schedule I.

Department of Agriculture, Forestry Division.

STROPHANTHUS LICENCE.

Licence subject to "The Forests Ordinance 1911" and any Rules made thereunder in favour of   to collect Strophanthus seed in $\frac{\text{Undemarcated}}{\text{Demarcated}}$ Forests within the area

known as   in the   Section or Sections of the   District.

Royalty at the rate of   per ℔. to be paid on all Strophanthus collected under this Licence.

For period from   to

Date of Issue

Station   Licensing Officer.

Schedule II.

Department of Agriculture, Forestry Division.

STROPHANTHUS TRANSIT PASS.

Permission is hereby granted to   to remove from the   District pounds of Strophanthus collected in the said district under Licence No.

    Royalty amounting to   has been paid this   day of   191 , on the above mentioned quantity of Strophanthus.

Station   District Resident

203/1913,—30th August.

Notice.

Under Section 3.

Notified that the following area of land shall be a Demarcated Forest and that the provisions of the above Ordinance in regard to Demarcated Forests shall apply to the said area.

The said area is bounded as follows :—

Commencing on the right bank of the Mlungusi river at the point where it is crossed by the Naisi road the boundary shall follow the right bank of the Mlungusi river up stream to the point where the water channel leaves the stream; thence it shall be carried along the water channel to the point where it crosses the Plateau road; thence it shall be carried along the Plateau road to its extreme western point; thence it shall be carried in a straight line on a bearing of 290° from magnetic north to the Lisanjala river; thence it shall be carried along the left bank of the Lisanjala river upstream to its source; thence it shall be carried along the British Central Africa Company's boundary in a northerly direction for a distance of 2 miles; thence it shall be carried in a straight line in a north-easterly direction to Domasi peak; thence it shall be carried in a northerly direction to the source of the Chifundi stream; thence it shall follow the boundary of the Church of Scotland Domasi Mission estate to the point where it is crossed by the road leading from Domasi to Zomba; thence it shall be carried along this road in a southerly direction to the point where it is crossed by the African Transcontinental telegraph line; thence it shall be carried along the route of the said telegraph line, in a south-westerly direction, until it reaches the Church of Scotland Naming'asi estate; thence it shall be carried along the boundaries of the said estate in a northerly, westerly, and southerly direction until it reaches the Naisi road; thence it shall be carried along the Naisi road to the point of commencement.

No. 16 of 1912.

PLANTS PROTECTION.

Proclamation.

5/1913,—31st January.

By the Acting Governor-in-Council :—

WHEREAS by Section 3 of the above Ordinance, it is provided that the Governor-in-Council may by Proclamation to be published in the *Gazette* absolutely or conditionally prohibit the importation directly or indirectly from any country or place named in such Proclamation of any plant or any earth or soil or any article packed therewith or any package or other article or thing which in the opinion of the Governor-in-Council is likely to be a means of introducing any plant disease into the Protectorate,

AND WHEREAS it has been made to appear to me that the importation of cotton plants with the following exceptions should be absolutely prohibited :

Exceptions :—

(1). Cotton plants grown in Egypt :

(2). Cotton plants imported for experimental purposes by the Director of Agriculture and packed in double bags or tins,

AND WHEREAS it has been further made to appear to me that all plants permitted to be imported should be imported subject to certain conditions ;

NOW THEREFORE by virtue of the powers in me as Acting Governor-in-Council vested as aforesaid I DO HEREBY declare and proclaim that the importation of cotton plants with the exceptions as aforesaid shall be and is HEREBY absolutely prohibited.

AND FURTHER that the importation of all plants permitted to be imported shall be imported subject to the following conditions :—

1. Every package containing plants imported into the Protectorate through the medium of the Post shall contain a statement containing the full names of the kind and variety, the country of origin, and the name and address of the person or firm supplying such plants together with any certificate which may be prescribed by Schedules A or B. Such package shall be delivered by the Postal Department to the Agricultural Department, Zomba, for inspection, and disinfection, if necessary. Such package shall, if in order, be delivered to the Post Office to be forwarded to the addressee without further postal charge. Any package of plants which does not contain the requisite statement and certificate shall be liable to be confiscated or otherwise dealt with as the Agricultural Authority may determine.

2. When plants are intended to be imported otherwise than through the medium of the post, a statement containing the full names and the kind and variety, the country of origin and the name and address of the person or firm supplying such plants together with any certificate which may be prescribed by Schedules A or B shall be posted to the Comptroller of Customs. Such statement and certificate shall be dispatched by the consignor in sufficient time to enable it to reach the Comptroller of Customs one month in advance of the consignment. Plants which reach the Port of Entry, for which the necessary statement and certificate have not been received, shall be detained, pending the receipt of the statement and certificate as aforesaid and if such are not received within one month subsequent to the arrival of the plants the whole consignment shall be liable to be confiscated or otherwise dealt with as the Agricultural Authority may determine. When plants are imported by persons entering the Protectorate, the importer shall declare the same to the Customs Officer, giving the information required above, and producing the certificate which may be prescribed by Schedules A or B. In the event of the statement and certificate being in order, all plants shall be disinfected, if considered necessary by the Agricultural Authority at the Port of Entry, and allowed to proceed. Should any statement or certificate prove to be incorrect, the whole consignment shall be liable to be confiscated.

3. All plants shall be securely packed, and should any package become so damaged in the course of transit as to render it possible that any plant may escape therefrom, such package and any plant therein or therefrom, may at the discretion of the Agricultural Authority be confiscated.

Schedule A.

The importation of plants of the following kinds shall be accompanied by a certificate from the Official Agricultural Authority of the countries from which the plants originated to the effect that they have been grown in areas known to be free from diseases or pests which characteristically attack such plants :—

Rubber of all Varieties	
Cacao	
Cocoanuts	
Rice	From all Countries.
Tobacco	
Potatoes	

Schedule B.

The importation of plants of the following kinds shall be subject to the permission of the Agricultural Authority being first had and obtained.

Coffee	
Tea	From all Countries.

No. 7 of 1910.

COTTON.

7/1913,—31st January.

Rules.

Under Section 3.

1. Every landowner and person planting cotton in the Protectorate shall uproot and burn all cotton bushes on his land or planted by him before the last day of October next following the date of planting of such bushes. Provided that this Rule shall not apply to the Lower Shire, Ruo and West Shire Districts.

Destruction of old bushes.

2. Every landowner and person planting cotton in the Lower Shire, Ruo and West Shire Districts shall uproot and burn all cotton bushes on his land or planted by him in these Districts before the last day of December next following the date of planting of such bushes.

Time for destruction in Lower Shire, Ruo and West Shire Districts.

3. Any bushes not uprooted and burnt in accordance with these Rules may be uprooted and burnt by order of the Director of Agriculture or of the District Resident. In the event of this being done the landowner and the person who planted the bushes shall be jointly and severally liable for any expense occasioned by such uprooting and burning in addition to their liability to the penalties prescribed for a breach of the Ordinance.

Cotton bushes may be destroyed by Government.

4. All native grown cotton produced upon Crown lands from seed issued by Government shall be ginned in the Protectorate.

Cotton to be ginned in the Protectorate.

5. All cotton seed issued by Government to natives is issued subject to the condition that Government retains the right to any seed obtained from the crop which is the product of the seed issued. Every licensee purchasing native grown cotton produced upon Crown lands from seed issued by Government, before selling, giving or otherwise disposing of such seed after ginning, shall obtain a certificate from the Director of Agriculture that such seed is not required by Government, and if the Director of Agriculture shall intimate that such seed or any part thereof is required by Government the licensee shall hold the quantity specified at the disposal of Government.

Reservation of seed to Government.

Approval of Director of Agriculture.

6. No cotton seed shall be issued to natives until it has been approved by the Director of Agriculture.

Authority for distribution of seed.

7. Nò person except a person authorized by the Governor, shall distribute seed to natives for cultivation on Crown lands. Applications for such authority shall be made in the first instance to the Director of Agriculture.

Licence to purchase.

8. No person shall purchase native grown cotton being the production of seed distributed for cultivation on Crown lands, unless he shall previously have been licensed so to do under these Rules.

Form of licence.

9. A licence shall be in the form prescribed by the Governor and shall expire on the thirty-first day of March next following the date of issue. Every such licence shall be obtainable from the District Resident of the District in which the purchase is to be made.

Duty on licence.

10. The duty chargeable on a licence shall be ten shillings.

Place of purchase.

11. No licence shall authorize a licensee to purchase native grown cotton in a place other than the place stated in the licence.

Establishment of markets.

12. For the purpose of the sale of native grown cotton markets shall be established by Government in native cotton growing districts.

Market tolls.

13. Purchasers of native grown cotton shall pay market tolls at the rate of 3d. per cwt. of seed cotton purchased: Such tolls shall be paid to the District Resident of the District to which his licence applies concurrently with the submission of the monthly return referred to in Rule 14 hereof.

Monthly Returns.

14. Every licensee shall on the last day of each month make a return to the District Resident of the District to which his licence applies, shewing the total weight of native grown cotton from Crown lands purchased by him during the month and the price which he paid for such cotton.

Inspection of cotton purchased.

15. All native grown cotton from Crown lands purchased by a licensee may be inspected at any reasonable time by the District Resident, the Director of Agriculture, or by an officer of the Agricultural Department or by any officer appointed by the Governor, and such licensee shall give all such information as to the place where and the person by whom such cotton was grown or sold or ginned or otherwise as the said inspecting officer shall require and the licensee be able to afford.

Cancellation of licence.

16. A licence may be cancelled on conviction of the licensee of a breach of any of these Rules.

A new licence shall not be issued to any person whose licence has been so cancelled except by the express authority of the Governor.

17. Any person committing a breach of any of these Rules shall be liable on conviction to a fine not exceeding five pounds or in default of payment to imprisonment for a term not exceeding one month.

Penalty for breach of Rules.

199/1913,—30th August.

1. Rule 1 of the Rules made under the above Ordinance and published in the Gazette of 31st January, 1913, shall not apply to the North Nyasa District.

Non-application of Rule.

2. Every landowner and person planting cotton in the North Nyasa District shall uproot and burn all cotton bushes on his land or planted by him before the last day of December next following the date of planting of such bushes.

Destruction of old bushes in North Nyasa District.

No. 2 of 1911.

GAME.

Proclamation.

Under Section 38.   *178/1912,—31st October.*

By the Governor in Council.

WHEREAS it has been made to appear to me expedient that the operation of the above Ordinance, with the exception that elephants (female or young) and all the birds mentioned in Schedule I to the Ordinance shall not be hunted, killed or captured, in so far as it relates to natives should be suspended in respect of the portion of the Dowa Sub-district* of the Lilongwe District the boundaries of which are as described in a notice No. 213 dated the 30th December, 1911, and published in the *Gazette* of that date,

     NOW THEREFORE I DO HEREBY proclaim and declare that the operation of the said Ordinance, subject to the exception as aforesaid in so far as it relates to natives shall be and is HEREBY suspended in respect of the portion of the Dowa Sub-district* of the Lilongwe District hereinbefore described until further notice: Provided that if elephants be killed in pursuance of the provisions of this Proclamation the tusks thereof shall be deemed to be the property of the Government.

Form of Licences.

Under Section 24 (1).   *77/1911,—31st May.*
No.   NYASALAND PROTECTORATE.

VISITOR'S LICENCE " A," £10.

This Licence is not transferable and must be produced when called for by an officer of the Protectorate Government.

                ISSUED AT
                DATE

       (*Name in full*) the undersigned, of (*Address*)
is hereby licensed to hunt, kill or capture the wild animals mentioned in Schedule III of the Game Ordinance, 1911, specified on the back hereof, within the NYASALAND PROTECTORATE for the period from the date of issue of this Licence until the 31st day of March, 19 , subject to the provisions and restrictions of " THE GAME ORDINANCE, 1911."

     This Licence does not entitle the holder to hunt, kill or capture any animals whatsoever within a Game Reserve.

       AMOUNT DEPOSITED OR THE AMOUNT OF THE SECURITY GIVEN £

                Signature of Issuing Officer
                Signature of Licensee
       REMARKS :

---

* Now Dowa District.

Schedule III.

Animals a limited number of which may be killed or captured under a Visitor's or Protectorate licence :

		No. allowed.
1.	Buffalo	6
2.	Hippopotamus	4
3.	Eland	6
4.	Gnu, Wildebeest (except white-tailed species) ..	6
5.	Zebra (other than Mountain Zebra)	6
6.	Antelopes and Gazelles .—	
	Class A.—Sable	6
	Roan	6
	Kudu	6
	Class B.—Any other species in all ..	30
7.	Colobus and other Fur Monkeys	6
8.	Aard Vark (Orycteropus)	2
9.	Egret	10
10.	Wart Hog	10

No.   Nyasaland Protectorate.

PROTECTORATE LICENCE " B." £2.

This Licence is not transferable and must be produced when called for by an officer of the Protectorate Government.

Issued at
Date

(*Name in full*) the undersigned, of (*Address*)
is hereby licensed to hunt, kill or capture the wild animals mentioned in Schedule III of the Game Ordinance, 1911, specified on the back hereof, within the Nyasaland Protectorate for the period from the date of issue of this Licence until the 31st day of March, 19   , subject to the provisions and restrictions of "The Game Ordinance, 1911."

This licence does not entitle the holder to hunt, kill or capture any animals whatsoever within a Game Reserve.

Amount Deposited or the Amount of the Security given £
Signature of Issuing Officer
Signature of Licensee
Remarks.

Schedule III.

Animals a limited number of which may be killed or captured under a Protectorate licence :

		No. allowed.
1.	Buffalo	6
2.	Hippopotamus	4
3.	Eland	6
4.	Gnu, Wildebeest (except white-tailed species) ...	6
5.	Zebra (other than Mountain Zebra)	6

6. Antelopes and Gazelles :—
     CLASS A.—Sable ... ...: 6
              Roan 6
              Kudu 6
     CLASS B.—Any other species in all 30
7. Colobus and other Fur Monkeys 6
8. Aard Vark (Orycteropus) 2
9. Egret 10
10. Wart Hog 10

No.   NYASALAND PROTECTORATE.

ADDITIONAL LICENCE "C." £10.

This Licence is not transferable and must be produced when called for by an officer of the Protectorate Government.

ISSUED AT
DATE

(Name in full) the undersigned, of *(Address)* having taken out Licence "A" * or "B" No.   at   on the   19 , is hereby licensed to hunt, kill or capture ONE ELEPHANT within the Nyasaland Protectorate during the period from the date of issue of this Licence until the 31st day of March, 19 , subject to the provisions and restrictions of "THE GAME ORDINANCE, 1911."

This Licence does not entitle the holder to hunt, kill or capture any animals whatsoever within a Game Reserve.

       Signature of Issuing Officer
       Signature of Licensee
       REMARKS .

* *If "A" issued strike out "B" and vice versa.*

No.   NYASALAND PROTECTORATE.

ADDITIONAL LICENCE "D," £20.

This Licence is not transferable and must be produced when called for by an officer of the Protectorate Government.

ISSUED AT
DATE

(Name in full) the undersigned, of *(Address)* having taken out Licence "A" * or "B" No.   at   on the   19 , and having already killed one elephant under Licence "C" No.   is hereby licensed to hunt, kill or capture   ELEPHANT within the Nyasaland Protectorate during the period from the date of issue of this Licence until the 31st day of March, 19 , subject to the provisions and restrictions of "THE GAME ORDINANCE, 1911."

This Licence does not entitle the holder to hunt, kill or capture any animals whatsoever within a Game Reserve.

       Signature of Issuing Officer
       Signature of Licensee
       REMARKS;

NOTE.—This licence entitles the holder to hunt, kill or capture a total of two elephants during the year ending on the 31st March, 19   When one elephant has already been killed under a licence "C" previously issued to the licensee only one additional elephant can be shot under this licence.

* *Strike out if not required.*

No.   NYASALAND PROTECTORATE.

ADDITIONAL LICENCE "E," £40.

This Licence is not transferable and must be produced when called for by an officer of the Protectorate Government.

ISSUED AT

DATE

(Name in full) the undersigned, of *(Address)* having taken out Licence "A" or * "B" No.   at   on the   19 , and having already killed   Elephant under Licence "C" No.   or "D" No.
is hereby licensed to hunt, kill or capture   ELEPHANT within the Nyasaland Protectorate during the period from the date of issue of this Licence until the 31st day of March, 19 , subject to the provisions and restrictions of "THE GAME ORDINANCE 1911."

This Licence does not entitle the holder to hunt, kill or capture any animals whatsoever within a Game Reserve.

Signature of Issuing Officer
Signature of Licensee

REMARKS:—

NOTE.—This Licence entitles the holder to hunt, kill or capture not more than a total of three elephants during the year ending on the 31st March, 19 , less the number of elephants already killed under a licence "C" and or "D."

* *Alter according to circumstances.*

No.   NYASALAND PROTECTORATE.

ADDITIONAL LICENCE "F," £60.

This Licence is not transferable and must be produced when called for by an officer of the Protectorate Government.

ISSUED AT   .

DATE

(Name in full) the undersigned, of *(Address)* having taken out Licence "A" * or "B" No.   at   on the   19 , and having already killed   Elephant under Licence "C" No.   or "D" No.   or "E" No.   is hereby licensed to hunt, kill or capture   ELEPHANT within the Nyasaland Protectorate during the period from the date of issue of this Licence until the 31st day of March, 19 , subject to the provisions and restrictions of THE GAME ORDINANCE, 1911."

This Licence does not entitle the holder to hunt, kill or capture any animals whatsoever within a Game Reserve.

Signature of Officer
Signature of Licensee

REMARKS:

NOTE.—This licence entitles the holder to hunt, kill or capture a total of four elephants during the year ending on the 31st March, 19 , less the number of elephants already killed under Licences "C," "D," or "E."

* *Alter according to circumstances.*

206. *Game.*

No.   Nyasaland Protectorate.

NATIVE LICENCE " G," £1.

This Licence is not transferable and must be produced when called for by an officer of the Protectorate Government.

Issued at

Date

(*Name in full*) the undersigned, of (*Address*)
is hereby licensed to hunt, kill or capture the wild animals as detailed hereunder within the   District during the period from the date of issue of this Licence until the 31st day of March, 19   , subject to the following conditions :—

This Licence does not entitle the holder to hunt, kill or capture any animals whatsoever within a Game Reserve
Animals
Conditions
Remarks

Signature of Issuing Officer
Signature of Licensee

No.   Nyasaland Protectorate.

SPECIAL LICENCE " H."

This Licence is not transferable and must be produced when called for by an officer of the Protectorate Government.

Chief Secretary's Office,
Zomba,   191

(*Name in full*) the undersigned, of (*Address*)
is hereby licensed to hunt, kill or capture the wild animals as detailed hereunder within the   District during the period from the date of issue of this Licence until the 31st day of March, 19   , subject to the following conditions :—

This Licence does not entitle the holder to hunt, kill or capture any animals whatsoever within a Game Reserve.
Animals
Conditions
Remarks

By Command:
Chief Secretary.

Signature of Licensee.

No. 2 of 1913.

PUBLIC ROADS.

R u l e s.

81/1914,—29th April.

Traffic on Public Roads.

Under Section 9.

1. These Rules apply to all carts, wagons, lorries or other vehicles used for the transport of goods or produce and whether drawn by animals or propelled by other power (hereinafter termed "vehicle") and to all public roads as defined by the Ordinance.

Application of Rules.

2. (1). Every vehicle employed upon or traversing a public road shall have the owner's name legibly painted in English in letters not less than 3 inches high upon the front or near side of it. Provided that, on application to the Resident of the District in which the owner of a vehicle resides, such owner may obtain a registered mark or number, which mark or number may be used in lieu of his name upon vehicles belonging to him. Every registered mark when applied to a vehicle shall be painted upon it or upon a board or plate affixed to it on the front or near side of the vehicle in white letters or figures not less than four inches in height upon a black or dark coloured background. No fee shall be charged in respect of the registration of a mark or of the certificate of the Resident issued with regard to it.

Identification of vehicle.

Registered marks.

(2). The tare of every vehicle shall be ascertained and painted legibly upon it in a conspicuous part or, where a registered mark or number is affixed, then alongside or below such mark or number.

Tare of vehicle to be indicated.

3. The following provisions shall apply to all vehicles in use on a public road :—

Provisions as to :—
Wheels.

(*a*). The minimum diameter of any wheel shall be 2 feet 6 inches.

(*b*). The minimum width of tyre of any wheel (except in the case of pneumatic tyres or tyres of soft material) shall be 4 inches.

Tyres.

(*c*). With the minimum wheel diameter and tyre width stated in (*a*) and (*b*) the axle weight shall not exceed 16 cwt ;

Axle weights.

but such weight may be increased in the ratio of 2 cwt. in respect of each additional 3 inches in diameter of wheel or half inch in width of tyre.

Limit of axle weight.

4. No vehicle the aggregate axle weight of which exceeds 8 tons shall use any public road ; and when necessary for the protection of any bridge the load with the vehicle shall be reduced to such a weight as may be intimated by the Director of Public Works by notice affixed to the bridge before any vehicle crosses it.

Maximum load on bridges.

Locking of wheels.

5. Except in cases of emergency, proof of which shall lie on the driver, no wheel of any vehicle shall be so fixed as to prevent it revolving while the vehicle is in motion.

Camping and lighting fires on roads.

6. No person shall camp or light a fire on any public road or permit any person under his control to do so.

Placing of obstructions on public roads.

7. No person shall deposit or permit any person under his control to deposit any stone, log or other obstruction upon a public road ; and any stone or other thing used temporarily in scotching the wheels of a vehicle while at rest on any public road shall be removed therefrom so soon as the vehicle moves on.

Rules as to outspanning vehicle.

8. On outspanning :—(1) The vehicle shall be drawn to the near side of the road in the direction in which it is proceeding in. such a position as not to obstruct the passage of other vehicles upon the road ; and, between the hours of sunset and sunrise, shall carry upon it a light in such a position that it may be seen by any person approaching the vehicle from either direction upon the road.

Lights.

(2). All animals outspanned shall be removed to such a distance and there be so tethered or otherwise restrained that they shall not be able to stray upon the road.

Animals.
Lights on vehicle in motion.

9. Every vehicle traversing a public road between the hours of sunset and sunrise shall carry an efficient light or lights in such position that the presence of the .vehicle may be detected by any person approaching it upon the road from either direction.

Rule of road.

10. (1). A vehicle passing another going in an opposite direction shall keep to the left side of the road.

(2). A vehicle overtaking another shall pass it by keeping to the right of it.

Damage to surface and obstruction of passage on road.

11. No person shall drag any timber or other thing upon a public road in such manner as to impair its surface or obstruct the passage of persons or vehicles upon it.

Straying and driven animals.

12. No person shall allow any animal in his charge to stray upon a public road or drive animals thereon without a sufficiency of drovers to control their movements so that they do not impede the passage of persons or vehicles upon the road.

13. These Rules (with the exception of Rule 3) shall come into force on the 1st day of July, 1914.

Rule 3 shall come into force on the 1st day of January, 1916. *

Date to come into force.

---

* Rule 13 as amended by Notice of 2nd December, 1914 (No. 259/1914.)

No. 6 of 1914.

COPYRIGHT.

R u l e s.

59/1914,—31st March.

1. The Notice in writing to be given to the Comptroller of Customs under section 2 of the Copyright Ordinance, 1914, by the owner of the copyright in any book or other printed work in which copyright subsists under the said Ordinance, or his agent who is desirous that copies thereof printed or reprinted out of the Protectorate shall not be imported into the Protectorate, shall be in the Form No. 1 in the Schedule hereto or as near thereto as circumstances permit.

2. The notice in writing to be given to the Comptroller of Customs under Section 2 of the Copyright Ordinance, 1914, by the owner of the copyright in any work (other than a book or other printed work) in which copyright subsists under the said Ordinance or his agent who is desirous that copies thereof made out of the Protectorate shall not be imported into the Protectorate may be either a general notice in the Form No. 2 in the Schedule hereto or as near thereto as circumstances permit or a special notice in the Form No. 3 in the same Schedule relating to a particular importation.

3. Every notice given in pursuance of these rules in the Form No. 1 or No. 2 in the Schedule hereto shall be accompanied by a statutory declaration in the Form No. 4 in the same Schedule.

4. Before any article which appears, or is alleged to be a copy of a work to which a notice applies is detained, or any further proceedings with a view to the forfeiture thereof under the law relating to the Customs are taken, the person who signed the notice whether as owner or agent shall, if required so to do, give to the Comptroller of Customs in writing such further information and evidence, verified if so required by a statutory declaration, as he considers necessary to satisfy him that the article in question is liable to detention and forfeiture.

5. In the case of any detention in consequence of a notice in the Form No. 3 given to the Comptroller of Customs the person who signed the notice whether as owner or agent must if so required deposit with the Comptroller of Customs or other Officer of Customs at the port or place of detention a sum of money sufficient in the opinion of that Officer to cover any expense which may be incurred in the examination required by reason of his notice of the goods detained, and if upon the examination of the goods the said Comptroller or other Officer is satisfied that there is no ground for their detention, they will be delivered.

6. If any goods are placed under detention in consequence of any notice given in pursuance of these Rules, the Comptroller of Customs may require the person who signed the notice to give an undertaking in writing to reimburse him all expenses and damages incurred in respect of the detention, and of any proceedings for forfeiture [subsequently taken if such an undertaking has not already been given, and may also require him within four days after the detention to enter into a bond with two approved sureties in such form and for such amount as the said Comptroller of Customs may require.

7. Any deposit of money previously made will be returned on the completion of the bond.

8. In these Rules—

"Owner of the Copyright" has the same meaning as in section 2 of the Copyright Ordinance, 1914.

"Book or other printed work" means every part or division of a book, pamphlet, sheet of letterpress, sheet of music, map, plan, chart, or table separately published.

The Schedule.

Form No. 1.

NOTICE

RELATING TO COPYRIGHT BOOKS AND OTHER PRINTED WORKS.

To the Comptroller of Customs.

I,   of
hereby give you notice that copyright in the original work (1) mentioned in the Schedule hereto now subsists under the Copyright Act, 1911, and that (2)   the owner of the copyright in the said work (1)   and that (3)   desirous that copies of the said work (1)   printed or reprinted out of the Protectorate shall not be imported into the Protectorate.

        Dated this   · day of   , 19 .

             (Signature)
              (4)

1.—or works.
2.—If notice is given by the owner insert "I am"; if given by an agent insert name of owner and the word " is."
3.—"I am " or " be is."
4.—If an agent insert " Agent of owner."

Schedule.

Title of Book (5)
Description of printed work, if not a book
Full name of Author or Authors
Whether Author or Authors alive, if not, date of death
When and where (6) book or printed work first published

5.—The notice may apply to a number of books or printed works in which case the particulars in the Schedule must be given as respects each book or printed work.
6.—It is sufficient to state the country of first publication.

Form No. 2.

NOTICE

RELATING TO COPYRIGHT WORKS, OTHER THAN BOOKS OR OTHER PRINTED WORKS.

To the Comptroller of Customs.

I,   of

1.—If notice is given by the owner insert "I am," if given by an agent, insert name of owner and the word "is."

2.—"I am," or "he is."

3.—If an agent insert "Agent of Owner."

hereby given you notice that copyright in the original work mentioned in the Schedule hereto now subsists under the Copyright Act, 1911, and that (1)   the owner of the copyright in the said work, and that (2)   desirous that copies of the said work made out of the Protectorate shall not be imported into the Protectorate.

Dated the   day of   , 19 .

(Signature)

(3)

Schedule.

Title of Work (if any)
Full description of Work
Initials or Marks (if any) usually placed on copies of work
Full name of Author or Authors
Whether Author or Authors alive, if not, date of death
When and where (4) work first published
If work not published :—

4.—It is sufficient to state the country of first publication.

Whether Author British Subject or not

If not a British subject, name of country in which Author was resident, or domiciled at date of the making of the work

In the case of photographs, phonographic records and music rolls, date of making the original negative or original plate

---

Form No. 3.

NOTICE

RELATING TO A PARTICULAR IMPORTATION.

To the Comptroller of Customs.

I,   of

1.—Or agent for the owner.

hereby give you notice that I am the owner (1)
of the copyright in a certain original work as to which copyright now subsists under the Copyright Act, 1911, and that the undermentioned goods, that is to say, (2)

2.—Describe the goods, number of packages, marks used, and any other particulars necessary for their identification.
* Or Sub-Port
3.—Describe the ship, and give name or indication.
4.—State if the goods are copies of the original work made out of the United Kingdom, or how otherwise the goods are liable to detention and forfeiture.

are about to be imported into the *Port of   on or about the day of   next in the (3)   from

That such goods are liable to detention and forfeiture as being (4)

and I request that the said goods may be detained and dealt with accordingly, and I hereby undertake to reimburse the Comptroller of Customs all expenses and damages to be incurred in respect of the detention and of any proceedings for forfeiture which may be subsequently taken.

5.—If an agent insert "Agent of owner."

Dated this   day of   . , 19 .

(Signature)

(5)

Form No. 4.

STATUTORY DECLARATION.

I,

of

do solemnly and sincerely declare that the contents of the Notice hereto
annexed are true, and I make this solemn declaration conscientiously
believing the same to be true and by virtue of the Provisions of the
Statutory Declarations Act, 1835.

Declared by the above- named   at

this   day of   , 19 ,

Before me,   a Commissioner for Oaths.

No. 5 of 1913.

NATIVE LUNATICS.

144/1913,—2nd June.

Appointments.

Under Section 4.

(1). *To be Superintendent of the Central Lunatic Asylum, Zomba :—*

The Officer for the time being Commanding the Troops.

(2). *To be Deputy Superintendent of the Central Lunatic Asylum, Zomba :—*

The Deputy Superintendent of the Central Prison, Zomba.

INDEX.